THE
THERAPEUTIC USE OF SELF
IN COUNSELLING & PSYCHOTHERAPY

Sara Miller McCune founded SAGE Publishing in 1965 to support the dissemination of usable knowledge and educate a global community. SAGE publishes more than 1000 journals and over 800 new books each year, spanning a wide range of subject areas. Our growing selection of library products includes archives, data, case studies and video. SAGE remains majority owned by our founder and after her lifetime will become owned by a charitable trust that secures the company's continued independence.

Los Angeles I London I New Delhi I Singapore I Washington DC I Melbourne

THE
THERAPEUTIC USE OF SELF
IN COUNSELLING & PSYCHOTHERAPY

LINDA FINLAY

⑤SAGE

Los Angeles | London | New Delhi
Singapore | Washington DC | Melbourne

ⓈSAGE

Los Angeles | London | New Delhi
Singapore | Washington DC | Melbourne

SAGE Publications Ltd
1 Oliver's Yard
55 City Road
London EC1Y 1SP

SAGE Publications Inc.
2455 Teller Road
Thousand Oaks, California 91320

SAGE Publications India Pvt Ltd
B 1/I 1 Mohan Cooperative Industrial Area
Mathura Road
New Delhi 110 044

SAGE Publications Asia-Pacific Pte Ltd
3 Church Street
#10-04 Samsung Hub
Singapore 049483

Editor: Susannah Trefgarne
Assistant editor: Ruth Lilly
Production editor: Rachel Burrows
Cover design: Naomi Robinson
Typeset by: KnowledgeWorks Global Ltd.

Library of Congress Control Number: 2021941861

British Library Cataloguing in Publication data

A catalogue record for this book is available from the
British Library

ISBN 978-1-5297-6146-7
ISBN 978-1-5297-6145-0 (pbk)

CONTENTS

ABOUT THE AUTHOR

Dr Linda Finlay is a relational-centred, existential Integrative Psychotherapist and Supervisor (UKCP registered) in private practice. She also teaches psychology and counselling at the Open University (UK) and works as a freelance academic consultant. She has published many books and articles on therapy, reflexivity, healthcare and phenomenological research. Her most recent books are psychotherapeutically focused: *Relational Integrative Psychotherapy: Engaging Process and Theory in Practice* (Wiley) and *Practical Ethics: A Relational Approach* (SAGE). She is currently Editor of the *European Journal for Qualitative Research in Psychotherapy*.

PREFACE

'Therapeutic use of self' is a slippery, elusive concept, one that can be likened to mist rather than something we can grab hold of. It is hard to explain, yet being so central to the therapy project, it is vital that we try to grasp it as best we can. This book is my attempt to capture, examine and understand the processes involved.

There are many books about therapeutic techniques, procedures and skills – about therapists' *doing*. But what of therapists' way of *being* with clients? Who exactly am I, as the therapist? What matters to me? How different is my private self from my therapist self? Is my social out-in-the-world self (the self that might encounter clients outside the therapy room) different again? Do I even have a 'self' that can be specified? (Some would argue that all we have is a process of *self-ing* – a coming into being when-in-relationship.)

These existential questions about our way of being, as a therapist and as a person, concern our nature, what we bring to our relationships and how we are in the world. They point to our 'realness' (authentically being 'me') as distinct from our 'playing a role'.

More concretely, we can talk about our professional/therapist way-of-being as our *therapeutic use of self*. This is the 'self'[1] we employ during therapy: the self that allows us to be in relation with a client with genuine concern, curiosity and caring attention. Dewane (2006, p. 543) defines use of self as the 'melding' of the professional self (including training, knowledge, techniques) with the personal self (personality traits, beliefs, life experience). She argues that it is a 'hallmark of skilled practice'.

But how we are with one client is invariably different from how we are with another. Our way of being – at least in part – depends on the relational–social context, the specific situation, the therapeutic approach we're adopting and the individuals involved. It is also influenced by how we're feeling at that moment and how present we are – just as it's shaped by how our client is feeling and how present they are. Sometimes we can be aware, choiceful and strategic about our way of being. At other times, our being is simply an expression of the way we are, the way we find ourselves being, at any particular moment. I therefore believe that it is important to move towards a view of the therapeutic use of self as a dynamic, ethical and reflexive process that is profoundly relational.

Book structure

Following the initial chapter, which introduces the idea of the 'therapeutic use of self', eight chapters each focus on a particular facet of therapeutic being. A final synthesising chapter recognises that those facets interlink in practice and how our use of self takes place in a relational–social context. Each chapter offers numerous examples from practice and interweaves theoretical and empirical research references. Key ideas are highlighted in Practical application, Research and Case example boxes.

Many of the case illustrations offered are extracted from previously published material. Others are constructed, fictionalised stories based on composites drawn from my own work as a therapist and supervisor, or are accounts given to me by colleagues or clients.

The chapters follow a similar structure. Each starts with its specific focus and ends with a case study, critical reflections, discussion questions for students/tutors, and recommended resources (in addition to references given in each chapter). These latter sections acknowledge the considerable ongoing debate in the field and the huge diversity of practice.

The book does not claim to be definitive or comprehensive, nor does it advocate any specific 'right' way of being or of approaching therapy based on particular theoretical preferences. As McWilliams, a psychodynamic therapist, says: 'I have known many very good therapists, and I am struck by how different they are from one another' (cited in Kottler and Carlson, 2014, p. 22). The mystery of our Being will always be – at least partly – out of reach. It cannot be captured and fixed; there will always be *more*.

That said, we have choices about the approaches we take and it's important for us to critically reflect on our practice. Here I take the lead from Loewenthal's (2015) persuasive argument that, given we have fields of 'critical psychiatry' and 'critical psychology', we now need to engage 'critical psychotherapy' to challenge norms in the era of managed care (see: https://critical psychotherapy.wordpress.com/2015/06/28/welcome/).

My hope is that you will dwell with the many examples, quotations and experiences presented in the pages that follow. Perhaps you will catch glimpses here and there of new ways of being in your therapy practice. Perhaps something will resonate with your own experience or stir you to think about your own preferred ways of being and doing.

Above all, I invite you to use my words as a springboard: as a means to open up and discover what's important to you about your own therapist being. And if you disagree with my suggested approach, I encourage you to own your difference and create your own path ahead.

Note

1. I put the 'self' in inverted commas to highlight the point that it is a contested concept. In this book, I skirt around the philosophical debates about whether a self even exists by focusing more on the notion of 'being-in-relationship' and how our self fluidly responds to another. We are different with different clients, just as they are different with us compared with how they would be with another therapist. In this sense, I am privileging the phenomenological/gestalt view of self as constituted by relational contexts, instead of being an entity in itself.

ACKNOWLEDGEMENTS

Many people have helped with the evolution of this book. I could not possibly have written it without regularly consulting others for their different perspectives and affirmations. A huge thank you goes to my friends and colleagues who have given me wise feedback on chapter drafts.

Throughout the book I've offered extensive quotations from many sources. I've chosen them because I think they are powerful and/or articulate a point especially well. It is also important, I believe, for readers to be exposed to different voices and viewpoints. Some quotations have come directly from colleagues (therapists and clients) who have so generously offered the gift of their stories to me. Other quotations have come from published sources. I remain grateful to these respected colleagues whose work I have drawn heavily upon. You have all been – and continue to be – my teachers.

I am especially grateful to Susan Ram for her expert transformational editing and to Mel Wilder whose supportive presence nourishes me and helps me to process my ideas.

Finally, in terms of the publication process, I need to acknowledge that some material has been reproduced from already published sources. I am grateful to Sage for allowing me to reproduce chunks of material from Finlay (2019) *Practical Ethics in Counselling and Psychotherapy: A Relational Approach* (notably in Chapters 2, 3 and 7). Further material (particularly in Chapters 2 and 4) has been drawn from Finlay (2016a) *Relational Integrative Psychotherapy: Processes and Theory in Practice*, reproduced here with kind permission of Wiley-Blackwell Publishers. The section on presence in Chapter 3, including Figure 3.1, has been largely taken from Finlay (2016b), 'Therapeutic presence' as embodied, relational 'being', *International Journal of Psychotherapy*, 20 (2), with thanks to the journal's Editor, Courtney Young. Finally, the case studies of Gillian (Chapter 5) and Alex (Chapter 7) have been reproduced from Finlay (2015), Sensing and making sense: embodying metaphor in relational-centred psychotherapy,

The Humanistic Psychologist, 43 (4), 338–53, with grateful thanks to APA and the Editor, Scott Churchill.

For this current book, special gratitude needs to be extended to Susannah Trefgarne (Commissioning Editor) who helped me to shape its direction; to Ruth Lilly (Assistant Editor) who guided me through the permissions process, and also to Rachel Burrows (Production Editor) along with the rest of the publishing team and reviewers for seeing the manuscript through to publication. Of course, any misunderstandings and mistakes within this book are mine alone.

ONE

THERAPEUTIC USE OF SELF

The person of the therapist is the center point around which successful therapy revolves. (Satir, 2000, p. 25)

What do our therapeutic relationships with clients involve? How do we create a safe space for clients to go exploring? What are we *doing* when we show clients respect and caring, attuned attention or when we challenge them to grow? How is our way of *being* with clients therapeutic?

These questions around 'doing' and 'being' all relate to the idea of therapeutic use of self which can be defined as:

A therapist's thoughtful, deliberate effort to use their self as a tool, one which embodies a self-aware therapeutic way of being in the service of clients and the client-therapist relationship.

This chapter begins by expanding on this definition. It then moves on to examine how we adapt our use of self, develop a therapeutic alliance and promote 'contact-in-relationship' as our approach shifts in different clinical/ theoretical and cultural contexts. The point emphasised is that our use of self and our therapeutic choices (for doing and being) depend on the relational and cultural context, and demand a level of self-awareness. A fluid responsiveness is required, enabling the therapist to attune to the type of contact each client can accept at any given moment. Therapeutic use of self is not something that is predetermined and fixed – it is a process that emerges, moment-to-moment, in response to another.

The chapter concludes with a case study, along with critical reflections, discussion questions and resources – a pattern followed across the rest of the book.

Defining 'use of self'

Therapeutic use of self is the self-aware intertwining of both our *profes-sional* self (the one that uses knowledge, skills and techniques) and our *personal* self (which arises from our history, beliefs/values, personality and embodied lived experience). It involves our therapeutic practices that we've learned and our particular way of maintaining a caring, attuned, holding presence. In other words, therapeutic use of self involves the totality of our being and doing; it is present in our every intervention (see Box 1.1).

The concept of 'therapeutic use of self' first gained traction in the latter half of the twentieth century when practitioners in various healthcare fields took it up. For example, Mosey, an occupational therapist, defined use of self as:

> A planned interaction with another person in order to alleviate fear or anxiety, provide reassurance, obtain necessary information, provide infor-mation, give advice, and assist the other individual to gain more apprecia-tion of, more expression of, and more functional use of his or her latent inner resources. (Mosey, 1986, p. 199)

Box 1.1 Research: therapeutic use of self

Sleater and Scheiner (2020) conducted semi-structured interviews with humanistic and integrative therapists about their lived experience of the use of self. They analysed the transcripts and developed a model based on three themes:

1. Connection is the use of oneself to develop and cultivate a therapeutic attachment– for instance, through self-disclosure (which can be overt, inadvertent or unconscious). There is a balance to be struck between spontaneously being oneself and thoughtfully tailoring disclosures, depending on the circumstances and counter-transferences involved.
2. Awareness involves being attuned to what passes between therapist and client in the relationship (embodied or unconscious). Such attune-ment is grounded in mutuality and awareness of vulnerability. With experience, therapists learn to use the self in such a way as to become authentically involved and emotionally vulnerable, while also maintain-ing appropriate boundaries.
3. Wellness involves the requirement for therapists to take care of them-selves in order to be able to effectively use themselves. It helps to have an expanded awareness of our compassionate 'internal supervisor', to keep track of and enable healthy decisions.

Virginia Satir (1967) was perhaps the first to fully articulate its relevance to psychotherapy. In different writings throughout the 1980s, she challenged practitioners to shift from being merely skilled 'technicians' (whose primary focus is on skills and techniques) or 'clinicians' (who combine skills with practice-acquired wisdom) to become 'magicians' who use skills, practise wisdom and the use of self. In other words, she was urging therapists to move beyond just 'doing' to embrace 'being' by becoming more self-aware and attending to the therapeutic use of self:

> I have learned that when I am fully present with the patient or family, I can move therapeutically with much greater ease. I can simultaneously reach the depths to which I need to go, and at the same time honor the fragility, the power, and the sacredness of life in the other. When I am in touch with myself, my feelings, my thoughts, with what I see and hear, I am growing toward becoming a more integrated self. I am more congruent, I am more "whole," and I am able to make greater contact with the other person. (Satir, [1987] 2013, p. 25)

Satir goes on to liken the therapist's use of self to a musical instrument that requires care, fine tuning and sensitive handling when played:

> I think of the instrument as the self of the therapist: how complete one is as a person, how well one cares for oneself, how well one is tuned in to oneself, and how competent one is at one's craft. (Satir, 2013, p. 25)

Adapting and adjusting therapeutic responses

Research consistently emphasises the importance of adapting therapy to the individual. 'The clinical reality is that no single psychotherapy is effective for all patients and situations no matter how good it is for some' (Norcross and Wampold, 2018, p. 1893).

As therapists, we make deliberate choices about how and when to intervene. We continuously adapt and pace the levels of care, formality, spontaneity, emotionality, challenge, support, self-disclosure, intimacy, control and directiveness we offer (see Figure 1.1).

Early in the therapeutic relationship, we might listen in a reserved, empathic way as part of engaging a client in therapy. Then, as therapy develops, we might raise the element of challenge by adopting a more muscular, directive approach. These subtle moment-to-moment adjustments also occur when we meet clients outside the therapy context (at the supermarket, say, or on social media). How should we be? How much of ourselves should we show?

In an introductory contracting session, we may be quite formal and boundaried to show that we are a trustworthy 'professional'. Later, we might

Empathic support ⟷ Challenge

Separation, distance ⟷ Connection, intimacy

Self-containment ⟷ Self-disclosure

Non-directive permissiveness ⟷ Directive control

Formality ⟷ Spontaneity

Slowing stillness ⟷ Activating vibrancy

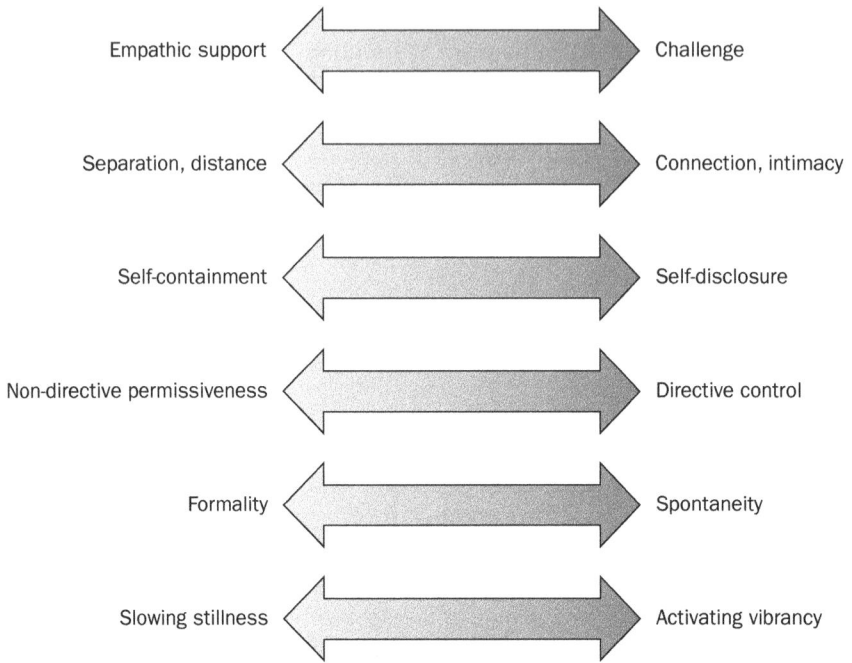

Figure 1.1   Choices of therapeutic 'use of self'

reveal more of ourselves as a 'person' as trust and intimacy grow. Sometimes, we find ourselves being lively and activating; at other times, our pacing may be slower in order to offer clients a space of stillness. For instance, Erskine (2020b) describes his therapeutic relationship with 'Violet' where he changed his approach to become 'softer and quieter' and *be* with her in her silence. This allowed her to be more present to herself. That he changed in response to her was pivotal as it demonstrated to Violet that she could have had an impact on her world.

There's no magic formula here. It's about exercising our professional judgement, minute-by-minute, in response to what we responsively assess is needed.

There is always choice. While our actual *doing* (our intervention) may derive from science, the choices we make regarding the timing, manner, balance and intensity of our intervention are all rooted in our *being* and in our 'art'.

From science we have learned that certain interventions work well with certain people. Norcross and Wampold (2018) summarise the evidence base concerning relationships and responsiveness, and suggest that a complementary style of interaction can be helpful – for instance, less directiveness is beneficial for highly reactive/resistant clients, while more guidance and direction is needed for less reactive clients. Research also favours direct responses to specific client requests concerning therapy preferences, including cultural adaptations. However, research consistently shows the importance of adapting therapy and responding authentically and sensitively to each person individually, depending on their needs. There are no easy recipes; our art is in the choice and balance of ingredients.

In the dialogue in Box 1.2, the therapist initially contains his (potentially destructive) responses, holding himself back in order to enable the client to be more present. Recognising that something delicate is emerging, he doesn't want to inhibit Jenny's process by inserting his own reactions too strongly or quickly. 'Among the ways that any clinician can do harm is to impose her or his viewpoint on the client rather than supporting the client to develop the viewpoint(s) that serves the client's therapy goals and life commitments' (Reinkraut, 2008, pp. 20–1). Then, the therapist becomes more present himself when disclosing that he is open to her anger. He

---

Box 1.2 Case example: adapting responses

Jenny (client): When I woke up this morning, I didn't really want to come to therapy.

Therapist: (*Initially, the therapist feels some irritation and wants to say, 'If you don't want to be here, you don't need to come.' But he has enough self-awareness to contain this reaction – which he recognises as coming from a rejected child place – to stay with Jenny's experience.*)

What was happening for you in that moment?

Jenny: Often I wake up feeling angry, I want to say 'no', I just want to stay in bed and do what *I* want to do. But then my grown-up responsible part of me gives me a shake and reminds me what I 'should' be doing. I knew I needed to be here.

Therapist: (*He notes that she sees that responsible part as 'adult' whereas he believes it's Jenny's 'good girl' part. He doesn't correct her or share his different interpretation. He stays with her experience and just reflects back.*)

I'm hearing that part of you didn't want to be here; but another part got you moving and told you to be responsible and go to therapy.

Jenny: Of course I want to be here. I really value you and our work together.

Therapist: And what about that angry part? Are you open to working with that part a bit more?

(*Jenny nods hesitantly, so the therapist proceeds gently, not wishing to overwhelm or scare her further.*)

I noticed that when you initially described your waking angry part you had your fists closed. Can you do that for me now and really try to exaggerate that moment?

(*Both therapist and client hold their fists up tightly like boxers. The therapist does it with her to normalise it and 'be-with' her in that place.*)

Initially, her arms are still a bit loose and floppy, and she looks feeble. He encourages her to put some 'muscle' and force into them. He provocatively – but gently – pushes against her arm until she holds her fists strongly.)

If those fists could be talking, what would they say?

(Conscious of the risk that Jenny might be experiencing him as being too aggressive like her father, he keeps his tone curious and gentle. Later, he will recognise that he occasionally comes across too forcefully, which elicits her compliance, and he wonders if at those points he is inadvertently replaying her history. He takes his initial irritated response to supervision.)

Jenny: (**Hesitantly**) Go away? I'll fight you if you try to make me.

Therapist: Can you say that again with more conviction? 'Go away. I'll fight you if you try to make me!'

(Therapist mirrors Jenny's behaviour and words but takes out the questioning tone and invites her to say it again more loudly.)

Jenny: Go away! I'll fight you if you try to make me!

Therapist: What's happening for you right now? You're looking thoughtful.

Jenny: I'm feeling strong. And I'm remembering my childhood. My father and brother used to fight like this all the time. I couldn't stand up to them. I never did this. When I tried, I was punished and told 'girls don't fight'. I'd end up hiding in my wardrobe.

Therapist: *(Now the therapist is feeling compassion for the 'good', scared little girl who was never allowed to express herself.)* Like you told yourself not to be angry this morning?

(Jenny nods slowly with this new insight.)

But what if I said that I'm okay with you expressing your anger here and that I like to see it?

Jenny: It's all right for me to be angry?

(The therapist smiles softly and nods encouragingly.)

Now there's a new concept!

carefully reflects back Jenny's words, all the time becoming more directive as he coaches her to express herself.

We can borrow the concept of 'titration' from the field of chemistry to better understand how we adapt our use of self and constantly make subtle adjustments. Titration involves continuously measuring and adjusting a concentration of a substance, one drop at a time, to bring about a given effect. The 'substance' in the case of therapy is our self. (The client too will be engaged in their own titration, adapting their response with us.)

The somatic therapist, Peter Levine, explains how he engages titration with his trauma work by exposing a client slowly to increasing amounts of trauma-related distress to build up their tolerance:

I started to develop a systematic approach where the person could gradually access these energies and these body sensations ... [a] little bit at a time. It's a process that I call titration ... The image that I use is that of mixing an acid and a base together. If you put them together, there can be an explosion. But if you take it one drop at a time, there is a little fizzle and eventually the system neutralizes ... I use this analogy to describe one of the techniques I use in my work with trauma patients. You're not actually exposing the person to a trauma—you're restoring the responses that were overwhelmed, which is what led to the trauma in the first place. (quotation from Levine in Yalom and Yalom, 2010)

Building the therapeutic alliance

Research has repeatedly demonstrated a robust relationship between therapy outcomes and the therapeutic alliance (emerging collaborative partnership). Relational factors are central to therapy's effectiveness (Cooper, 2008) and the working alliance is often predictive of therapy outcomes (Norcross, 2011; Norcross and Karpiak, 2017). The better the relationship, the better the outcomes, regardless of therapy approach/modality, client characteristics, culture/country and so on (see Box 1.3).

Box 1.3 Research: alliance and treatment outcomes

Flückiger et al. (2018) offer a major meta-analysis of 295 independent studies published over 40 years (mostly from North American and European countries), encompassing more than 30,000 patients engaged in in-person or internet-based psychotherapy. The relation between alliance and outcomes was investigated using a three-level meta-analysis. The results suggest that mutual collaboration and negotiated partnership between therapist and client are hugely significant aspects of psychotherapy across various approaches. The benefits of a strong working alliance for therapy appear to apply irrespective of outcome measures, treatment approaches, patient characteristics and national setting; they apply whether therapy is in-person or internet-mediated. Therapeutic success can be reliably predicted when there is agreement on therapy goals and when therapists respond early to client's motivational readiness to engage or change. A strong alliance is found to result from negotiation and also from prompt action to address any ruptures in the alliance. The authors recommend regular assessments of the alliance during therapy, arguing that this can help pick up unsatisfactory progress and the possibility of premature terminations.

The therapeutic alliance can be understood as the mutual partnership that, while emerging over time, is also infused with each moment of therapy. It expresses itself as a warm emotional bond where the therapist is responsive and encourages collaboration. Enacted in different ways, it reveals itself in the form of mutual respect and trust. As therapy unfolds, the client feels seen and supported; they sense that the therapist is on their side.

The process of building the alliance starts with contracting. Here, aims/goals/processes are agreed and key information is given about the collaborative responsibility for the therapy. The client needs to have a sense of what they are aiming for.

Lack of progress or improvement after the first few appointments should act as a warning to therapists, encouraging them to broaden the discussion with the client about the nature of the goals and processes of therapy (Miller et al., 2005). Forming a solid therapeutic relationship is crucial, for it enables therapist and client to work together through those more challenging moments of therapy when one or other wants to withdraw (Finlay, 2016a, 2019).

The dialogue in Box 1.4 shows the therapist and client discussing the client's use of a 'food-thought-feelings diary'. With alliance-building to the fore, the therapist attempts to move forward with the scheduled treatment plan, but realises she needs to engage the client by responding more directly to the client's concerns and mutually exploring obstacles, without losing track of the therapy focus/goals.

Box 1.4 Case example: adapting to engage

Therapist: So how did you manage with writing your food diary last week?

Client: Well, I did it the first day and then somehow it didn't happen. I couldn't see the point if I'm honest. I just don't have the time. I know my diet is s***.

Therapist: Yes, it's hard to write your diary when you have so much going on. I'm sorry I didn't make the point of doing it clear enough last week. It's not about examining your diet as such; it's more about seeing if there are any patterns to your bingeing.

Client: Well, I already know that it happens in the evening after work when I'm tired and just slump in front of the TV after my meal. Then it starts.

Therapist: Your bingeing? (*Client nods.*) Every night?

Client: Maybe two nights a week it's really bad; two nights maybe are good. The rest of the time I overeat but don't do a major binge.

Therapist: What does a 'major binge' look like?

Client: umm ... It's a little embarrassing.

Therapist: I'm not judging you, just trying to understand your experience.

> Client: Well ... um ... last night it was six mince pies and ... um ... a 2-litre tub of ice-cream.
>
> Therapist: Have you any idea what triggered that impulse last night and what you felt before, during and after?
>
> Client: After I hated myself. Before and during, I didn't really feel anything – just the craving.
>
> Therapist: The fact that you don't binge every night suggests that something else is probably going on for you when you get that craving. That's one of the things we need to try to figure out together. It's possible that feeling suddenly angry/frustrated or anxious could trigger the binge.
>
> Client: I dunno. Never thought about it like that.
>
> Therapist: Given you're finding writing the whole diary a pain, how about just jotting down any thoughts and feelings you have just at the point when you become aware that you have a craving to binge? Would you be able to do that – just for one week?
>
> Client: I guess so. That sounds more doable.
>
> Therapist: What might stop you doing it?
>
> Client: I may not know what to say.
>
> Therapist: Just a sentence or two about your thinking or feeling would be good, even if it's 'I'm feeling blank'.

Contact-in-relationship

Our use of self is not something we *do* to the client. Instead, it emerges within the specific relationship and evolves as we adapt – over time – to the client's needs and the relational context while they adapt to us. This distinguishes our work from that of digital 'therapist bots' – robots – which formulaically follow predetermined protocols and lack the self-awareness to adjust the approach taken.

What is beneficial for one client could be problematic, even harmful, for another. Reaching out to comfort someone by holding their hand can be experienced as a lovely, supportive gesture. But in another context, or with another individual, it could be interpreted as patronising, invasive or even threatening. While a forceful challenge may help inspire a client to break with past patterns and behave differently, it could also nudge a client into a freeze or flight response. Our art involves attuning to the needs of both client and the therapeutic relationship towards evaluating when and how to intervene (see Box 1.5).

The judgements we make regarding our levels of closeness/distance flow from attending to the therapeutic relationship *and* responding to the client's cluster of relational, developmental and social needs. At any given moment,

---

Box 1.5 Practical application: titrating levels of intervention

Wosket (2017) offers five levels of intervention, all of them dependent on the degree of mutuality of disclosure the client can tolerate and benefit from. Underpinning this logic is the notion that there is no 'right' intervention. Rather, we try to attune ourselves to the needs of a specific client and choose the degree of relationality and disclosure that is likely to be most helpful. Which option we choose depends on our own way of being (and level of self-awareness) and the relational context.

Level 1 = You haven't said as much, but I wonder if you are feeling quite vulnerable today …

Level 2 = It seems hard for you to talk about your feelings today and yet I sense that you are upset …

Level 3 = I notice we're not talking about your feelings today and when that's happened before it's often when you have been very frightened or very sad. If you're feeling like that today, I'd like to help if I can …

Level 4 = It's hard for me to listen to you talk like this when I feel that your words may be covering up a lot of sadness and loneliness. I know that sometimes it's difficult for you to let me see you're upset and to let yourself be comforted there …

Level 5 = I feel like I want to gather you up in my arms and comfort you. (2017, pp. 55–6)

---

we need to determine how open or closed to making a connection the client is, whether internally (with themselves) or externally (with the therapist) (Erskine, 2015). The aim is a dual one: to facilitate contact with the client and also to enable the client to be in-relationship with different parts of themselves. This is what is meant by 'contact-in-relationship' through attunement, involvement and empathy (Erskine et al., 1999; Moursund and Erskine, 2004).[1]

Therapy begins as we attune to the client's needs. This includes recognising what areas they are open to exploring initially. Our access to their experience at this point is through the relationship and how we're experiencing them. For example, are they pushing us away or are they asking for something? Then, as (mutual) trust builds, the work inches progressively into more painful or difficult areas. The client is encouraged to connect more deeply with both the therapist and with their own relational needs.

Box 1.6 Case example: contact-in-relationship

Client: My father was like a Nazi; we were all terrified of him. I remember that I was strange already back then. I started to avoid social contacts and had my own world ... In my world, everything was fine.

Therapist: You were strange?

Client: Yes, I felt different from others. I didn't tell you about my inner world. For a long time I felt that you would think I am crazy and will put me in a psychiatric hospital.

Therapist: So you were very afraid of your father, who was often drunk and violent. And at that time you started to live on the other side where everything was OK. So this 'other world' in which everything was fine helped you to survive and keep you sane in the 'insane world'.

(*The therapist acknowledges and validates the client's coping mechanisms, which promotes the client's awareness and acceptance.*)

Client: Yes, it helped me to survive, definitely.

Therapist: (*With a kind and compassionate voice*) Let's appreciate this strategy of a five-year-old that helped you to survive.

(*Another validation, which helps the client to experience self-compassion.*)

Client: I feel touched; I never thought about this in this way ...

Therapist: Maybe this strategy was the most clever strategy to survive in a family where there was no one to hold on to ... (*short pause*) What do you feel now?

(*The therapist conveys the normalisation of the client's past coping strategy.*)

Client: Feel like I would embrace this younger part of me ... telling him I love him and care for him.

Therapist: Just do this; take your time.

Client: (*Crying*) I feel sad for what I have gone through ... (*Pause*) Now I understand that having my own world actually saved my life ... I also understand that I am not there any more. I am safe now. (Žvelc & Žvelc, 2021, pp. 139–40)

This contact-in-relationship is demonstrated in the dialogue in Box 1.6, where the therapist takes a compassionate approach to encourage the client to connect with a younger part of themselves (Žvelc and Žvelc, 2021). At the start, the pace is slow; the therapist listens, attunes and validates the client's experience and offers time for reflection (attunement). This enables the client to contact their grief and acknowledge the value of their own coping mechanisms. By compassionately asking about the client's way of coping and surviving (enquiry), the therapist is modelling acceptance and being present to the grief, which in turn encourages the client to honour (or even let go of) their protective mechanisms (involvement). By 'normalising' what has happened, the therapist helps the client appreciate and embrace the defensive strategies which have helped them cope. (NB: Italics changed from the original.)

Theoretical influences on use of self

Different theoretical frameworks dictate different types of 'doing' in therapy and promote specific ways of 'being'. For example, in traditional psychoanalysis, therapists typically adopt a neutral stance, receiving projections and transferences, which they then interpret. Cognitive-behavioural therapists take a more directive, psychoeducational coaching approach. Person-centred humanistic therapists are more non-directive and open, bringing their personhood to the fore as they embrace empathetic affirmation while practitioners who lean towards gestalt and existential work may be more directive and/or disclosing of their own reactions.

In practice, such theoretical differences lose their sharpness when therapists take a developmental–relational, systemic and/or integrative (or pluralistic) stance. A contemporary relational, body-focused psychodynamic therapist is likely to have more in common with an existentially orientated humanistic therapist than a traditional Freudian one. A relational cognitive behavioural therapist (CBT) would probably find more commonality with a humanistic/psychodynamic transactional analyst who works with the 'Adult' ego state, instead of another CBT practitioner who follows set protocols.

Research backs up this notion that theoretical modalities do not necessarily determine the therapist's style. Reupert (2008), an Australian researcher and family therapist, interviewed sixteen participants from various theoretical backgrounds (including psychoanalysis, CBT, humanistic therapy, and family therapy) to explore what they brought of themselves to the therapeutic encounter. Some participants described suppressing all personal aspects of self and using their professional parts only, while others identified the self as an inevitable presence permeating every aspect of their work. Interestingly, use of self did not seem to depend on the therapeutic approach they espoused.

Rowan and Jacobs (2002) identify three ways in which the self can be used in therapy: instrumental, authentic and transpersonal. These form a continuum that cuts across traditional theoretical boundaries. In each 'possibility', different assumptions are made regarding the therapist's level of self-awareness and the depth of relational connection with the client.

- The *instrumental self* sees the therapist applying skills and manualised treatments and techniques in goal-orientated ways. Cognitive-behavioural and systemic practitioners, and those engaged in brief therapy, primarily engage this mode, although others (including psychodynamic therapists) can also work this way.

- The *authentic self* involves more spontaneous person-to-person interactions, with active, mutual exploration, self-disclosure and acknowledgement of the co-created therapeutic relationship. While humanistic approaches most clearly engage this way of being, so do other relational-orientated therapies.
- The *transpersonal self* represents therapists who are attentive to what happens 'between and beyond' their own self and that of the client. The therapist tries to let go of assumptions about therapeutic goals to focus on merged boundaries. For example, they might explore the notion of 'collective unconscious', or the idea of 'deep empathy', or the spiritual concept of 'altered states of consciousness'. Some psychoanalytic and existential practitioners operate at this 'soulful' level, as do systemic practitioners who work with intergenerational processes.

Cultural influences on the use of self

When therapeutic use of self is seen through a sociocultural or diversity/ difference lens, wider issues concerning professional ethics come into focus.

First, there is the impact of our own cultural background on our values, assumptions and behaviours – for instance, how our values/beliefs lead us to dress and behave in certain ways. But it goes deeper. Perhaps these values lead us to be drawn to or avoid working with certain groups of people. Are you aware of any lurking prejudices you might have about the client's sexuality, ethnicity, race, class, religion, appearance, lifestyle habits, disability and cultural beliefs?

Second, with a sociocultural lens, it's clear that it is insufficient to simply treat the individual in isolation. Instead, we must see the individual in their wider social contexts (be that family, friends, work, culture) and adapt our treatments accordingly. At the very least, appreciating the context gives us an idea of what is going to be meaningful and realistic for the person to aim for.

To give a specific example, we might wish to titrate our levels of intimacy and use of touch. But is touch going to be acceptable to the client? How might they react? Is touch with the opposite sex taboo (given their age, family history, upbringing and both ethnic and class background)? It also works the other way. Might you feel uncomfortable with a new client who tries to hug you goodbye or sends you kisses in a text? These aren't just individual preferences. It's about cultural norms (both the therapy/institutional culture and in the wider society). As Amari (2020, p. 9) notes, a 'relational use of self' involves a 'network of relationships in which practitioners and clients are embedded'.

Therapists are expected to be ambassadors for diversity, inclusion and social justice; there is an ethical obligation[2] to become more aware of the experiences of marginalised groups of people, be sensitive and respectful of others, and to challenge inequalities and discrimination. As these ideas are enshrined in most (if not all) professional codes of practice, we are invited to embrace them in our therapeutic use of self. In their statement on diversity and equalities, for instance, The United Kingdom Council for Psychotherapy (UKCP) states its mission to promote:

> an active engagement with difference ... that allows competing and diverse ideas and perspectives on what it means to be human to be considered, respected, and valued. UKCP is committed to addressing issues of prejudice and discrimination in relation to the mental well being, political belief, gender and gender identity, sexual preference or orientation, disability, marital or partnership status, race, nationality, ethnic origin, heritage identity, religious or spiritual identity, age or socio-economic class of individuals and groups. (UKCP, 2017)

In other words, we are professionally obliged to cultivate a reflexive awareness of our attitudes, developing a cultural sensitivity and some cultural knowledge regarding each client we see (see Box 1.7). We might even be called to engage explicitly in anti-oppressive practice. We need to do this,

---

Box 1.7 Practical application: cultivating cultural competence

The aim of cultural competence is to increase awareness of difference/diversity while minimising cultural barriers in communications with clients and colleagues. While it is impossible to fully understand every client's cultural background, it is still possible to show sensitivity to, and openness about, what seems important to them. The following research-supported guidelines (adapted from Soto et al., 2019) may be helpful:

1. Explore the impact of each client's cultural background/experience trying to actively learn their perspectives.
2. See the individual in their complexity rather than reducing them to stereotypes.
3. Aim to understand both internal and external struggles which are created by different social identities (gender, race, ethnicity, religion, sexuality ...).
4. Ensure therapy adapts to clients' cultural identities/values.
5. Cultivate awareness of own cultural values, assumptions and potential prejudices. Assume your cultural perspective is different from the client's.
6. Consult colleagues who have the specific cultural experience/knowledge to help interventions be more culturally appropriate.
7. Conduct therapy in the client's preferred language (maybe utilising interpreters with appropriate training/cultural knowledge).

not out of a political correctness, but because it concerns our ethical integrity and humanity in relationships both inside and outside the therapy room. And it's also worth noting that Norcross and Wampold have thoroughly reviewed the evidence base and conclude that 'therapists expressing cultural humility and … cultural responsiveness [show] markedly improve[d] client engagement, retention, and eventual treatment outcome' (2018, p. 1902).

Case study

Ania is a single mother with a four-year-old daughter called Zofia. Polish by birth, she immigrated to the UK and married a British man who left her when she was pregnant. Without social support, it was challenging for Ania to bring up her little girl alone. She was helped by a network of new friends she made at a mother-and-toddler group. When the Coronavirus pandemic and 'lockdown' hit, Ania and her child became isolated and mutually dependent. When lockdown was lifted and it was time for Zofia to start going to nursery school, Zofia refused to go. Her behaviour became problematic: she began wetting the bed and had frequent tantrums. Ania herself became anxious and felt a failure as a mother. She approached her local women's Counselling Centre and was given ten sessions of weekly individual counselling. The columns below shows the progress of the therapy and the counsellor's use of self at the different stages.

Table 1.1

The Story of Ania's Therapy	Analysis of Therapeutic Use of Self
Contracting: In their initial phone call to arrange an appointment, the counsellor offers Ania the choice between online and in-person work. Ania expresses her preference for online counselling, explaining that she's still anxious about going outside into the world. However, she also admits to feeling quite anxious about going online as she isn't technologically savvy. The counsellor talks her through the process, and they have a quick try-out of Zoom to make sure she knows what is required.	*Therapist use of self can be seen from the first moment of contracting when care is taken to contract for online work. Her* ***attuned attentiveness*** *to Ania's needs concerning her worries about both going outside and doing online work is important.* *The counsellor needs to feel comfortable with online work too.*
During contracting, care is taken to ensure that Ania has a safe, private therapy space at home. It is agreed that Zofia could be looked after by the next-door neighbour an hour a week. As this would be the first time in several months that mother and daughter are apart, this step alone proves a helpful therapy intervention. They initially contract for five sessions, with the aim of reviewing Ania's progress at the end of that period when they will decide whether to continue for a further five sessions.	*The counsellor understands the importance of Ania having a safe, private space at home to work in. She is creative when she takes the slightly unusual step of inviting Ania to have a quick 'go' at Zoom before the first session of therapy. She does this in order to reduce Ania's anxiety.*

(Continued)

Table 1.1   (Continued)

The Story of Ania's Therapy	Analysis of Therapeutic Use of Self
Weeks 1–2: In the first session, the counsellor listens empathically to Ania's story and the challenges she has faced as a single mother. Together, they recognise the ways in which Ania's current anxiety and profound loneliness are related to the existential threat posed by Coronavirus and the recent isolation of lockdown.	*The counsellor's 'use of self' here is largely* **'instrumental'**. *The aim is to build the alliance and modify behaviours given the problematic environment. While a problem-solving, psychoeducational approach is adopted, the therapist still maintains an empathetic, relational stance which moves into an* **'authentic'** *approach.*
The counsellor's initial formulation centres on the 'understandable separation anxiety' experienced by both mother and daughter, who (the counsellor suggests) have become overly attached (enmeshed?). Together they devise a programme that encourages Ania and Zofia to spend increasing periods apart over the next few weeks. The counsellor suggests that Zofia attends a play group and spends time with different friends.	
Week 3: Ania expresses fear of going outside in the world post-lockdown and the counsellor offers some anxiety management and self-care advice.	*The counsellor is careful to be compassionate rather than judgemental. She seeks to counteract Ania's sense that she is somehow 'at fault' for creating the separation issues. She takes care to 'normalise' Ania's experience. As part of her relational stance (in 'authentic' mode), the counsellor admits to having anxieties herself. The timing of this normalising self-disclosure is important. Rather than share this information about herself at the start of therapy, she waited until she was more confident about how the disclosure would be received.*
Ania then starts to cry in response to feeling that the therapist is being so nice to her and that she doesn't deserve it. She feels 'at fault'; she sees herself as a bad mother who has 'caused' the separation anxiety in her child. The counsellor emphasises that many parents are likely to be experiencing some separation anxieties at this time. She encourages Ania to connect more with her friends from the mother-and-toddlers group. She also briefly shares her own fears of going outside to public areas.	
Week 4: Over time, it becomes easier for mother and daughter to be apart. The counsellor and Ania discuss creative ways to introduce the idea of nursery school to Zofia and to associate it with positive things. They decide it would be helpful to walk past the nursery gates each day on the way to the park and talk about the fun things Zofia will be doing when she starts going again in a few months' time.	*The counsellor and Ania have formed a good alliance and, at this point, are working well together to explore the problems and solutions.*
On their fifth session review, Ania expresses feeling grateful and that she definitely wants to continue for the remaining five sessions. She shares that she doesn't know how she's going to manage without the support of her therapist once their work together is over. Concerned that Ania might be getting too dependent on her, the counsellor suggests that it might be helpful to have the remaining sessions every other week, so that Ania can gain confidence in her own coping abilities.	*Increasingly, the counsellor is encouraging Ania to draw on her own resources and ideas for problem solving.* *The counsellor tries to manage the risk of Ania becoming too dependent on her by engaging some distancing strategies. Suggesting that the latter sessions should take place every two weeks helps Ania to become more self-reliant.*
Sessions 6–10 and ending: In the last five sessions, the focus is on consolidation of the progress made with Zofia's (and Ania's) independence and socialisation. They continue to work on developing Ania's resources to cope and consider ways she can live a more fulfilled life.	*The celebration of Zofie's and Ania's progress offers important validation. By focusing on her wider social supports and life-after-therapy, Ania is reminded of her ability to manage without her therapist.*
Ending: In the last session, Ania and the counsellor review their therapy experience and celebrate Ania's progress in managing both her own anxiety and the separation from her daughter. They talk about the future and how Ania can continue to use her self-care and anxiety management resources.	

Critical reflections

> Expertise is less about mastering the therapy method and more about the relationship, responsiveness, and commitment to improvement. (Norcross and Karpiak, 2017, p. 73)

This chapter has emphasised the complexity of our therapeutic use of self, highlighting how we negotiate complex relational–social boundaries between client and therapist. The science and art of therapy are expressed in the clinical judgements we make regarding when and how to intervene as we fluidly engage varying levels of support/challenge; separation/distance; connection/intimacy; self-containment/self-disclosure; non-directiveness/directiveness, and more.

As I reflect on the complexity of this process, I am awed by the artful way we continually negotiate subtle experiential and relational layers. I am reminded about Storr's words that 'psychotherapy will always remain more of an art than a science' (1990, p. 69).

When we 'go with the relational flow' and trust the therapeutic process, the use of self is like Satir's deft playing of a finely tuned musical instrument. Together, client and therapist find themselves immersed in a duet of co-created music. Yet, while moments of connection can feel magical, our craft skills and strategic techniques can be reflected upon, observed and learned as the micro-communications identified in the case study above.

If we are using ourselves as our primary tool of therapy, it is critically important for us to be reflexively self-aware of our being and doing (see Box 1.8) and to examine our approach with an ethical–professional lens. Without such awareness, therapists run the risk of reproducing reductionist,

---

Box 1.8 Practical application: reflecting on one's self in therapy

Thinking about your own practice, it's worth taking time to reflect on how you use your self. Hint: think about your *being* and *doing*. You may find the following self-inventory questions helpful (adapted from Edwards and Bess, 1998; Dewane, 2006):

- Why do I like being a therapist? What personal needs are met?
- What special qualities or abilities do I offer clients?
- How do my beliefs affect the way I work?
- What traumas or life challenges have shaped my worldview and might be triggered in work with clients?

- How easy is it for me to just 'be with' clients and not rush into 'doing' or 'performing'?
- How does my theoretical model of practice influence my work?
- How do I adjust my levels of intimacy, disclosure, spontaneity, support and challenge with different clients?
- How do I react if a client resists, or is critical of, their work with me?

habitual, routinised ways of working. Even worse, therapists' needs and power dynamics may be unhealthily acted out, turning care into harm, and we don't want therapy to repeat patterns from individuals' histories of manipulation, violence and/or powerlessness (Finlay, 2019).

Part of what we need to factor in with our use of self is the wider relational–social context. It's not just about responding to the individual. We need to recognise the complexity and impact of the client's social–cultural identities and how that mixes with ours. If we are to play ourselves like a musical instrument, we need to consider the person we are in a duet with, and understand the acoustics of where the music is to be played.

In short, we need to move away from a view of the use of self as an internal/individual act towards seeing it as a dynamic, ethical and reflexive process that is profoundly relational (Amari, 2020).

Discussion questions

1. 'Use of self is both our "science" and our "art".' What does this mean?
2. Write five statements starting with 'I am' describing the nature of your being when you are with clients. Analyse how you show these being aspects in your everyday doing practice.
3. How different are you in different contexts? For example, how does your 'being' change when you are with different individual clients who have different backgrounds; or when you encounter a client in a different public space; or when you work in-person versus online?

Resources

Book: *The Therapeutic Use of Self* by Val Wosket. Classic, seminal book exploring the topic.

Book: *On Being a Master Therapist* by Jeffrey Kottler and Jon Carlson. Compelling read as these master therapists dialogue in an informal, brutally frank way while drawing on a wealth of resources. They nail the key ingredients for being an accomplished therapist.

Book: *Integrative Psychotherapy: The Art and Science of Relationship* by Janet Moursund and Richard Erskine. Readable text which beautifully explains the theory/practice of integrative therapy focused on the therapeutic relationship. The verbatim transcript of a therapy session demonstrates their ideas in practice.

Lecture: The role of self in psychotherapy (presented by Brandy Klingman). Available at: www.youtube.com/watch?v=ooOGOgTgSOU

Video: Interview with Irvin Yalom on the Art of psychotherapy. Available at: www.youtube.com/watch?v=ZdTFqpltd8I (I recommend watching any/all of his demonstration videos).

Notes

1. The model here is an integrative psychotherapy one, drawing on several theories, including transactional analysis and developmental theory.Other therapists drawing from different theoretical approaches may understand the process differently. For example, some gestaltists use the concept of 'contact' slightly differently.
2. We also have legal obligations. For instance, in the UK, the Equality Act of 2010 prohibits unlawful discrimination, harassment and victimisation.

TWO

BEING WELCOMING

A therapeutic practice which does not feature hospitality at its core is not ethical. (Manu Bazzano, 2015)

Therapy literature discusses the concept of hospitality in various ways, even if the word 'hospitality' is not used. More typically, the therapeutic relationship and therapist presence are described as 'welcoming', 'respectful' and 'inviting'. Therapists strive to create safe, therapeutic spaces where clients feel held, accepted, affirmed, supported, resourced, empathised with – and challenged to grow.

I actually like the concept of 'therapist-as-host', which captures a sense of gift-giving, and our striving for openness, attentiveness and the importance we attach to respecting, caring for and honouring the other. Above all else, we want to create a safe, boundaried yet spacious, permission-giving space, one that allows vulnerability and offers some hope (Finlay, 2019).

This chapter starts by exploring how we might *be* – and what it is we *do* – when welcoming clients into therapy. It then moves on to consider how we set about creating (physical and emotional) spaces, that are both safe and welcoming. Following the template set up in Chapter 1, it ends with a case study, critical reflections and discussion questions.

Welcoming clients into therapy

At the heart of a welcoming attitude to the Other is a willingness to attune and be responsive to his or her unique needs and wants. If we welcomed a guest into our home with a drink, we would find out what he or she specifically wants – we would not offer every guest coffee, two sugars, no milk. A welcoming attitude also means being responsive to the changing needs or wants of the Other. (Cooper, 2009, pp. 122–3)

Welcoming happens the first moment we invite a prospective client into the therapy, whether it's on the phone, by email, etc. When they eventually come into our therapy space, we then try to be appropriately warm and welcoming: a gracious, generous 'host' offering a special kind of spacious hospitality:

> The guest ... client comes seeking sanctuary, a safe place of protection where wounds can be carefully cleansed and healed. But where is the sanctuary, if not fundamentally in the heart of the host or therapist who is willing to face this living encounter and courageously open to it? (Kapitan, 2003, p. 74)

When a client first walks into our therapy room, they bring with them uncertainty, confusion and all their defensive structures. Why should they trust us? Why should they take the risk of exposing themselves to a relative stranger? What might enable them to open up, face their inner demons and join us in a process of exploration and discovery? What might stop them from committing to therapy? (Finlay, 2019).

Of course, much depends on the individuals concerned and the context. There are no set recipes to follow; different therapists evolve their own style of hospitality (or not).

In my own practice, I try to be warm and solicitous. I'll often begin by offering the prospective client coffee or tea (in addition to the fresh glass of water already waiting) and invite them to sit down.[1] Then I'll attempt to reassure them – for example, by acknowledging that first sessions are challenging, while emphasising my concern/interest in hearing their story. I try to listen deeply to their narrative in order to learn what is causing them to seek therapy. Because my work is usually long-term, my initial focus tends to be on developing the relationship needed before a client is ready to engage with in-depth work. This means that I avoid having a battery of 'assessment questions' lined up ready to be fired at them, although, of course, I check out priorities and safety/risk issues. I also make a point of leaving the formal contracting until our first hour is finished. Therapists doing brief therapy work are likely to be more focused and instrumental in this assessment session.

Moursund and Erskine remind us of the importance of 'tuning into' clients' needs:

> The client needs to know that his [sic] therapist is trustworthy and competent and has his best interests at heart ... He needs to know that he will be neither humiliated nor pathologized as he begins to reveal his most secret thoughts and feelings. (Moursund and Erskine, 2004, p. 109)

In the therapy context, hospitality reaches beyond courteous behaviour and towards attentiveness, openness and in-depth listening; it's about focused space/time and generosity of spirit. Henri Nouwen, a Dutch priest, scholar and healer, defines this hospitality as:

> The creation of a free space where the stranger can enter and become a friend instead of an enemy ... Hospitality is not to change people, but to offer them space where change can take place ... [leaving] open a wide spectrum of options for choice and commitment. (Nouwen, 1998, p. 49)

Nouwen proposes the creation of 'a friendly emptiness', where the other is 'free to sing their own songs, speak their own languages, dance their own dances' (1998, p. 49). Perhaps a new client, unfamiliar with the process of therapy, just wants to 'spill out' their story as soon as they arrive.

We might allow them that space before gently inviting or suggesting other possibilities. Similarly, for the client who expects us to 'get on with it' and 'sort' them out, we would acknowledge their need, while explaining what possibilities are realistically on offer.

This free space is not without paradoxes. 'Hospitality only really begins to happen', says Brown et al. (2011) 'when we press up against its limits'. The philosopher Derrida (2000) recognises how that hospitality is only possible when a host is 'master' in their own house. By being so, the host can set limits to safely contain their guests, and avoid being overrun by them. As Derrida notes, 'absolute' hospitality in the form of unconditional opening up of one's home while not asking for anything in return is excessive and unhelpful. Instead, psychotherapists need to embrace what Derrida calls 'practical hospitality'.

Pickering offers a revealing account of the limits of analytic hospitality:

> A patient, Amy, continually dreams of being in a waiting room, hotel foyer, at a train-station or bus stop, an in-between-place. Life feels like something not yet begun, yet at the same time is slipping away, out of grasp. Amy longs for a room in which she can stay put, be safe and simply be. She finds this in the therapy room and so hates leaving. She takes a long time to gather up her belongings and I become concerned lest the next patient arrives disturbing her session ... The act of hospitality has a limitation and Amy is acutely aware of this. (Pickering, 2019, p. 32)

When a client comes into your therapy space, are you aware of trying to create a welcoming atmosphere? Do you take their coat or offer a drink? Do you invite them to be seated or allow them to choose which chair they would prefer? What rituals do you engage to help your client (and yourself) feel more at ease and to show your attentiveness?

Box 2.1 Practical application: therapist hospitality

1. I felt at home with my therapist because he was at home with me. I am a Sikh who wears a turban. When we first met, my (white) therapist indicated that he had noticed I was a Sikh. I could tell he understood something about that. In fact, he has visited India more than I have! Just one week before someone made the mistake of assuming I was Muslim. They didn't realise how offended I was. But this therapist understood. I particularly appreciated the way he asked me how important my religion and being a British Punjabi was to me. I was able to explain that my family and community ties were important but that I wasn't devout. While alcohol is prohibited with some members of my community, most of my family/friends are very Westernised and liberal and I freely drink alcohol. My therapist didn't make assumptions and make me feel uncomfortable.

2. My supervisor always moves her clock to a place of my choosing so that I can see it better and has a cup of coffee waiting for me. In her simple act of preparing for my arrival and in the way she remembers my preferences (e.g., to keep control of my timekeeping), I feel cared for.

Our action – or inaction – matters as it carries meaning about the way we care for, and about, our clients. In Box 2.1, two clients describe what is important to them about their therapists' hospitality.

Welcoming physical spaces

First and foremost, a safe, welcoming physical space is one where privacy and confidentiality are assured. On no account should clients be put in a situation where they worry that someone outside could overhear. Otherwise, what makes a welcoming space depends on individual preferences and what is possible given the context. (Therapists working in agencies may have little choice about the physical environment they offer clients. Similarly, working remotely is a challenge because the therapy space is no longer under the control of the therapist-host – see Chapter 6.)

If some degree of choice is possible, there are five key areas to consider:

- **Decor** While research offers no consensus on the decor best suited to therapy sessions, both therapists and clients seem to lean towards environments that are calm, soft, warm, peaceful and welcoming (as opposed to harsh, cold, clinical, soulless and strictly functional (see Box 2.2).

> ## Box 2.2 Research: desirable counselling spaces?
>
> Nasar and Devlin (2011) found that softness, personalisation and order in counselling settings affects clients' experience of their therapist, including their perceived expertness, trustworthiness, and social attractiveness. Thirty colour photographs of psychotherapists' offices were viewed from the client's perspective. Ratings were obtained about the quality of care and comfort expected in each office (Study 1) and how qualified, bold and friendly the therapist in the office would be (Study 2). Additional studies examined the likelihood of choosing a therapist based on their office, and about what came to mind about the office, the therapist and the patient experience. The quality of care, comfort, therapist boldness, qualifications of the therapist and the likelihood that one would choose a therapist based on the office improved with more softness/personalisation and orderliness in the office.

- **Comfort for the client** Again, clients vary when it comes to what is 'comfortable'. While a soft chair one can sink into may be experienced as cosy, it can also be viewed as too informal. A choice of seating would be ideal. Research (e.g. Pearson and Wilson, 2012) suggests that seating with a view of the outside world (garden, space, nature) may offer clients relief from an intense focus on their inner worlds.
- **Safety issues** Attention to physical safety issues is further evidence of the therapist's caring attitude. We need to be aware of the dangers of slippery floors or steps, poor lighting, rough paths, or dirty, dusty or unsafe furniture. During pandemics, extra care needs to be taken with equipment and hygiene. Caring that clients do not get harmed, as distinct from being defensive about the possibility of being sued, is part of our hospitality.
- **Implicit communication** Artwork, soft furnishings and personal objects all communicate (implicitly and explicitly) something about the therapist and the work ahead. There's a balance to be struck. While a dingy, musty-smelling room may convey neglect, an overly 'perfect' space may be difficult for a client to relax in (Finlay, 2019). While most therapists tend to avoid personal self-disclosure – for example, family photographs on show – many favour the display of professional books. Research has shown that the display of credentials creates a more positive judgement of therapists by clients (Devlin et al., 2009).
- **Comfort for the therapist** Pearson and Wilson (2012) make the important point that since therapists are in their therapy room for hours at a time, they too need the room to be comfortable, grounding, and both emotionally and intellectually nourishing.

Welcoming emotional spaces

There are a number of subtle ways in which we can set about creating safe, welcoming emotional spaces for our clients, be it in-person or online (see also Chapter 6). It's important to recognise that what feels trustworthy (or threatening) varies from one individual to another at the outset. One client might find professional formality and neutrality reassuring; another might feel ill at ease with such an approach. While some clients readily relax into the (metaphorical) arms of a loving and nurturing therapist, others might find this engulfing or troubling. Whereas one client might feel safer and more at ease in an anonymous group, another might feel exposed and per-haps fearful of other group members' judgements.

The spirit of hospitality means ensuring that every time a client enters the therapy space, efforts are made to enable them to feel comfortable and trust the professional who demonstrates grace. Defining grace, Dobrin points to the Three Graces of Greek and Roman mythology, the sister god-desses who dispensed charm and beauty, bringing happiness through gen-tleness and refinement. He explains the concept further with reference to different religious traditions:

> In Judaism, grace is the spontaneous gift of affection, mercy and compas-sion. In Christianity, those who have been blessed by God are said to have received God's grace. In Chinese philosophy, when the heart feels empathy, in particular for the oppressed, a person has been touched by grace.

A gracious person is a graceful person, someone who at least attempts to not hurt others' feelings with clumsy words or thoughtless deeds. To live in grace is to walk lightly and leave the world blessed by your presence. (Dobrin, 2014)

Therapist's grace may, according to Heron, involve five attributes: warm concern for and acceptance of the other; openness and attunement to the other's experiential reality; a grasp of what the other needs for his or her essential flourishing; an ability to facilitate the realisation of such needs in the right manner and at the right time; and an authentic presence. 'This combination of concern, empathy, prescience, facilitation and genuineness is ... the spiritual heritage of mankind' (Heron, 2001, p. 11).

Erskine explains what graciousness involves in practice:

> Graciousness is built on respect ... Graciousness opens the possibility for dialogue through an honoring of the other's inherent "OKness." It is the real expression of "I'm OK, You're OK." We express graciousness through ... [the way we] emotionally talk to each other ... [it]is not about content but about the tone of voice, the cadence, and the affect that characterizes about 90% of our communication. (Erskine, 2008, p. 34)

In practice, a safe, welcoming emotional space is enabled through:

- the practical element of professional contracting;
- the attitudinal element of showing the client inviting acceptance;
- social recognition of clients' cultural heritage and values.

Contracting

Contracts have legal, practical and ethical functions. They're a concrete symbol of the hospitality offered and the intention to contain the therapy process safely and professionally. Simultaneously, the client makes a formal commitment to therapy.

In general terms, the contract (be it written or verbal) allows therapeutic boundaries to be agreed, set and maintained. The aim is to negotiate the terms under which therapy will unfold. Fees, the range or limits of confidentiality, and general arrangements regarding the timing and cancelling of appointments, all need to be established, along with various implicit and explicit procedures relevant to the context (private practice, public healthcare or the voluntary sector). It's also important to agree on the provisional focus and envisaged length of therapy, since both will have a major influence on the type of work attempted (Finlay, 2019). Contracts 'allow everyone involved to share aims, hopes and preferences' (Amis, 2017, p. 44).

Research findings (e.g. Cooper, 2008) stress the value of clear contracting, agreed goals and processes and key information-giving to ensure mutual responsibility for the therapy. The client needs to have a sense of what they are aiming for and what's allowed and/or welcomed. A solid therapeutic alliance acts as a platform on which therapist and client continue working together, even at those more challenging moments of therapy when one or other might want to withdraw. The contract offers a way of ensuring a holding–containing–boundaried frame, as Clarkson acknowledges:

> Punctuality, cooperation and variations in timing, changes in schedule, vacations, holidays and unavoidable absences need honest and appropriate explorations to ensure that the *vas* – the container of psychotherapy – is not leaking or damaged. (Clarkson, 2003, p. 56)

A key contracting consideration is confidentiality. Through appropriately phrased sections of the contract, therapists make a firm commitment not to share information or data relating to their client without that client's consent (or without sound legal or ethical justification). Clients need to have trust that what they say will be respectfully held in confidence.

The issue of data protection is relevant, too. The General Data Protection Regulation (GDPR) requires that the way we process (access, use, store, destroy) and use personal data/notes is both transparent and under the client's control. Personal data held on an individual belongs to that individual and, given that clients/supervisees have the right to see *any* data we hold about them, care needs to be taken to ensure that any notes written are respectful. Such data includes personal details, such as addresses and other information on the contract plus any clinical notes that might be written as an aide-memoire relevant to the progression of the work (Finlay, 2019).

Inviting acceptance

Clients also need to be confident that whatever they say (with some limits) will be welcomed and not rejected. As therapists, we help build such confidence by welcoming the client's expressions of vulnerability with compassion and without judgement. We do so when we show that we value their way of being and when we acknowledge them as someone who is trying to manage challenging circumstances. If a client is to learn to accept and value themselves, then their therapist needs to model the way (see Box 2.3).

Box 2.3 Practical application: critical judgement or professional care?

Consider the two vignettes below, which recognise how the critical judgements we make may not be experienced as entirely welcoming. Note also the value in being curious and non-judgemental about the therapist's process as well:

1. A client discloses that they hear critical voices. The therapist assumes the client is having auditory hallucinations. Out of concern that the client might be entering a psychotic episode, he immediately asks risk assessment questions about the client's mental state and psychiatric history and then abruptly suggests that therapy is inappropriate at this time and refers the client back to the GP.

   Comment: Here, the therapist is not exactly welcoming of the client's revelations about hearing critical voices. Instead, he seems to jump into making assumptions – an approach more in line with a reductionist medical model framework. It can be argued that rushing to make a medical diagnosis runs the risk of missing the person behind the label. 'When we totalize others, when we reduce them to objects of our knowledge, i.e. to easily labelled categories and stereotypes, we have violated their inherent worth as good in themselves' (Sayre and Kunz, 2005, p. 227). The therapist could have taken some time to explore what the client meant by 'critical voices' and to do 'justice to the way clients live their lives, rather than to ... focus on particular symptoms' (van Deurzen and Adams, 2011, p. 1).

On the other hand, perhaps the therapist was drawing on some real expertise enabling him to recognise that the client's immediate need was for a proper psychiatric assessment. Alternatively, the therapist might be admitting that he did not have sufficient knowledge to work with these issues. Or perhaps this particular therapy service explicitly barred people with severe and enduring mental health problems. In these alternative circumstances, referring the client onwards may be a caring, ethical, responsible act.

2. A client, aged 30, discloses her history of having been a sex worker throughout her teenage years. The therapist is somewhat shocked but tries not to show her negative judgement. She quickly moves away from exploration of the client's past to ask about her current situation. The therapist is reassured when the client says she is now in a committed, fulfilling relationship and is no longer offering sex for money, and that her husband/partner accepts her history. The therapist expresses some relief that the client has made different choices and is now in a 'healthy' relationship.

Comment: In trying to focus on the positive aspects of the client's current situation, the therapist failed to welcome the client's past self into the session. The therapist appears to assume that the client had choices about being a sex worker, and as a result rather dismisses the client's traumatic history and its context. The client, in turn, is likely to have picked up the therapist's negative, even judgemental, reactions. She may well feel that the therapist will not be able to handle – let alone appreciate – the realities of her life. It is possible the client herself feels some shame and disgust about her past actions, making it harder to bring herself into the room and begin the process of owning these parts.

It's also possible that the therapist was attuning correctly to the client, recognising she was not yet ready to talk about a traumatic past and wanted to different present to be acknowledged. Or perhaps the therapist herself was somehow triggered and was perhaps reminded of her own shame re: past sexual behaviour.

Carl Rogers, perhaps the most famous proponent of non-judgemental acceptance, explains:

In the therapeutic relationship, where all of herself was accepted, she could discover that it was safe to communicate ... that she did not need to

be lonely and isolated, that another could understand and share the meaning of her experience. She would discover, too, that in this process she had
made friends with herself – that her body, her feelings, and her desires
were not enemy aliens but friendly and constructive parts of herself.
(Rogers, 1980, p. 178)

While few therapists commit to person-centred 'non-judgemental unconditional positive regard', most would see a place for respectful acceptance and curiosity. For instance, in Acceptance and Commitment Therapy
(ACT) – a version of CBT – clients are helped to stop avoiding, denying
and/or struggling with less welcome aspects of their emotions/behaviour,
and accept that these feelings are understandable responses. With this
understanding, clients can begin to commit to making necessary changes
in their behaviour.

It is not necessary to accept or condone problematic behaviour. Rather,
the therapist offers a compassionate view of the client as a person and
attempts to avoid imposing their own values. For instance, the therapist
might ask: 'What do you need … (e.g to soothe or motivate yourself)?' or
'How would you treat a friend in this same situation?' (Germer, 2021). Such
interventions encourage the client towards a loving awareness and acceptance of themselves.

Recognition of cultural difference

As different norms, values and practices can be found across cultures (e.g.
family, class, ethnic, institutional contexts), there is a need to be respectful
when working with people from different backgrounds. The extent of eye
contact, touch, emotional expressiveness, body proximity and movement,
etc., will all be influenced by the backgrounds of both therapist and client.
As part of being welcoming, culturally sensitive therapists will try to ensure
the client isn't made to feel too uncomfortable within the therapy context
and will strive to be respectful of the other's traditions. For instance, I
would hold back from initiating touch (even handshakes) with most clients
while being prepared to follow their lead.

Atiyeh is a counsellor in the US who works with refugees who recognises
the importance of culturally sensitive hospitality. She describes trying to
offer the spirit of 'Syrian hospitality' in communicating a warm welcome.

I try to hold on to an empathy for how culture shock feels and to encourage that empathy among my supervisees. I have an appreciation for my
father's story because I currently work at a Jewish agency expressing
Jewish values by resettling Middle Eastern refugees. I have a first-hand
experience of the power of this work to bridge cultural boundaries.

As the Syrian refugee crisis continues, refugees are forced to flee their communities and are placed in third countries for resettlement when there is no opportunity to return home. In the United States, a network of non-profit agencies is responsible for meeting families at the airport, securing housing and providing basic services and cultural orientation. I have learned that we can accomplish these steps either by checking off the boxes or by approaching these refugee families with the same spirit of hospitality and welcoming that they most likely would afford to us. Doing so demonstrates respect and honour and eases the culture shock of being in a new country. (Atiyeh, 2017)

Case study

Hospitality isn't just about greeting the person in a welcoming way. It's about welcoming in the client's process and expressions with grace, curiosity and compassion. The hope is that, in time, clients will be able to welcome unwanted or unacknowledged parts of themselves.

In the following illustration, a spirit of hospitality is embodied in the explicit invitation to the client to be present to whatever is emerging in their body. The therapist models a spacious mindful awareness, inviting expression and acceptance of whatever is arising.

Therapist: When you think about the event with your boss, what do you feel in your body now?

Client: … like some dark feeling. I am not sure what it is.

Therapist: Allow yourself to be with it. Make space for it. (*The therapist is promoting acceptance of experience.*)

Client: (*Mindful awareness*) It is like a bullet in my stomach … Like something old and painful.

Therapist: Mm-hm. Observe and be curious …

Client: (*Mindful awareness*) Now came an event from childhood. When I was five years old, my father wanted me to eat up all of this disgusting vegetable soup. I resisted and then I was beaten.

Therapist: OK, just observe it and be aware of your breathing.

Client: (*Mindful awareness*) I feel anger … Like the bullet was this anger, which stayed in me.

Therapist: Allow yourself to be with whatever comes.

Client: (*Mindful awareness*) Just now I've had a picture, that bullet came from my stomach and I throw it into my father. I feel angry. I would like to tell him what I should have told him long ago.

Therapist: Trust your intuition and go with whatever comes.

Client: 'You had no right …' (in an angry tone). (Žvelc and Žvelc, 2021, p. 193)

Critical reflections

One of my early lessons concerning therapist hospitality came from Freud. When a hungry patient (the so-called 'Rat-Man') showed up at his clinic, Freud began the session by offering him food. Freud's spontaneous gesture is worth remembering. If a client comes in and is feeling weak from not having eaten all day, the relational–ethical – *human* – thing to do is to offer at least a drink and perhaps a biscuit. Similarly, I know of a therapy service for refugees and asylum seekers which lays out a free buffet of food in the waiting room each day for those needing food (Finlay, 2019). Some would challenge these acts as messing with norms of practice (boundaries designed to ensure client safety). What is your view?

Reading Atiyeh's blog (2017) about her own refugee work reminded me how hospitality works both ways. We are hosts, but we are also *guests* in clients' lives. So, we need to knock respectfully at the client's metaphorical 'front door', waiting to be invited in rather than barging in and throwing our weight (advice, opinions) around.

It's worth considering your cultural values further regarding the importance of hospitality. Some therapists are very attentive to it; others don't seem to consider it at all. For me, with my particular cultural background, it feels important to welcome the person graciously. Hopefully, that welcome is maintained in the way I strive to listen carefully, with curiosity and compassion, throughout the rest of therapy.

Of course, it's not always so easy to do in practice. It can be hard to attune to the precise level of openness and hospitality the client can handle. Some clients can find too much attentiveness overwhelming and, feeling unworthy, become uncomfortable. Clients' experience of our care in such situations can provide a fruitful conversation further into therapy.

I began this chapter with the metaphor of the therapist-as-host and I'm ending with the idea of the therapist-as-guest. Pushing these metaphors further, think about the exchange of gifts that occurs when we go to other people's homes. As guests, we bring gifts – and receive from our hosts multiple gifts in return: food, drink, conversation, conviviality. I think the idea of mutual giving and receiving of gifts is one to import into therapy (ensuring, of course, levels of gift-giving are both appropriate and ethical – see Finlay, 2019). I certainly feel inspired and nourished by my clients who bring me the 'gift' of their selves; the giving is not just one way. 'In the context of hospitality, guest and host can reveal their most precious gifts and bring new life to each other' (Nouwen, 1998, p. 44).

I'll leave the last words of this chapter to Pickering's (2019) beautifully phrased thoughts on the ethics of hospitality within her own psychoanalytic practice (see Box 2.4).

Box 2.4 Practical application: putting hospitality into practice

How do I put the ethic of analytic hospitality into practice? Before each patient arrives, I make sure that the outer environment is ready for that particular patient, taking into consideration individual needs and, where possible, individual preferences. Then I sit in my chair. I take a moment to examine my conscience, to ensure my motivation is altruistic and not contaminated by hidden ulterior motives. Then I do simple breathing meditation ... to clear my mind to be open, empty and receptive to this particular patient, to be fully present in the here and now.

Like Abraham sitting in the noon-day sun by his tent, I await the arrival of the angelic stranger, the inherent alterity and divinity within every patient. I greet that person with an attitude of hospitality for the unknowable stranger, with the courtesy of *agape* and motivation of compassion. I seek to avoid prejudging the person based on the last time we met, but instead await the emergence of who and how they are in this given encounter. Every moment is unique, ... unprecedented and unrepeatable. (2019, p. 44)

Discussion questions

1. Thinking about your own practice, consider the ways you might embody your welcoming of clients.
2. Are there circumstances when you believe therapists should give something more than, or in addition to, therapy?
3. Where are the limits to your own hospitality? Are there any types of behaviour or response you are not prepared to accept?

Resources

Book: In my book *Practical Ethics: A Relational Approach* (Finlay, 2019), I argue that the therapeutic relationship is fundamentally concerned with ethics. Chapter 5 specifically engages how to create a welcoming hospitable space and to contract ethically.

Academic paper: Welcoming the Other: actualising the humanistic ethic at the core of counselling psychology practice by Mick Cooper.

Blog: Creative spaces: inside 25 counselling & psychotherapy rooms by Jodie Gale. Available at: https://jodiegale.com/creative-spaces-inside-25-counselling-psychotherapy-rooms/

Blog: Bringing Syrian hospitality into your counseling practice by Shadin Atiyeh, 8 November 2017. Available at: https://ct.counseling. org/2017/11/bringing-syrian-hospitality-counseling-practice/

Website: Lots of information, videos and resources about Acceptance and Commitment Therapy (ACT) and mindfulness: https://positivepsychology .com/act-acceptance-and-commitment-therapy/

Note

1. If therapy is online, I try to check that clients are comfortably seated in a private space with a drink handy.

THREE

BEING OPEN AND PRESENT

Our existential journey requires us to be prepared to be touched and shaken by what we find on the way ... It is only with such an attitude of openness and wonder that we can encounter the impenetrable mysteries, which take us beyond our own preoccupations and sorrows and ... make us rediscover life. (van Deurzen-Smith, 1997, p. 5)

Being open and present (i.e. opening ourselves to whatever is emerging moment-to-moment in the therapeutic encounter) is central to our work as therapists (Schneider, 2008; McWilliams, 2017). We strive to hold our assumptions, hopes and expectations lightly in order to be present to new possibilities. We try to avoid serving up 'knowing' explanations and solutions, ready to be awed and surprised as we touch – and are touched by – the other. We place our trust in the therapeutic process and aim to be energetically present, inviting, alive to creative possibilities, and ready to share ourselves as we join with our client and go exploring.

This chapter first explains that being open involves being both unknowing and open to wonder and curiosity. Then presence is explored, considering also the specific role played by therapist self-disclosure. A third section deals with the specific process of bracketing, which can be understood as a way of engaging openness and presence.

These three processes are multi-layered, complex and contested. They do not readily slot together – for instance, it could be argued that bracketing and self-disclosure are in contradiction with one another. Therapists differ in the degree to which we favour and draw on each of these elements, making for considerable variation across therapeutic practice. My hope is that the examples given will help spur your own thinking about how you engage openness and presence. The chapter ends, as usual, with a case study, reflections and questions.

Being open

Being open can be understood as:

- being unknowing;
- being open to wonder and curiosity.

Being unknowing

In openness, we navigate the ambiguous spaces between knowing and not knowing. Larner, a family therapist, describes the paradox here: that while we possess professional power and knowledge, we can choose to suspend both elements as part of being open to the contribution of the client and engaging therapeutic dialogue:

> I 'put forward' ideas, interpretations, hunches, truths (for me), possible steps or strategies for change etc., as my way of knowing and making meaning but always as part of the therapeutic conversation. I always defer to the client's wisdom and knowledge in a simultaneous reverence and irreverence for theory. (Larner, 1995, p. 209)

When therapists are open, they have an open mind and stance that is ready to be moved and receive whatever presents itself in the moment, rather than making assumptions (McWilliams, 2017). This receptivity involves curiosity and an unknowing, or at least uncertain, way of being. Here, therapists 'exercise an expertise in asking questions from a position of "not knowing" rather than asking questions that are informed by method and that demand specific answers' (Anderson and Goolishian 1992, p. 28). The aim is to ask questions that enable clients' self-discovery so they can make their own choices and find their own way through their situation. This stance avoids squeezing the person into predetermined categories of problem and solution.

Yet, we 'know' stuff (e.g. about mental health and psychological processes) and it can be hard to put this knowledge aside. Therapists' knowledge and understanding can be a critical support and resource for the client. We can't deny that clients stand to benefit from our theoretical depth, experience and expertise (and in any case, it may be important to hold on to it). But therapist expertise (high levels of ability/skill, professional competence and effectiveness) is hard to measure and study (Hill et al., 2017).

While some therapists may be less concerned about being unknowing, they still enact different versions of openness – for example, by showing curiosity or bracketing easy assumptions. Therapists who work psychoanalytically might lean on attachment theory (their 'knowing'), but they are likely to be trying to make sense of what emerging relational–developmental processes might mean (McWilliams, 2017). There is an openness to any projections that might appear; if spotted, these can be brought more clearly into awareness and eventually gently returned to the client in a safely contained, manageable form.

And while some CBT practitioners engage a more 'knowing' psychoeducational process, those who practise mindfulness along with CBT embrace openness to whatever emerges in the moment. Cigolla and Brown (2011), for instance, have explored therapists' use of mindfulness as an aware, present-centred, compassionately curious, empathic, accepting way of being. Similarly, others have focused on how mindfulness explicitly encourages both client and therapist to be present and through modelling meditation techniques to help the client become more aware of thoughts and feelings so as to better manage them (Segal et al., 2013).

At a practical level, when we engage psychoeducation with clients, we draw on our professional knowledge in order to convey and teach, and it matters how we do this. The work can be done in patronising, directive (telling) ways that can disempower the client; or it can take the form of invitation, of mutually and openly exploring possibilities.

At times, sharing knowledge/insights derived from theory becomes a psychoeducational element of therapy. For example, I might teach a client the 'PAC model' from transactional analysis; clients often find this interesting and relevant. The art comes in *how* such teaching is done. Rather than saying 'this is how I analyse you', it is better if clients can be invited to identify with and apply what the theory is saying to themselves. This way we hear their perspective, interpretations and meanings, rather than placing our own knowing (and ego) to the fore.

Being open to wonder and curiosity

Part of therapist openness is an attitude of *opening themselves* to wonder and curiosity (van Deurzen-Smith, 1997). It's a letting go of expectations and trying to control the course of therapy and of being open to the unexpected. One therapist expresses this as:

> Creating space and openness, allowing things to be, to create a non-judgemental atmosphere where he can learn to trust his voice and feel free to speak his mind. Somehow my client senses this is what I "want" from him. To be heard without criticism or reprimand. (Seth, 2017, p. 82)

In turn, that attitude is modelled for clients who, too, may learn to wonder, be curious about their own process, and become ready to be impacted by the other, to embrace unexpected possibilities.

Yalom (n.d.) puts his finger on it when he declares that he approaches all his patients with a 'sense of wonderment at the story that will unfold'. Hycner describes his sense of wonder thus:

> If I'm not amazed at least once during a session, that's an indication to me that I'm either "burned out," or I'm not in touch with a larger sense of what is going on for this person, and between us. (Hycner, 1991, p. 112)

Van Deurzen, Yalom and Hycner are all existential psychotherapists who celebrate the importance of wonder in therapy. This wonder involves a radical openness that can be seen in the way therapists are:

- alive to possibilities and the unexpected, open to being 'awed' (Schneider, 2008);
- receptive to the client as a *person* with a history;
- rejecting of any reductionist gaze or categories, and of the certainties of therapist's interpretations/understandings;
- available to be impacted by the client;
- prepared to open their own self to confront existential givens.

Yet somehow this list does not quite capture the ineffable quality of what is involved in our being open. When they arise in therapy, moments of wonder and curiosity have an awe-full, even spiritual, dimension. This receptive openness is the opposite of being a technical problem-solver (McWilliams, 2017).

Concrete examples of such moments may help capture the experience better. Seth (2017) (see Box 3.1) researched therapists' lived experience of wonder in therapy. A therapist–participant describes a transformative moment of mutual, wordless connection. Interestingly, the moment was triggered by something outside the therapy space: an external phenomenon that impacted the therapist, his client (Kara) and their relationship:

> Something in her eyes and mouth had changed, her facial muscles relaxed. She moved in her chair as if relieving stiffness and her face moved to a half smile. Her eyes were fixed on something outside my window and she moved her hand to point to something. I looked through the window.
>
> In a small tree near the window a flock of long-tailed tits, a big flock of tiny pink and black animated baubles were filling the tree as they fluttered around from one branch to another. I smiled because of the magical charm of that sight and turning to Kara I found her grinning at me. Kara looked younger, her eyes were wide with wonder, she made short gurgles of laughter and for the first time she looked straight into my eyes. She had opened to the world for the first time in my presence and simultaneously I had opened to her a little more, she knew my smile. Time had stopped as we shared something of ourselves that no amount of words could express adequately. (quoted from Seth, 2017, p. 87)

Box 3.1 Research: Psychotherapists' wonder

Seth (2017) engaged an in-depth hermeneutic phenomenological exploration of existential psychotherapists' lived experience of wonder, its meaning
and the conditions for its emergence as a phenomenon in a clinical context.
Eight existential psychotherapists and counselling psychologists participated in the study. Following van Manen's (2014) hermeneutic phenomenology of practice, participants wrote a description of a concrete experience
about wonder in clinical practice and then were interviewed.

Three interconnected overarching themes were identified around:
1. the experience of wonder as a state of **openness** (in which the therapist
dwells in unknowing); 2. the embodied, deeply relational dimension of
wonder (where therapists opened to being fully present); 3. how wonder is
a profoundly renewing experience, a birthing place for new knowledge and
therapeutic discovery. The deep, mutual relational connection highlighted
ethical dimensions of wonder reminiscent of Buber's *I–Thou* relating,
Emmanuel Levinas's *Alterity of the Other* and Irigaray's *Maternal Philosophy
of Breath*.

I would like to end this section – as Seth ends her thesis – with an observation by Carl Rogers:

> People are just as wonderful as sunsets if you let them be. When I look at
> a sunset, I don't find myself saying, 'Soften the orange a bit on the right
> hand corner.' I don't try to control a sunset. I watch with awe as it unfolds.
> (Rogers, 1969, p. 236)

Being present

Presence is a mysterious process and hard to describe because of its
fluid, ineffable nature and ability to manifest itself in different ways.
While mostly associated with humanistic approaches to therapy, presence is increasingly seen across all modalities as a helpful – if not
essential – therapeutic way of being. A general consensus is the understanding that therapeutic presence (as distinct from, say, the 'stage presence' of an actor or politician) involves being grounded in one's own
embodied self in order to 'receive' the client's experience (Geller and
Greenberg, 2002, see Box 3.2). Figure 3.1 presents a trans-theoretical
model of presence as embodied, relational being involving six intertwined dimensions (Finlay, 2016b).

Box 3.2 Research: presence

Geller and Greenberg's (2002, 2012; Geller et al., 2012) extensive research has shown empirically how psychotherapeutic presence can promote a positive therapeutic alliance and therefore effective practice. Their model of presence comprises three domains: 1. preparing the ground for presence (pre-session and in life); 2. process of presence (inwardly attending, receptivity and extending/contact); 3. experience of presence (immersion, expansion, grounding and being with/for client).[1] This model subsequently evolved into the development of a self-report measure (a research tool): the Therapeutic Presence Inventory (TPI). The TPI comprises two versions – one from the therapist's perspective and the other from the client's; both have been found to be valid and reliable (Geller et al., 2010) and are being used in further research studies. For instance, Geller et al. (2010) found that therapist-rated therapeutic presence predicts clients' perceptions of empathy, congruence and unconditional regard.

Geller and Porges (2014) have studied neurophysiological mechanisms. Their results suggest that cultivating presence enables both client and therapist to enter a physiological state that supports feelings of safety and optimal relational conditions for growth and change. They offer a concrete neurophysiological description of how presence emerges (and can be nurtured) interpersonally, including by regulating presence via the vagus system.[2]

Erskine's (2021) 'relational needs' work (along with that of others) attests to the importance of being solidly grounded, attuned, aware, responsive in order for the client to feel adequately held and attended to. It can also be powerful for the client to see they have impacted the therapist. The less the therapist is present, the more anxiety-provoking the situation is likely to be for the client, who may feel shame and/or abandonment in the face of therapist withdrawal or perceived lack of interest. In turn, the client is likely to want to withdraw and/or dissociate.

In other words, the presence of the therapist invites the client to be present. More specifically, Germer (2021) advocates a self-compassionate presence to encourage the client to accept themselves with compassion. How this is done varies according to the individual and to the theoretical framework adopted, and this is the focus of the rest of this section. A further subsection highlights the dilemma about therapist self-disclosure as part of presence.

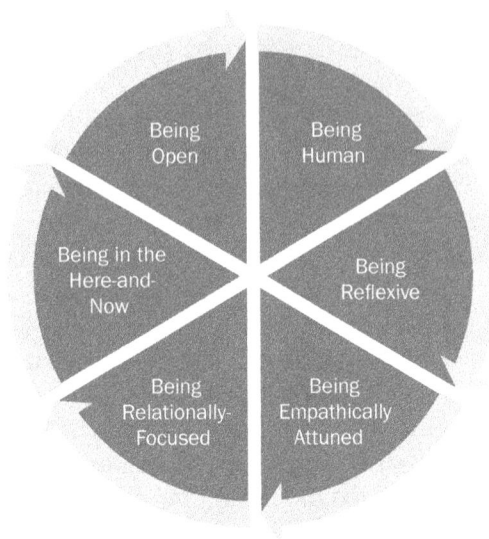

Figure 3.1   Therapist being as presence

Humanistic variants

Gestalt literature offers deep, sustained descriptions of the process of presence. A number of commentators, notably Hycner and Jacobs, have built on the significant work of the phenomenological philosopher Buber ([1923] 1958, [1951] 1965) and his ideas about how therapists engage the twin dialogical processes of Presence and Inclusion.

Buber's focus on presence arose out of his overwhelming experience of absence, which led to a search for a presence that would not let him down. Buber called for 'genuine communication' in the dialogic relationship where the therapist holds their 'ground in a way that is contactful' (Yontef, 1993, p. 35). He highlighted how 'being present' and 'presence' are intertwined processes towards I–Thou[3] relating. When we have the courage to be fully present, we are met and affirmed by the other through what Hycner calls an 'embrace of gazes' (in Hycner and Jacobs, 1995, p. 9). In being present, the therapist gives up any instrumental desire to control and be validated, seeking instead a more intimate encounter based on being-with the client. The hope is that the client will experience this as the therapist offering an affirmative solidness in which the client can be held and witnessed in a safe, trustworthy way. This, in turn, enables the client to be as present to their self as possible (Finlay, 2016a, b).

Chidiac and Denham-Vaughan (2007) offer an account of presence in gestalt practice, describing it as 'energetic availability' and 'fluid responsiveness'. 'I notice you noticing me, and I feel seen' (p. 10). They argue for presence as a 'moment-to-moment disciplined awareness' and the thera-peutic use of the 'authentic process self' as the vehicle for change (p. 17). Like other gestaltists, they also discuss the need for therapists to titrate their presence in the service of the client. Being too present – for example, through excessive self-disclosure – can result in the client feeling over-whelmed or diminished. Restricting presence (perhaps through too much retroflection), can result in the client believing that the therapist is not engaged or interested. Both 'miscalculations' can elicit shame and discom-fort in the client.

Presence has also been explored in some depth in the wider human-istic literature. In the field of person-centred theory, Rogers, towards the end of his life, began to articulate presence as the foundational dimension underlying his three core conditions of congruence, unconditional posi-tive regard and empathy. He wondered if he had over-emphasised the core conditions and under-acknowledged presence. Elsewhere, Rogers (1986) has described presence as those times when he is closest to his inner self and in a slightly altered state of consciousness: moments when intuitive spontaneous responses emerge seem particularly impactful/valuable to the client.

With emotion-focused therapy, the therapist is a witness and a compas-sionately validating presence – one who offers a corrective emotional expe-rience (Greenberg, 2015). Together, therapist and client embrace strategies that promote emotional awareness, acceptance, expression, regulation and transformation geared towards both strengthening the client's sense of self and creating new meaning.

In the existential world, Bugental (1978), May (1983), Schneider (2008) and Yalom (2002) have all been active in highlighting the importance of the process. Other experiential and person-centred theorist-practitioners similarly insist on the centrality of presence. Mearns and Cooper (2005) and Knox et al. (2013), among others, have discussed presence as a neces-sary element of working at relational depth, as linked to embodied empa-thy, and as being a 'solid grounded "Otherness"' (Mearns and Cooper, 2005, p. 9).

Interestingly, different theorists and practitioners refer to being present to different aspects, even as they agree on the need to be in the 'here-and-now'. And there are variations: Bugental, for instance, is more present to *intra*personal factors, while Yalom attends more explicitly to *inter*personal processes (Krug, 2009).

Relational–integrative approaches

Compared with traditional insight-orientated psychoanalysis, there has been a move towards therapists embodying a more intimate, personal analytic presence in the relational psychoanalytic field. With a growing emphasis on the mutuality of the therapeutic relationship, the therapist is seen as need-ing to be present both to the client and to their own feelings (which may offer important clues to the client's unconscious experience). Therapists are encouraged to foster a client's sense of self by maintaining an affirming, holding, relationally responsive presence.

Therapist presence is a transitional one, suggests Casement (1985), which potentially offers space for clients to grow (much like the mother who is non-intrusively present with her playing child). The therapist can be invoked by the client as a presence (a transferential figure) or can be used by the client – for instance, to represent an absence. The therapist's pres-ence is at once intimate and distant.

Stern (2004) focuses on the value of staying open in the present phe-nomenological moment. He recommends resisting the temptation to jump quickly into making interpretations, an action which may pull the client into their past. Instead, he argues that therapists need to be present *to* the present moment, understood as an intersubjective, meaning-making dyad. Similarly, Atwood and Stolorow (2014) offer their philosophically-based, intersubjective take on psychoanalysis which sees the therapy relationship as an intersection of two subjectivities and therapist's presence as a rela-tional home for emotional pain and existential vulnerability.

In the field of integrative psychotherapy, the work of Erskine and his colleagues stands out for its emphasis on the role of presence (e.g. Erskine, 2015; Moursund and Erskine, 2004). Their work draws on transactional analysis, behaviourism, gestalt, systemic and developmental-attachment theory. They note a duality to presence: a simultaneous attending both to the client and to self (in terms of being emotionally available and self-aware). The therapist decentres from their own needs, making the client's process the primary focus. Here the therapist is mindful of the client's expe-rience, watching every little gesture, listening to each word or being with the client's silence. At the same time the therapist's history, relational needs and sensitivities, theoretical stance and professional experience all enter into building therapeutic presence (Erskine, 2011).

Our professional artistry often comes down as much to the timing of interventions as to what we actually say. The key question is: at what point (if at all) should we stop being accepting and interrupt clients' reflections by inserting (asserting?) our presence? There is a tricky balance to be found between overwhelming or intruding upon the client with our presence and modelling authentic presence.

Box 3.3 offers an illustrative dialogue from a therapy session where a client was talking about his shame and lack of confidence at work. In this excerpt, the therapist asserts their presence in several ways. They inter-rupt and challenge the client while self-disclosing their actual response and revealing vulnerability. As the therapist becomes more present, the client is enabled to gain awareness of his projections and assumptions that others

---

Box 3.3 Case example: being present

Client: You're probably thinking I should have been more assertive, but it didn't feel the right time and she was ...

Therapist: (*interrupting*) Can I ask you to pause a minute? It seems you're saying that *I* think you should have been more assertive. I actually think you were brave to have challenged your colleague. I couldn't have done that. And it wasn't the right time to be more assertive.

Client: You don't think I wimped out?

Therapist: No, I'm curious about what led you to think that of me?

Client: Dunno. I just assumed.

Therapist: Who has said this to you in the past?

Client: My father. He was always telling me I was 'wet and weak' and that I should be more of a 'man'.

Therapist: Do you think you might have been seeing your father in me?

---

are going to be critical. In Box 3.4 the therapist (Dave Mearns) demonstrates an openness and acceptance of the client while also being challengingly real in his use of words.

Box 3.4 Case example: being an accepting–challenging presence

Dominic 1: I shouldn't have come today. I'll go away if you like.

Dave 1: Because you've been drinking?

Dominic 2: Yeah – I've been drinking.

Dave 2: Do you *want* to go or do you *want* to stay?

Dominic 3: I wouldn't mind staying.

Dave 3: I would like that too ...

Dominic 5: How do you feel about me ... now ... here?

Dave 5: Dom, I want to tell you that I feel absolutely *nothing* about the fact that you've been drinking. But you asked how I felt about you, now, here (*pauses*). I feel ... a bit ... scared.

Dominic 6: Scared?

Dave 6: It surprises me too ... I guess it *does* matter to me that you've been drinking ... I'm scared in case we have to start again. ...

Dominic 7: Like it matters to you?

Dave 7: Yes it does, Dom.

Dominic 8: Like this isn't just a 'game' to you?

Dave 8: I think you *know* that, Dom. In fact, I *know* you know that, Dom.

Dominic 9: Yes, 'sober me' knows it, but does 'drunk me'?

Dave 9: *I don't know. Does he? Do you?*

Dominic 10: Big question. Maybe I need another vodka before I can answer that.

Dave 10: Dom, *be* here, be here *drunk*, but don't play fucking games with me. Neither you nor I deserve that. (Mearns and Cooper, 2005, p. 73)

Therapist self-disclosure

Patricia DeYoung (2003, p. 47) describes presence in terms of being 'deeply real': 'At the heart of relational therapy,' she says, 'there is the therapist's commitment to be present, with caring and focus, in the relationship.' Self-disclosure is part of this process of being present as a real, authentic human being who is capable of showing emotion and empathy. Sharing personal feelings/experience/process may help *normalise* the client's experience, deepen the therapeutic relationship, and offer alternative perspectives. However, judgement is required when deciding whether, how and when to self-disclose (Clarkson, 2003; Amis, 2017; Finlay, 2019).

The principal argument against self-disclosure is that a shift in the focus from client to therapist during a session has the potential to violate boundaries. A therapist who over-discloses risks being overwhelming in their presence. In addition, self-disclosure increases the therapist's vulnerability and opens us to being manipulated. Self-disclosure also makes an uneasy bedfellow when we are trying to bracket or make ourselves more neutral so as to be more present for the client.

It can help to recognise there are different forms of self-disclosure – inadvertent or intentional. Inadvertent disclosure occurs constantly and occurs from the first moment of contact through our website listings, telephone/texting/emailing manner, therapy room decor, our dress, first handshake and so on. Therapist disclosure is more than instrumental performance in pursuit of client growth.

When it comes to intentional disclosure, we can distinguish between the *non-immediate* self-disclosure of sharing one's personal history versus the *immediate* sharing thoughts/feelings that are arising in the moment. The latter is often the favoured form as it can be relational and can also be a way of revealing the therapist's presence in the therapy room (Audet and

---

Box 3.5 Case example: to disclose or not

In one session I could not bear the intensity of my own grief which was being stimulated by my patient's mourning. I defensively distanced myself from her experience. She noticed the subtle change in my demeanour and asked what had happened. I explained what I was feeling and she became upset and angry. She said she felt undermined in her grief, as if I was telling her my grief was more important than hers and that she should now abandon herself to shore me up. I was surprised. She knew I was grieving. I thought my speaking of it would create a meeting of greater intimacy between us. Only recently we have begun to understand some of the roots of her experience of the interaction; her mother used to be abusive to her and then later apologize, saying she was just having a bad day. My patient heard her mother's 'confession' as a plea to forgive and, most importantly, *forget* the injury my patient had suffered. My patient worried I wanted the same thing. For my part, in retrospect, I do think I was turning to her to meet my need for comfort and solace. This is a patient for whom I feel great fondness and a desire for more closeness. Thus, I think there as a confluence of her fear of usurpation *and* my intrusion of my neediness into her session. (Jacobs, in Hycner and Jacobs, 1995, pp. 228–9. Included by kind permission of the authors.)

Everall, 2010). The case example in Box 3.5 illustrates the challenge posed by self-disclosure and delicate balancing required.

Research (see Box 3.6) indicates that disclosures can be beneficial or problematic. Writing in a Nordic context, Berg et al. (2017) show self-disclosure as a complex, multifaceted phenomenon. While participants believe disclosure enhances client well-being, shows care and normalises the client's experience, therapists recognise risks, including how it can backfire and they can feel vulnerable and regret opening up. Ziv-Beiman and Shahar (2016) highlight how therapist disclosure can be a clinical error when patients feel impinged upon.

All depends on the nature of the disclosure, the specific relational social context and the theoretical framework adopted. Therapist disclosure, offered with the aim of raising the client's self-awareness, occurs more frequently in humanistic-integrative contexts, and less frequently in traditional psychoanalytic practice (where the therapist is more of a 'blank slate') and in brief psychoeducational or CBT work, where disclosures are perhaps less relevant (Finlay, 2019).

Perhaps the biggest challenge is to work out, moment to moment, *when* to disclose or contain ourselves. This is where the role of bracketing comes to the fore – the subject of the next section.

Box 3.6 Research: therapist self-disclosure

Henretty and Levitt (2010) reviewed the literature and found that approximately 90 per cent of therapists self-disclose to clients. They found that therapist self-disclosure appears to encourage more client disclosure when used infrequently and at a relatively low-to-moderate intimacy level, and that receiving therapist disclosures enhanced clients' ratings of therapists' warmth.

Pinto-Coelho et al. (2016) carried out a mixed-methods study of 185 occurrences of therapist disclosure during psychotherapy sessions. Their findings revealed that clients rated disclosures of feeling/insight as more intimate and of a higher quality than disclosures of fact, and that more disclosure was positively related to client-rated working alliance.

Ziv-Beiman (2013), writing in an Israeli context, conducted an extensive empirical and theoretical review and single case study. She found therapist disclosure to be a potentially powerful therapeutic tool, beneficial to the alliance and integration. She recommended low-to-mild frequency of 'immediate' self-disclosures.

'Bracketing'

Bracketing is a concept from phenomenological philosophy and means putting previous understandings/assumptions into metaphorical brackets which can be held aside – reflexively, in awareness.

In practice, we bracket many aspects:

- **Our knowing** By not jumping to conclusions and by holding lightly to interpretations or judgements about someone's mental state.
- **Truth (or otherwise) of what the client is saying** For instance, if a client tells us their dream, we don't say, 'It was only a dream, it wasn't real'. Instead, we acknowledge that the dream was experientially real for that person. So, we attend to dream as we would any recounting of experience in so-called 'real' life.
- **Our feelings/needs** Foregrounding clients' interests, we try to avoid unduly leaking our emotions (or at least minimise their negative impact), so as not to drown our clients. It is destructive, exploitative and unethical for the therapist to use the client's therapy for their own support.
- **Cultural assumptions and values** If a person says they feel themselves to be a woman in a man's body or want to engage in certain kinky sexual practices outside of our beliefs or cultural norms, we respect their preference and bracket our own values (see Box 3.7 for guidelines on cultural competence – openness and respect – in reference to gender and sexuality). (Finlay, forthcoming)

Box 3.7 Practical application: tips for culturally competent work across gender, sexual and relationship diversity (GSRD)

Given the impact of gender, sexuality and relationship diversity (GSRD)[4] on mental health, it's important to explore clients' values/understandings while bracketing our own. It's about respecting diversity (e.g. recognising that polygamy and arranged marriages are more common than monogamy and romantic-love marriages in cultures around the world [Barker 2017–2019]).

- Be aware of your biases and the limits of your expertise. If you are concerned that you may not have the openness and expertise to work with a particular client, refer to somebody who does where possible.
- Do not expect clients to educate you about their gender, sexuality or relationship style in the sessions they are paying you for. Be prepared to do your homework, guided by the client where relevant. Therapy time should not be used for your CPD and building your cultural competency.
- Respect clients' gender, sexuality and relationship style, and be open to the diversity of ways in which they may, or may not, self-identify and/or practise these. Do not make assumptions based on limited information – e.g. about pronoun or sexual identity.
- Be careful not to implicitly or explicitly reinforce the pathologisation or stigmatisation of a client's sexuality, gender or relationship style.
- Be aware that not all supervisors will necessarily have expertise on GSRD issues ... It can be useful to access additional formal and/or peer supervision on top of your regular supervision in relation to a particular client or client group. (Barker, 2017–2019, p. 59)

The process of bracketing is beset with misunderstanding. Some make the mistake of seeing bracketing as a way of being unbiased or objective. However, it is better understood as non-judgemental focused openness. As such, it involves trying to see clients and their lives with 'fresh eyes' (Finlay, 2008, p. 29; 2016a). Seen in this way, bracketing is enacted alongside a genuine, mindful sense of curiosity and compassion. As therapists, we strive to maintain a genuinely unknowing stance in which we remain modest about our claims to understanding. We try to bracket what we might know or assume, in order to be present to what is emerging in the here and now.

Engaging a phenomenological attitude, we strive to leave our worlds behind and enter into our clients' worlds in order to reflect on their meanings and experience. This attitude involves a special attentiveness that dwells with the situations the client describes and listens out for (even magnifies) details. This attitude is as free from value judgements and theoretical con-structs as is possible. We try instead – at least in the first instance – to focus on the meaning of the situation purely as it presents to our client (Wertz, 2005).

While bracketing is mostly practised by existential-phenomenological therapists, those in other modalities enact their versions. For instance, psy-choanalyst Bion has argued that therapists should work without desire or memory and with a quiet mind open to making contact with clients' uncon-scious communications. '"Forget" what you know and "forget" what you want, get rid of your desires, anticipations and also your memories so that there will be a chance of hearing these very faint sounds that are buried in this mass of noise' (Bion, 2005, p. 17). Winnicott agrees when he advocates a 'not knowing' stance:

> The patient's creativity can be only too easily stolen by a therapist who knows too much. It does not really matter, of course, how much the thera-pist knows provided he can hide this knowledge, or refrain from advertising what he knows. (Winnicott, 1971, p. 67)

Whatever the theoretical framework adopted, what is called for is an espe-cially attentive attitude of non-judgemental, curious receptivity, and both an emptying of the self while being present in the moment, in order to be filled by the other and what is occurring between. While it's not easy to let go into this space, the results can be rewarding (Finlay, forthcoming).

Case study

In the following case study, the therapist's openness is demonstrated by acceptance of the client and her different life choices; her presence (includ-ing self-disclosure) is contained and titrated to allow space for the client's expressions.

Caitlin, aged 15, has a history of self-harm, acting out behaviour and school truancy. She was referred by a school counsellor to a Children's and Young People's mental health service for long-term therapy. Her mother reported that Caitlin's behavioural problems had been escalating over the last year and that she had been 'hanging around with a bad crowd' and is 'now out of control'.

On first meeting Caitlin, the psychotherapist saw a pale girl with black dyed hair, dressed in a loose long-sleeved black top, who talked and acted tough. Initially, she was aggressively sullen and told the therapist to 'f*** off'. The therapist responded mildly, asking if she felt annoyed at being forced to come to the clinic, noting that most people found the first session challenging in terms of having to share private information with a stranger.

Caitlin seemed to relax a bit hearing this, but she didn't speak.

The therapist tried another tack when it was clear that Caitlin wasn't going to talk: 'The counsellor at school said that he thought you weren't happy and that it would be better to have a space that was completely removed from your school and home life to get some support.'

'Can you get my mother and school off my back? I wanna be free to do my own thing,' was Caitlin's response.

'We might be able to help with that a bit. But until I know more, it's hard to know,' the therapist replied. Recognising that Caitlin was still finding it hard to express herself, she commented on what looked to be a new tattoo on the back of her hand. 'New tattoo? Is it a picture of a dragon?'

Catlin rolled up her sleeve to allow the therapist to see the full length of the dragon. The therapist noted evidence of old scarring, but she didn't comment on this; nor did she disclose that she personally disliked tattoos. Instead, she simply and honestly said, 'It's a beautiful piece of artwork.'

Caitlin then shared that she had got several new tattoos and facial piercings this last year. She said she was proud of her 'ink and studs' and was 'planning lots more' all over her body and face. She checked to see if her therapist looked shocked. The therapist was shocked but contained her response, keeping her facial expression bland to support Caitlin to open up.

As the therapist drew her out, Caitlin talked about only feeling happy when she was 'hanging out' with her friends smoking weed and drinking alcohol. When Caitlin said that her therapist (aged 60) wouldn't understand that's what young people these days did, the therapist grinned. She shared that she herself had been a 'bit wild' in her teenage years, but did not give details. She noted the possibility of a child protection issue but held back, needing more information.

When asked about her family, Caitlin said that none of them cared about her and she could do what she liked. Her parents had divorced when she was 6, and she had gone to live with her father (her mother was an alcoholic). That arrangement broke down when her father married again when Caitlin was 10. She describes her stepmother as an 'evil bitch who was always yelling at me'. When Caitlin was 13, she went back to live with her mother, but the mother's new partner makes lewd comments to Caitlin (out of the mother's earshot) which made her feel uncomfortable.

It took a few sessions before Caitlin shared her long history of self-harm. The therapist learned that she had started cutting when her stepmother came on the scene. She began with her forearms, then switched to her upper thighs, concealing her actions. Caitlin found it hard to express herself and say why she self-cut. The therapist explained that people cut for all sorts of reasons, including to express pain, self-punish, protest, feel a sense of control, feel something, get a high, give themselves self-care, and so on.

The therapist bracketed her professional formulations about Caitlin's history of attachment and why Caitlin might be cutting. She encouraged Caitlin to explore what it meant to her. In time, Caitlin recognised that it was her 'secret pleasure', that each cut was like a 'memorial that talks' to her and that she always felt calmer afterwards when cleaning her wounds. The therapist was touched, awed, by how Caitlin seemed to use her cutting as a way to have a subtly caring relationship with herself rather than it being 'self-abuse'.

The therapist reflected back Caitlin's sense that she was unimportant and disclosed her sadness that it seemed Caitlin had been betrayed by both parents. Together, they noted how difficult it was for Caitlin to share her upset and express her anger against her parents and their partners. Caitlin carried on with her weekly one-to-one sessions, using them well to express herself, and eventually she agreed to take part in some family therapy.

Critical reflections

Lumping two different processes of openness and presence together in this chapter may have been ill-advised, but it shows the complexity of the relational dance we engage.

Openness and presence are paradoxically linked. For instance, sometimes, we open to the other and make ourselves *less* present to enable the client to be more present. At other times, we make ourselves *more* present – perhaps by self-disclosing – to show our openness to the other. Sometimes we need to become more present to our own experience to see the other; at other times we need to bracket our stuff to recognise the other's difference.

In other words, there are no easy formulas to follow, except to recognise that when we start being unduly judgemental or engage in pat responses and practised routines, we are probably not being as receptively open and respectively present as we could be.

This ambiguity is highlighted in an account of emergency psychological care (EPC) work in Brazil. The authors argue the need for the psychologist to be present to themselves *and* present in empathy *and* to decentre, in order to focus on the client. In this example, the therapist goes as far as to leave the room in order to help the client to be able to express themselves ...

> In one session, after a long silence and in full contact with what was happening, an EPC provider realized that the client had great difficulty describing what was troubling her. The provider decided to tell the client what he was feeling and told her that he had realized she was unable to speak – he did not make an assessment, did not judge, and did not speculate on possible causes. The client confirmed that perception and the provider asked whether it would be easier if she had some paper and pencil. The client accepted but, even then, she was unable to express herself and said it would be very difficult to do so with the care provider because she

felt she was being analyzed. The therapist asked whether she would be able to express herself if he left the room; her answer was yes. Thus, he said he would leave the room and would wait until she called him back. (Vieira et al., 2020, p. 4)

Coming across creative examples like this reminds me of the importance of lightly holding to one side our assumptions/knowing and cultural values, including any 'rules' (about how people should behave or how therapy must be) in order to be with whatever is emerging with the client. It's important to try to be open to being surprised, holding on to *unknowing*.

When we strive to enact openness, we resist making quick judgements about our clients and their behaviour. We also avoid reductionist categories with their tendency to objectify our clients – for example, by labelling someone as a diagnosis rather than as a person, or explaining them just in terms a particular personality style or defensive structure. While diagnosis can be informative, it's important to ask what we might miss if we view just through that lens. Using the lens of diagnosis, 'depression' may lead us to look within the person and miss seeing their depressing life circumstances. And is there a risk of unduly pathologising someone rather than recognising their way of being? For this reason, I prefer terms like 'neurodiverse' rather than 'autism', or descriptions such as 'struggles to regulate emotion/behaviour' rather than 'borderline personality disorder'. This is not just political correctness; it's about recognising that people are infinitely more complicated and contradictory than labels suggest, and we do clients a disservice if we foreclose on our assessments and understandings too quickly (Finlay, 2016a).

Yet there is a contradiction between therapeutic approaches that prize unknowing openness and those approaches required when working in mental health contexts where medical ideology (diagnosis and solution-focused treatment) dominates. There is a balance to be struck between employing our presence, power, judgement and expertise as therapists while holding knowledge lightly, being reasonably humble and modest about the extent to which we understand or 'know' the other. This is the important ingredient for me. Surely the client is the expert in their own life?

Holding on to unknowing is, of course, easier said than done. It takes discipline and courage to sit with uncertainty and not-knowing and letting go of power/control towards trusting the process of the therapy encounter (Finlay and Evans, 2009).

I myself often fall short and invariably end up regretting moments when I make a hasty judgement about a client's process or view them through the lens of some reductionist category. In such moments, I have allowed my openness and presence to flee the scene; I've retreated from the path of enabling my client to see themselves in a new light and visualise a future of fresh possibilities.

Discussion questions

1. Analyse the times when you've felt 'too much' for a client and have had to rein yourself in, and when you've felt overwhelmed, dominated or diminished by a client.
2. Consider what you are able to 'bracket' and what you can't; discuss the impact of this.
3. What are the limits of your values and cultural competencies to work appropriately across gender, sexual and relationship diversity?

Resources

Book: *Therapeutic Presence: A Mindful Approach to Effective Therapy* by Shari Geller and Leslie Greenberg. Comprehensive evidence-based exploration of presence plus practical, experiential exercises for cultivating presence.

Book: *Between Person and Person* by Richard Hycner. A lovely book unpacking Buber's dialogical philosophy in a practical, reader-friendly way.

Book: *Tales of Un-knowing* by Ernesto Spinelli. A book of compelling stories laying out therapeutic encounters and an existential therapist's reasonings.

Book: *Working at Relational Depth in Counselling and Psychotherapy* by Dave Mearns and Mick Cooper is a gentle scholarly yet human/humanistic exploration of what's involved in therapeutic encounters.

Video: Boundaries and managing self-disclosure (presented by Karen Hallam): www.youtube.com/watch?v=1BFkZhsTcik

---

Notes

1. Colosimo and Pos (2015) provide a 'rational' model involving four core modes of presence, each associated with concrete behaviours regarding how therapists can embody their presence – namely, being here, being now, being open and being-with.
2. Emotion regulation, social connection and flight/fight fear responses are managed by the vagal nerve system. Polyvagal theory suggests optimal therapeutic states emerge when the nervous system detects safety and defences are down-regulated. New neural pathways can then be encouraged.
3. In I–Thou, the therapist surrenders an instrumental desire for control or validation and eschews habitual ways of interacting that are found in instrumental I–It relationships. The I–Thou relationship is free from

judgement, narcissism, demands, possessiveness, objectification, greed and anticipation (Hycner, 1993).

4. The term 'GSRD' seems to be replacing the ever-lengthening list of sexual/gender categories including LGBTQI++. Currently, there are dozens of GSRD identities and terms to choose from, and increasingly young people see themselves on a spectrum and eschew binary categories (Barker, 2017–2019, p. 14).

FOUR

BEING EMPATHICALLY AND COMPASSIONATELY ATTUNED

Empathy is best offered with humility and held lightly, ready to be corrected. (Elliott et al., 2018, p. 406)

Research demonstrates how empathy, compassion and attunement are the foundations of the therapeutic use of self and how they are the most effective and powerful elements of the therapeutic relationship (Cooper, 2008). However, as processes they remain elusive. When we empathically and compassionately attune to another we gently sense, resonate with and stay with that individual in their experience. But their multi-dimensional nature, involving cognition, emotion, body and developmental–relational elements, makes them hard to describe. That different theorists define them in varied ways adds to the complexity: while some use the terms fluidly and interchangeably, others distinguish sharply between them.

Much depends upon the theoretical lens applied. Loosely speaking, person-centred therapists focus on 'empathy'; relational CBT and mindfulness practitioners home in on 'compassion', while relational psychoanalytic therapists favour 'attunement' and the provision of 'corrective emotional experiences'.[1] In practice, however, the use of self is layered – all therapists probably engage all elements but to different degrees.

This chapter will try to articulate more specifically how we engage empathy, compassion and attunement. The first three sections examine each of these processes in turn. The fourth section goes on to look at how they relationally intertwine in practice. Beyond technique, empathy, compassion and attunement are relational processes. It's our responsiveness to clients and our harmonic fit with them as we go exploring together. The chapter ends with the usual case study, reflections and questions.

Empathy

The term 'empathy' (from the German *Einfühlung*) means 'gently sensing another person in order to better appreciate their experience' – essentially, stepping into another's shoes. Rogers (1980, p. 142) described it as being sensitive to 'felt meanings which flow in the other person'. The process involves listening deeply to both the words and 'feeling tones' of the other:

> I hear a deep human cry that lies buried and unknown far below the surface of the person ... Can I hear the sounds and sense the shape of this other person's inner world? Can I resonate to what he is saying so deeply that I sense the meanings he is afraid of yet would like to communicate? (Rogers, 1980, p. 8)

In this quotation, Rogers shows how he opens himself to the unknown: that which is unknown, perhaps to both therapist and client.

Beyond technique, empathy is a relational process. When clients first enter therapy, they often struggle to articulate what exactly is troubling them. Their inner turmoil is expressed more often in feelings than in coherent thoughts and therapists move to check their meanings. 'Behind your words I'm hearing you say you've lost hope. Am I picking that up right?' Or, 'That's some burden you've been carrying. I'm guessing you feel robbed?' (Finlay, 2016a).

Rice and Greenberg describe the process thus:

> As clinicians we have encountered moments when a client was starting to express, often with great difficulty, some intense present emotional experience ... This seemed to be a time for the therapist to resonate empathically with the client's feelings, and to reflect them in their full intensity, without being scared, clearly and genuinely prizing the client. We found that when we were truly able to respond in this way at such times, clients were able to go deeper and deeper into their feelings until they seemed to 'touch rock bottom' and were able to start up again. Clients seemed to experience a sense of relief and wholeness ... This seemed to break the sense of isolation and fragmentation. (Rice and Greenberg, 1990, p. 407)

In such moments of relational depth (Mearns and Cooper, 2005), we empathically resonate with and attune to the whole of the client's being. We become immersed in their world. However, empathy isn't becoming fused with the client or projecting our own perspective. Instead, we try to be open to the client's Otherness. It's not, 'I know your experience of raging against your mother because I also hated mine'. Rather, it's about feeling awe in the face of the unfamiliar (Finlay, 2016a). Empathy involves shifting perspective: 'It's not what I would experience *as me* in your shoes; empathy is what I experience *as you* in your shoes' (Murphy and Dillon, 1998, p. 88). In other words, we need to step back and appreciate the other's difference and where they are. Casement explains this important point:

> Empathic identification is not enough, as it can limit a therapist to seeing what is familiar, or is similar to his [*sic*] own experience. Therapists therefore have to develop an openness to, and respect for, feelings and experiences that are quite unlike their own. (1985, p. 95)

Nine different facets of empathic knowing occur in therapy, suggests Hart (1999), on a continuum of 'external empathy' to 'deep empathy'. At one pole, the therapist is an observer, perceiving another's experience as if they were them. With deep empathy, there is a more direct intersubjective knowing where self–other can blur.

Similarly, Rowan (2002) identifies three levels of empathic use of self: instrumental, authentic and transpersonal.[2] At the instrumental level, therapists can learn sets of skills, including a basic, safe (defended) level of empathic listening skills. The authentic level links to Hart's 'deep empathy' and is where we enter the client's world and self–other boundaries are loosened (as seen with projective identification and other transferential dynamics). With the transpersonal, boundaries between therapist and client fall away and there is a transcendental, even spiritual 'linking' (Finlay, 2016a).[3]

Elliott et al. (2018) also identify different types of empathy, such as empathic reflection, empathic affirmation, empathic recognition, process empathy, empathic conjecture, exploratory empathy, evocative empathy, and so on (see Box 4.1). Whether some of these empathies could also be called compassion or attunement is up for debate.

Box 4.1 Case example: forms of empathy

'Rick' (a clinical amalgam) was a 30-year-old unmarried man from a family of unsympathetic high achievers. He presented saying that he was anxious and worried much of the time, and at his first appointment he was clearly agitated. At the beginning of therapy, Rick's therapist focused on building *rapport* using **empathic understanding** responses to validate the client's perspective. For example:

C: *I'm really in a panic* (anxious, looking plaintively at the therapist). *I feel anxious all the time. Sometimes it seems so bad, I really worry that I'm on the verge of a psychotic break. I'm afraid I'll completely fall apart. Nothing like this has ever happened to me before.*

T: *So feeling really, really anxious as if you might break down* (**empathic reflection**) – *it is just so hard to control and manage it* (**empathic affirmation**).

C: *Yes! I don't know myself any more. I feel so lost. The anxiety's like a big cloud that just takes over, and I can't even find myself in it any more. I don't even know what I want, what to trust ... I'm so lost.*

T: *So you feel so lost, like you don't even know yourself or what you want and need. No wonder you feel lost if it takes over like that. Anxiety can do that, ambushing us and taking over.*

C: (Client tearing up) *Yes, I do feel ambushed and confused* (sadly and thoughtfully).

The therapist's **empathic recognition** provided the client with a sense of being understood, building rapport and fostering a sense of safety that gradually helped the client move from agitation into reflective sadness. To facilitate this, the therapist began using more **exploratory empathy**, trying to get at the implicit or unspoken feelings in the client's narratives, including emerging experiences. For example:

T: *And I hear that this leaves you feeling, sort of, almost sad?* (**empathic conjecture**)

C: *Yes, this is such a familiar feeling ... I always felt lost as a kid. Everyone was always so busy – there was no place for me. My siblings were focused on their sports and academic achievements. I was the youngest so I was expected to tag along to their activities even though I hated it. It was so boring!*

T: *It sounds almost as if you felt like the odd one out in your family, like you didn't quite fit in somehow?* (**exploratory reflection**)

C: *Yes, very much so. There was so much going on. Mum was always busy with her activities or driving my siblings somewhere. I used to escape with my books and my music.*

To further amplify the client's experience, the therapist next used **evocative empathy**, attempting to bring the client's experience alive in the session using rich, evocative, concrete language, often with a probing, tentative quality. For example:

T: *So you felt forgotten somehow? I have an image of you as a little boy sitting alone in a corner curled up with your book as the people around you rushed to and fro.*

C: *Yes, I used to hide away and try to disappear* (client's voice breaks).

The therapist continued to facilitate the exploration of the client's inner experience using **process empathy** and **empathic conjectures**. For example, while watching Rick the therapist noticed that her client's voice shifted and that he looked very sad.

> **T:** *I noticed your voice changed just then* (**process reflection**). *You look very sad. Are you?* (**empathic conjecture**) *What is happening inside as you recall the busy household?* (**exploratory question**)
>
> **C:** *I feel like I cannot live up to their expectations. Even though I know I've got all this potential, I always feel there is something wrong with me.* (Elliott et al., 2018, p. 402; italics in original, bold is mine)
>
> *Included by kind permission of the American Psychological Association*

Compassion

One of the best-known definitions of compassion comes from the Dalai Lama, who describes it as 'a sensitivity to the suffering of self and others, with a deep commitment to try to relieve it' (1995, p. 16, cited in Gilbert, 2010). Lewin expands, arguing that, in compassion, we stay with clients' suffering and offer succour without smothering (Lewin, 1996). Compassion, he says, is the 'core value that animates psychotherapy and gives it soul and staying power' (1996, p. 28); Erskine (2020a) talks about compassion as what motivates therapists to attune to clients' relational needs. Germer (2021) promotes self-compassion to regulate emotions and encourage a radical acceptance of self/vulnerability.

Compassion is so prized that some have turned it into a therapy in itself, as, for instance, in Compassion Focused Therapy (CFT) (developed by Paul Gilbert, 2010). In this therapy, a compassionate orientation is offered to clients who learn to cultivate their own skills of compassion and self-compassion. This can help lead to feelings of self-acceptance, self-soothing, safety, comfort and calmness. These ideas similarly apply to therapists' self-care and use of supervision/internal supervisor.

Compassion is a 'higher order form of empathy', says Wosket (2017, p. 213), describing its emergence in stages. First, she is 'hit by' her feelings in response to what is going on for the client – for example, she may shudder or feel a lump in her throat or tears may well up. She may even be momentarily 'struck dumb' by the impact of that feeling. But then thinking sets in and this helps her give form to her feeling. She then shares this with her client, as in 'I felt like a weight fell on my chest as you described …' (p. 214). In this way, compassion becomes animated in the way therapists use themselves.

The key, for Wosket, is to stay congruent and authentic, and avoid falling into fake sympathy:

> My client is recalling in anguished words the relived agony of very early childhood abuse. He says: 'I can just see this tiny child with a blank face lying on the bed. It's overwhelming. I have this hollow inside me …' If I had attempted an empathic response to this, probably the best I could have

mustered would have been something like: 'You feel unbearable sadness and pain at seeing this image of yourself being hurt as a tiny child.' However this would be an incongruent response to the extent that I do not in any way know what it feels like, as a two-year-old, to be abused as my client has been abused and, further, it is not an intervention that genuinely conveys my own feelings which are, predominately, outrage and horror. I cannot understand or know what one person's unique and individual trauma is like and to make a pretence of so doing can be patronising and insulting. What I actually say to my client is: 'I cannot imagine what you feel when you look at that image of yourself as a two-year-old. When I think about a tiny child being hurt in that way I just wish I had been there to save you from it.' … He begins to weep and thereby takes a first small step towards the gargantuan task that lies ahead of mourning the murder of his childhood. (Wosket, 2017, p. 212)

Attunement

Musical metaphors like resonance, rhythm, duet and chorus come to mind when describing an attuned relationship (perhaps unsurprisingly given the 'tune' in at-tune). (Finlay, 2016a, p. 52)

Attunement means adjusting to another in sympathetic, synchronous relationship. Applied to therapy, it is our responsiveness to, and our harmonic fit with, clients. See Box 4.2, where Casement attunes to the client's deeper need for the therapist to recognise he doesn't understand.

The attuned therapist tunes into the emotional tone of the client. It involves being 'in sync' with the client, tracking subtle shifts and movements in their experience and then focusing selectively on what seems most alive for them. Like an attuned mother who notices a child's distress and offers comfort and soothing, the attuned therapist mediates emotion (Stern, 1985).

Erskine et al. (1999) describe how 'inquiry, attunement and involvement' are facets of the overall empathic frame within which the client's growth is nurtured. Attunement – conscious and out-of-awareness synchronising of the therapist and client process – is necessary to ensure a fit with the client's ongoing, moment-to-moment needs and processes. Beyond empathy, it's about kinaesthetically sensing and moving with the client in a contact-enhancing way. The authors identify and characterise the multiple, nuanced forms by which attunement can be expressed:

1. *Affective* attunement A three-level response: noticing and empathising with the client's affect; vicariously feeling and responding to the emotion; and communicating a response.

Box 4.2 Practical application: therapeutic attunement

When a patient who is speaking so quietly that he can hardly hear her, Casement senses that the near-inaudibility of her voice might offer a significant communication:

> I think there is something important about the way in which you are talking to me – talking so that I can hardly hear. I could again have asked you to speak louder. Instead I have realized that I will only pick up what you are trying to get across to me if I listen very carefully, as a mother might with her infant who does not have any words. And what I am sensing is that you are feeling that I am not in touch with you. I believe that this is what you need me to understand, that I am not at this moment understanding you. (Casement, 1990, p. 166)

At this point, the patient began to cry. When she could speak again, she replied: 'But you understood that you did not understand. That is what makes the difference' (1990, p. 166). Casement goes on to recognise the possibility that this patient's parents may have often assumed they had understood her when they had not.

---

2. *Cognitive* attunement Understanding the client's thinking and perspective, including their world view and meanings.
3. *Developmental* attunement Thinking developmentally and seeing/enabling the client's regression and attending to that 'child's' needs.
4. *Rhythmic* attunement Being responsive to the client's own rhythmic patterns. For example, where clients are slow thinkers, therapists will go more slowly or speak more simply and gently when the client is regressed. (Erskine et al., 1999)

Brains in synchrony

Accumulating neuroscientific evidence suggests that the infant's right brain hemisphere is involved in attachment and the mother's right hemisphere in comforting functions. The two right brain systems are seen to be mutually engaged in affective synchrony, creating a context of attuned resonance that results in a kind of right-brain to right-brain communion (Schore, 1994).

Other research[4] has focused on the idea of mirror neurons (ones that might explain behaviour such as flinching when we see someone wince in pain). These have been hypothesised – somewhat controversially – as underlying our ability to understand others and as forming the basis of empathy and other social skills.

Applying neuroscience to therapy, it appears that we work with our own and our client's left brains when we process cognitively, while right-to-right brain communication is involved with embodied empathic relational–developmental connection. Research on somatic countertransference suggests that the therapist may be decoding unconscious right brain communications (both conscious and unconscious) through felt somatic reactions (Schore, 2003).

The therapy process depends on accurate attunement … on reliable repetitions of right-brain interactions and resonances that help expand right-brain capacities. The right brain is the home of the capacities damaged by early relational trauma … Even for a highly functional adult, right-brain limitations are likely to become problems in emotional and interpersonal functioning. A person who can't solve personal and social problems in right-brain ways will come to rely on left-brain, explicit analytical reasoning. But left-brain analysis will only contain and manage, not solve, emotional and interpersonal problems (DeYoung, 2015, p. 63).

Empathetic, compassionate attunement as a relational process

The story in Box 4.3 shows Erskine demonstrating his layered attuned responsiveness and sensitivity to his client's needs. He engages his compassion by opening to his tears. But it is their interpersonal contact – the relational *between* – which is key.

Box 4.3 Case example: attuned responsiveness

Ruth was a mother of a 19-year-old boy who died in a car accident … I was not certain that she possessed the internal resources to say 'hello' through imagination; I sensed that it was too soon after her son's death. Instead … I had Ruth look me in the eye. I asked her to tell me all about her son. I wanted Ruth to experience my full emotional resonance with her feelings … of being a mother of a child who had just died …

She told me that he had been driving the car. He and three other boys had been drunk and they crashed into a store front. As I inquired about her feelings she expressed her anger at his frequent drinking of alcohol and his reckless driving … I … expressed how disturbing it is for a parent when children act irresponsibly …

> She told me about his brilliant school accomplishments, about the delightful things they did together in his early teenage years, and how loving he had been to her during divorce. I rejoiced with her ...
>
> She wept as she talked about his birth ... and the many instances of loving contact that they shared together. She told me how she admired her son for his many sport and academic accomplishments. Along with her I felt an appreciation of his many qualities. She could see the tears in my eyes as she recalled many special experiences that she and her son had together.
>
> The therapy of Ruth's grief was in our constant interpersonal contact ... Ruth's expression of each affect and my attuned responses – was essential in Ruth's finding some relief from her grief. (Erskine, 2015, p. 302)

The attainment of deeper, empathic, compassionate attunement requires us to let ourselves go into the process, to release our own Being in order to Be-with the other in the moment, to relinquish certainty and knowingness. It means allowing embodied feelings, thoughts, impressions and intuitions to appear in the space between. It involves permitting ourselves to be open and to be touched. It means welcoming whatever becomes figural in the moment. But this is a process of embodied intertwining, not a merging: we hold on to ourselves in order to respect the Otherness of the Other. It invites us to respond to the other and move to their rhythm as we go exploring together.

Wosket offers some quotations from clients who communicate their sense of being relationally held by their empathically, compassionately, attuned therapist, always prepared to go exploring with them:

> 'Even though you couldn't know how unbearable it was for me then, I felt you came there with me, rescued me, and brought me back.'
>
> 'I know you can't really understand what it was like for me but I sense that you have had losses too and so you know what it feels like.'
>
> 'Your eyes are very expressive. I can see you're upset and that helps me to feel cared for. If you care for me I might be worth caring about . . .'
>
> 'You held me in your arms when I was really upset – even though you sat on the other side of the room and never ever touched me.' (Wosket, 2017, p. 215)

As many authors agree, empathetic, compassionate attunement is not something we 'do' or 'provide', like giving medication. Instead, it is co-created relationally between a therapist who dwells with the client and tries to understand, and a client who tries to communicate and be understood.

Elliott et al. (2018) offer an extensive review and meta-analysis of the diverse and complicated research on empathy (and related therapist factors) and client outcomes. Results indicate that empathy is a moderately strong predictor of therapy outcome:[5] synthesising the research, the authors

Box 4.4 Research: synthesis of findings on empathy

- Empathy involves attuning to clients' experience, not simply reflecting back the content of their words.
- Therapists need to adjust their responses/understandings moment-to-moment towards sensing clients' emerging experience.
- It helps if therapists explicitly explore clients' experience of therapists' empathy rather than assuming that empathy has been shown. Client reports of therapist empathy predict treatment outcomes.
- Empathy is shown in therapists' listening, receptive attentive ways of being, not just in what they do.
- Empathy needs to be offered with humility, assumptions held lightly. The therapist needs to keep open to being corrected.
- Empathy is a co-created experience involving mutual communication.
- Empathy must be adapted to individuals. Some clients can find expressions of empathy too invasive or controlling.
- Empathy is not just a technique; it's part of being relational and offering authentic care. (Elliott et al., 2018)

Included by kind permission of the American Psychological Association

helpfully conclude with some tips about how to engage 'empathy' (in its different manifestations), which is summarised in Box 4.4.

Another facet of relationality is the cultural context (see Box 4.5). The way we enact our empathy/compassion/attunement is likely to differ,

Box 4.5 Research: cultural variations re: empathy

The vast majority of studies on empathy have been conducted on white participants (often college students) in Western cultures. Cross-cultural research on empathy is both complicated and contradictory.

On one hand, Cassels et al. (2010) studied Western students and suggest they have more empathy than Asian ones. Research by Ng and James (2013) suggests that Chinese clients may not consider therapist empathy a priority and do not necessarily know how to react to feeling-based empathic statements. Other relational factors, such as being non-judgemental and 'having a compassionate heart to help' in terms of engaging tasks beyond professional duty, may be more salient. Research by Goetz et al. (2010) suggests individualistic American participants were likely to express more compassion towards strangers, while collectivistic Chinese participants were more likely to express compassion towards members of their own group.

> On the other hand, the large-scale study of 104,365 participants across 63 countries conducted by Chopik et al. (2017) shows that collectivist countries were higher in empathy than individualistic ones. They also found that higher empathy countries also seem to have higher levels of agreeableness, conscientiousness, self-esteem, emotionality, subjective well-being and prosocial behaviour.

depending on the institutional context and our culture as well as the specific relationship involved. Much of the literature on empathy/attunement in therapy takes a Western perspective, so a broader cultural awareness is needed. The concept of cultural empathy prompts us to reach beyond the comfort zone of our individualistic perspectives and engage the relational and cultural context.

Case study

When she started therapy, Violet was a 52-year-old woman with a schizoid process who seemed depressed. Initially, she would spend her sessions going into great detail about her day-to-day life while avoiding talking about her feelings. The therapist (Richard Erskine) felt talked 'at' rather than 'to'.

> Just like Violet, I was not fully present. I was confused by her. I did not understand how she functioned. No wonder I periodically felt drowsy or found my mind wandering to other situations. It was evident to me that in the absence of any emotional connection between the two of us, I compensated by becoming more and more behavioral in my interventions. Eventually, I became aware of a parallel process: my focus on behaviour change mirrored both her mother's and husband's attempts to control her behaviour. My countertransference was in my wanting something to happen ... so I focused on expressive methods, cognitive understanding and behavioural change to ward off my worry about not being effective psychotherapist ... (Erskine, 2020b, p. 3)

Erskine realised he needed to change his approach. After some months of working with her, he began to understand there was a need to respect and be-with Violet in her 'quiet place' – a space involving long periods of silence where she self-stabilised and self-regulated. He recognised her need for him to be less invasive by gently reflecting back and describing her internal experience.

I invited Violet to withdraw to her 'safe bed'. There was about 15 minutes of silence wherein I caringly watched over her in the same way that I watched over my children as I sat by their bed at night when they were sick with a fever. I watched Violet's laboured breathing and the tension in her clenched hands. I made a statement: 'You must be so scared.' Violet nodded her head to indicate agreement ... A couple of minutes later I again said, '"It is important to have a safe hiding place."'. She again nodded her head. After another two minutes of silence I again said, '"It is so important to hide in your quiet place, particularly when you are sad."' She again nodded, her breathing returned to normal, she unclenched her hands.

When Violet opened her eyes she said my description of her internal experience was important because it meant that I understood her and that she was not all alone ... We discussed how my description of her internal sensations was different from her mother's and husband's criticizing definitions of her. She described my voice as 'tentative' and my tone soft, 'not a definite, authoritarian voice' that she was used to in her family. (Erskine, 2020b, p. 13)

Critical reflections

When I began counselling (back in the 1970s), I understood the critical differences between empathy and sympathy. I learned the technique of listening well and reflecting back empathetically. But only gradually was I able to develop an ability to empathically attune and be congruently relational, to open myself to feeling my own and other's pain in compassion. I saw how going beyond just technique (from 'doing' empathy to 'being' attuned empathically/compassionately) enabled the possibility for deeper embodied relational connection and healing. This embodied relationality is discussed further in the next chapter.

Of course, there are many times when I don't feel that attunement or – worse – when I actively misattune. Maybe I'm not sufficiently present and in the right space myself or, counter-transferentially, I get caught up in replaying dynamics of misattunement (as illustrated by Erskine's initial response to Violet, above). Or maybe my client is so enveloped in a cloud of dissociation that I simply cannot 'feel' them. At these times, it's important for me to engage empathically and compassionately with myself and try not to beat myself up that I'm not being a better, more attuned therapist.

One point I don't think I have stressed enough in this chapter is the dynamic, moving quality of our tuning into another and how we need to let ourselves go into the process. It's not a question of simply attuning empathically and compassionately to the client or not. Instead, we inevitably move into, out of and through different intensities of closeness and distance, between synergistic merger, rupture and repair. One moment we can feel a little distant and not well tuned in. In the next, we get impacted by something the client says or does and we open compassionately to them. We might then get drawn into an empathic identification so intense that there may be a sensation of merging (or confluence) with the client. We then regroup, recognising that it is important to differentiate and respect the Otherness of our client. There is a balance of feeling/sensing the other and ourselves as separate while tuning into what is being cocreated relationally.

While we can lose our own identity momentarily as we sink into the other, it is unlikely to help the client to join them in their pain; we need to hold onto ourselves and maintain a therapy perspective simultaneously. This is the key to Buber's notion of Inclusion:[6] 'You can see it, feel it, experience it from two sides. From your side, seeing him, observing him, knowing him, helping him – from your side and from his side (Buber, [1951] 1965, p. 171). In practice, then, we tend to move between levels of empathy, compassion and attunement while reflexively stepping back to reflect on what is happening in the process. Simultaneously being-with 'inside' and being 'outside', looking in, is not easily achieved – but that is the 'dance' we do (Finlay, 2016a).

I started this chapter with a musical metaphor, and I'd like to finish with one that emphasises the relational element of tuning in to another: as the music of the therapeutic relationship plays, it touches, evokes and heals:

Tuning in to the Other and to me, I also tune in to the between. It is as if I am listening intently and with all of me for a tune that is all of us (me, other and us). I listen to the tune being sung by the Other. I try and connect with the deeper song – the song of contact, meeting, connectedness, longing. (Finlay and Evans, 2009, p. 125)

Discussion questions

1. In differentiating between empathy, compassion and attunement, do you have a sense of prioritising one more than others in your work with clients? How might it vary at different points in the therapy?
2. When you are struggling with challenging emotions – for instance, grief – what do you need from different people?
3. Think about a specific time when you found it difficult to attune empathically and compassionately to a client. What factors arising relationally in the process (i.e. to do with the client, yourself and/or your relationship) might have contributed to your difficulty?

Resources

Book: *Beyond Empathy: A Therapy of Contact-in-Relationship* by Richard Erskine, Janet Moursund and Rebecca Trautmann. This best-selling book beautifully illuminates the theory/practice of relationally oriented integrative psychotherapy.

Book: Richard Erskine's (2015) rich compilation *Relational Patterns, Therapeutic Presence: Concepts and Practice of Integrative Psychotherapy* provides a convenient précis of his formative work.

Book: *The Healing Relationship in Gestalt Therapy* by Richard Hycner and Lynne Jacobs. A 'must read' book synthesising the theory of working relationally/dialogically with powerful illustrations.

Video: Chris Germer on self-compassion in therapy. Available at: www.compassionintherapy.com/stream/chris-germer-2/

Video: Carl Rogers on empathy. Available at: www.youtube.com/watch?v=iMi7uY83z-U

Notes

1. Alexander and French (1946) coined the term 'corrective emotional experiences' to describe the healing power of the therapeutic relationship within the context of psychoanalytic therapy. Since then, the concept has been broadened and applied across modalities (Castonguay et al., 2012).

2. These three modes of therapist empathic being apply across the theoretical spectrum. 'Instrumental empathy' can be used by all practitioners. Humanistic and psychoanalytic therapists utilise the deeper forms which cognitive-behavioural therapists usually wouldn't routinely engage.

3. Buber ([1951] 1965) referred to the 'between' space as 'interhuman' (where two people connect in their separateness and relatedness) through which we glimpse the eternal 'Thou'.

4. Elliott et al. (2018) summarise the neuroscientific findings around empathy, arguing that three main processes are involved: 1. the existence of an automatic, intuitive emotional simulation process that mirrors the emotional elements of the other's bodily experience, with brain activation centring in the limbic system; 2. a more deliberate, conceptual/cognitive, perspective-taking process located in the prefrontal and the temporal cortex; 3. the emotion-regulation process that people use to soothe their personal distress when vicariously experiencing the other person's pain or discomfort, allowing them to mobilise compassion and

helping behaviours (probably located in the orbitofrontal, prefrontal and parietal cortex).

5. Mean weighted r = .28 (p < .001; 95% confidence interval: .23 −.33; equivalent of d = .58) for 82 independent samples and 6,138 clients.

6. Buber was an Austrian-born Jewish theologian, educator and existential phenomenological philosopher. Buber saw empathy as one 'feeling' among many. In contrast, he regarded Inclusion as an attempt to experience the wholeness of another's experiencing while holding on to the centre of one's own existence.

FIVE

BEING EMBODIED

The most important thing in communication is hearing what isn't said. (Peter Drucker, interview with Moyers, 1989)

Our bodies play a profound role in the therapeutic use of self. We observe our client's body language, ever alert to our own visceral sensations and movements as we watch, sense, respond. Being aware of bodily processes offers an important interpretive conduit (explicit or transferential) which can become the basis of bodily-based interventions.

In the quotation below, Appel-Opper notes the significance of clients' and therapists' living bodies.

> The way the client enters the room, looks at us, sits, moves ... tell[s] us about their relational rhythms and melodies. Their bodies tell the story around them of how they were looked at, held and touched, whether they were comforted and encouraged or abused and mistreated.
>
> The living body uses a certain language: a motionless shoulder, a lost gaze, a way of looking for breath, a tenuous movement say something. As therapists we react physically to these body narratives. They reach us skin to skin, heart to heart, muscle to muscle with little or no mediation of a cognitive or reflexive process and we react to them in an unintentional way. With small movements: we step back, we hold our breath, we stretch, we look away, and suddenly we are cold. (Appel-Opper, 2012, p. 88)

This chapter sketches different ways in which our bodies may be used in therapy and implicitly invites therapists to become 'bodily literate' (Shaw, 2003). The first two sections focus on the way we observe and experience the client's body and our own therapist's body. The third section highlights the relational–social dimensions of our bodies and this is followed by a section outlining four somatic therapeutic interventions: raising body awareness; using the body to express emotion; being a body the client needs; and vagal regulation. The chapter ends with the usual case study, reflections and questions.

The client's body

To evaluate what a client might need from therapy, we gather information through objective observation of micro-communications and questioning and through continual subjective, embodied, intuitive sensings. These skills don't always come naturally; it takes time to develop and hone them.

When a client enters the room, an attentive therapist will absorb the gestalt, the whole, of the client's body language towards understanding the client's present experiential state(s). For instance:

- *Facial expressions* What is the client communicating or is their expression flat?
- *Movement* How stiff or relaxed is the client? Do they wriggle a lot or use significant gestures? What is their posture communicating?
- *Vocal aspects* Is it soft, loud, tentative, flat, emotional? Are there pauses or pressure of speech?
- *Eye contact* Does the client make and hold eye contact? Where does the client gaze?
- *Bodily process* How in tune with their body are they? Or are they disconnected? What embodied language (e.g. 'stomach churning') is used? (Joyce and Sills, 2018)

We pick up what clients both 'give' and 'give-off' (Goffman, 1990). We then use this information – holding any interpretations tentatively – to inform our responses. In the following quotation, a therapist describes her initial sensings of a new client:

> He slopes in, no eye-contact, head down, shoulders rounded, chest caved inwards. He's 40 years old going on 8. In his every movement, he enacts his bullied and beaten up boy-self. And I find myself responding. I want to tell him to stop slouching which asks everyone to beat him up. I catch myself. I realise, this is his father's perspective. Aware that I've fallen into the same trap, I move to soften my eyes.

Beyond observing client's non-verbal communications, therapists will also be alert to any mismatches. For instance, the client who says they are angry but smiles and speaks softly may be displaying some difficulty in owning that anger. Their behaviour may suggest a pattern of trying to please others and/or softening the emotional expression of their anger which they've learned is somehow 'unacceptable'. Working with that anger, the therapist might encourage the client to own their anger by promoting more congruent, muscular vocalisations of it.

Interestingly, online work changes what we can tune into about our clients' bodies. We tend not to see their whole body and lose micro-communicative cues like hand-wringing or a tapping foot. But we can train our focus on, and appreciation of, clients' facial expressions. Mitchell's (2020, p. 126) research into online therapy experience, for example, reveals the paradoxical closeness and distance created by the technology. Her therapist participants described the weird 'sense of magnification' which allowed for 'close observations of clients' facial expressions' while also creating the 'opportunity to mutually scrutinise or judge more closely'.

More important than the bodily messages given by a client (deliberately or inadvertently) is their lived bodily experience. How do they feel themselves to be? Tense, clumsy, sluggish, ugly, energised, graceful, grounded? We tune into this experiential tone by asking clients directly about their experience, but also interpretively through our own responses. Westland (2009) describes the subtlety of the process in Box 5.1.

Box 5.1 Case example: therapist–client bodily communication

Helen knows that she can run away from herself with flurries of words and ideas, and we have a working agreement for me to interrupt her, if she doesn't not "catch herself". She can find this very containing. Helen is describing a conversation with a health worker about her ailing father. She is getting lost in the story of who said what and her ideas of what his care should be. I begin to feel confused myself in the detail of the story. I breathe and come back to myself ... I start to recollect where I began to get confused, and my interest waned. As I am doing this Helen is feeling uncomfortable "something niggles and is upsetting". I suggest that she pauses in the narrative and brings awareness to what is happening in her body. She becomes more inward-focused and somewhat reflective. Her face begins to look "upset". I notice very tiny movements in her face, and let myself breathe fully. "Upsetness" seems to intensify in Helen. Waves of emotion come up Helen's body emanating from the abdomen, and she sobs deeply. Through the tears she cries "He is so lonely and distressed". I assume that she is talking about herself, her father and her relationship with me. Later on we talk together about this tapestry of meaning. (Westland, 2009)

The therapist's body

As we try to be aware of the meanings of clients' non-verbal communications, we also need to stay focused on our own bodily presentation and experience and this involves:

- being reflexively aware;
- engaging felt sense;
- working with somatic resonances (bodily counter-transferences).

Being reflexively aware

The starting point is to be reflexively aware of the messages we might be giving off to clients. When we hold a grounded and comfortably contactful posture, for example, we communicate that we are listening, available, ready to learn and open to being impacted by the client. Through our bodies we present ourselves as trustworthy people who care. Box 5.2 highlights different bodily modes we engage in as part of our therapeutic use of self.

Box 5.2 Research: therapists' lived bodily experience

Through body language … [and] touch they express support, comfort, warmth … They … hold and embrace their patients/clients, both physically and mentally, in order to give treatment and keep them safe. In these ways the therapists use the '**trusted-healer body**' as a therapeutic tool.

Behind the 'trusted-healer body' is a '**scientist-professional body**' which is more clinical, analytical and distant. This body carries keys … sits behind a desk. It also observes patients/clients – examines, probes, diagnoses. In these ways, therapists display status and power – a remote image they seek to counteract . . .

They have to be careful about when they use touch and how it will be received. They want to be friendly, trusted and attractive yet deny their '**sexual body**' as it contradicts their other bodies. For women therapists, their sexual body is additionally a **vulnerable body** that can be threatened and invaded. When they come to work, they prefer to leave this more personal body at home.

Finally, the therapists seek to nurture, reassure, enable and care. As patients/clients express their needs, so the therapists respond. But … their bodies can feel invaded, grabbed at and sucked dry. In this way, the therapists engage a '**mother body**' – one that can feel both loving and exhausted. (Finlay, 1998, pp. 247–8)

Engaging felt sense: 'Focusing'

In addition to being aware of what our bodies are doing, we can also tune into our bodily wisdom using what Gendlin (1981, 1996), a phenomenological philosopher and psychotherapist, calls 'Focusing'. Focusing attends to intuitive 'gut feelings' of either participant or therapist and involves dialoguing with the body. 'What might that body sensation be saying?' 'What does it need?' The insights arising (in words, images or metaphors) can sometimes trigger an 'Aha moment' – a sudden release of tension. A new way of capturing the experience in language is born.

But Focusing is more than a technique. It is a mindful, gently compassionate way of being which is respectful of one's body (our own or others'). It helps us to pay attention to our bodily experiencing at the threshold between what we are conscious of and what we are not quite aware of. Focusing enables us to tune into subtle bodily feelings that may be trying to tell us something. Time slows down, space opens up. Sensations, symbols and words emerge, fresh and alive. Now we are open to the wisdom of the body which will guide and surprise us (Finlay, 2014).

Gendlin argues that what comes from the bodily sensed edge of awareness has a special intricacy which involves more than body sensations:

> The body sense is unclear and vague at first, but if you pay attention it will open up into words or images and you experience a felt shift in your body. In the process of Focusing, one experiences a physical change in the way that the issue is being lived in the body ... The whole issue looks different and new solutions arise. (Gendlin, online source)

Working with somatic resonances (bodily counter-transferences)

Therapists' bodies can be a rich source of information, recovered via somatic resonances/countertransferences. Just think about the times in a session where you've suddenly and inexplicitly felt sleepy or tearful or experienced an unusual sensation in your body. Could you be embodying something meaningful about the client's experience?

The term 'somatic resonance' tends to be used in humanistic work, where it is seen as mutual empathic, kinaesthetic, energetic sensings. In psychoanalytic work, the term 'bodily countertransference' is more common, referring to an analyst's experiencing of a client's physical state (empathically or through projective identifications). In practice, relational body psychotherapists straddle both concepts, engaging resonance and also countertransference (Soth, 2018).

The gestalt 'eye' of Joyce and Sills offer this useful checklist to engage somatic resonance:

- What feelings and images do you have in response to the client in the first session?

- Who does he [*sic*] remind you of?
- What metaphor would you use to describe him (for example, like an express train, like a frightened animal)?
- What reactions do you have to your client's appearance (e.g. their clothes, hair, face, skin colour)?
- What has most impact on you as you listen to him (his voice tone, the rhythms of his speech)?
- What is your body resonance (for example, do you feel tense or relaxed, energized or passive as you sit with him)? (2018, p. 71)

Stone (2006) likens the psychoanalyst to a 'tuning fork' when describing embodied resonance in countertransference. He suggests that bodily reactions are more frequently involved when working with borderline, psychotic or severely narcissistic individuals where there has been severe childhood trauma and/or problems to do with sex, aggression or eating disorders (see Box 5.3).

Box 5.3 Practical application: somatic counter-transference

As I sit there I begin to feel a tightness in my chest and find it hard to breathe. Although I do not suffer from asthma, he does and I wonder if this is how it feels. The tightness increases, and it is hard to get enough air in or even to breathe out. I decide to break the silence and ask him how he is feeling. I do this as a way of trying to use what is happening to me in the countertransference, but mainly in the hope that if I say something I will be able to breathe again. He says he isn't feeling anything, and looks at me blankly through his thick lenses. My anxiety increases, I am becoming afraid I soon won't be able to breathe at all, and I blurt out, almost gasping, 'How does your chest feel?' He looks at me in shock, pulls his feet up, draws his legs up to his chest in a foetal position, and howls. As he starts to sob and weep I feel the tension run out of my chest, down through my solar plexus, and with relief I breathe in deeply and easily. He continues sobbing for the next 10 minutes until the end of the session. He is my last patient and he remains in my waiting room until he is able to get up and leave. Not a word has been spoken by him during this time.

Two days later he makes no mention of what occurred at the end of the previous session, and when at an apposite moment I refer to it, he has little memory of what happened, and he apparently had no feelings or thoughts while he was sobbing. For my part, I also had little idea what was going on beyond feeling empathically the pain and grief his body was expressing. (Stone, 2006, pp. 110–11)

The relational–social body

As the excerpts above show, it is vital to factor in both the relational and cultural context if we are to understand any bodily encounter, and it is worth probing both these aspects more deeply.

The relational body

The non-verbal dance of relationship is both subtle and impactful. Cooper emphasises the concept of 'embodied empathy' or attunement:

> The therapist is not resonating with specific thoughts, emotions or bodily sensations, but with the complete, gestalt-like mosaic of her client's embodied being. ... The whole of the therapist's body is alive in the interaction, moving and vibrating in tandem with the client's experiencing. (Cooper, 2001, p. 223)

We not only vibrate physically to the other, we also use our bodies to communicate, contain and hold the client (while striving not to invade or smother). Relational depth can even occur in silence with a glance, touch or shared smile (Mearns and Cooper, 2005). Stern (2004, cited in Mearns and Cooper, 2005) gives the example of a therapist who normally said goodbye by shaking hands with a client. However, on one occasion when the client was particularly sad, they had a deep moment of connection as the therapist clasped the client's hand in both of his. That vital moment was experienced as perhaps one of the most memorable moments of therapy.

Our bodies also touch and become touched (sometimes without actual physical contact). Our bodies impact others just as theirs impact us. This point is made in the following story, where the psychiatrist recognises her own non-verbal role in setting the agenda. (Mrs Jones is a patient seeking treatment for anxiety):

> When the topic of previous sexual abuse was mentioned by Mrs Jones, the treating psychiatrist observed that she herself appeared uncomfortable and subtly leaned back in the chair and crossed her own legs and arms. Immediately after this, Mrs Jones had abruptly changed the subject, stating 'But you don't want to hear about all that.'
>
> Reflecting on her own behavior, the treating psychiatrist realized that she did not comment on this and subsequently Mrs Jones discussed more superficial topics. She noted Mrs Jones had appeared considerably less animated and engaged in the session after the topic shifted to more mundane events.
>
> The psychiatrist reflected on how she felt during this particular session. She realized that she had been unsure how to explore the sexual assault at that

point because the patient appeared uncomfortable. She wondered if she might have been projecting her own concerns and discomfort about addressing such an anxiety-provoking topic onto Mrs Jones. (Foley and Gentile, 2010)

Going further, Susie Orbach (2004) highlights the mutual bodily transferences co-created within the therapeutic relationship. She highlights how our bodies that patients/clients see have been created through the relationship and represents their needs (symbolic and relational) rather than being the actual natural one, and vice versa.

Cultural bodies

Beyond the immediate relationship, the wider social context remains significant. Non-verbal communication is powerfully shaped by culture and traditions (see Box 5.4). Given that people's presentation, dress, mannerisms and behaviour cannot be separated from matters of family background, ethnicity, race, sex/gender and class, differences are likely to be of significance in meetings between therapist and client.

Box 5.4 Practical application: cultural diversity

Some non-verbal expressions are understood universally (such as a frown or smile); others are culturally influenced. Here are some differences that may be relevant when we're working with clients from other cultures:

Head nod A head nod in many societies signifies agreement/approval but in some cultures (like Balkan countries), a nod means 'no'. In the Indian subcontinent, a fluid head-rocking motion carries a range of (usually positive) meanings.

Facial expressions While expressing emotions facially is valued in the West, people in other parts of the world are often taught to practise more self-control. In certain cultures (those of East Asia, for example) smiling may signal something other than happiness, such as a face-saving cover-up. Eye contact can be seen as polite or a challenge.

Hand gestures In the many parts of the West, a hand wave is used for greetings and farewells. However, in parts of Europe and Latin America, it is also a signal for 'no', while the Italian 'goodbye' wave is similar to the British and American 'come here'. Handshaking is a common Western form of greeting, but other cultures may use other forms. Care also needs to be taken with the 'V' sign because it means different things across the world. (Rugsaken, 2006)

How a client perceives us, on the basis of their observation of our physical appearance, can hugely affect how they engage therapy (Symons, 2020). Research suggests, for instance, that a perceived difference in class can lead to difficulties (Balmforth, 2009) and that young people's perceptions of an overweight counsellor undermined the counsellor's professional credibility (Moller and Tischner, 2019).

While we need to avoid making stereotypical assumptions, it's important to be aware of the sociocultural implications of bodily being – both our own and that of clients. For example, the sex of both therapist and client needs to be understood as having both biological and social (gendered) consequences, some of which may impact the therapy relationship.

There are also the implicit cultural meanings communicated through our bodies, including how we carry our intergenerational history with us. Appel-Opper (2019), for instance, describes her sense of foreignness and lostness as a German therapist practising in the UK and how she had to learn the meanings of the 'English contact smile', which initially irritated her as she couldn't understand the intentions behind it. At the same time, having to find her feet in a new culture opened her to clients' stories of feeling 'othered'. She offers the following story of therapy with a depressed immigrant involving 'unfreezing' of emotions held in her tight shoulders:

> As soon as I open my mouth, she hears that I am not British. She asks, *"Where are you from?"* To which I reply, *"I am German."* When we sit down, she tells me that her English husband had died some years ago. In a sad voice, she adds, *"I am alone now."* As she says this, I feel a heaviness in my shoulders. From the corner of my eye, I see that her shoulders look and seem heavy, and are somehow held, not moving at all ... She explains that she is Italian. In the next sessions, we explore the fact that she had never been back to Italy ... I say in a soft voice, *"Your shoulders look a bit lost to me."* This intervention unfolds a bodily, and with this, a cultural dimension, in which Anna immediately recalls how her mother had always spoken with her arms and hands ... *"My parents are dead now, but both had been against my marriage to an Englishman."* Anna cries and says, "This was such a long time ago, why am I crying now?" Later on ... I ... move my shoulders up and down very slightly. I say, *"Can I present these tiny movements to your shoulders so that we both see how this might be for them?"* I recognize that her breathing becomes slightly deeper, and that she appears calm. Anna looks "touched," as if the movements had reached her younger Anna back in Italy while the Anna in the UK is fully present. After a few minutes ... I ask how her shoulders feel. She replies, *"I can feel my shoulders a bit more and I also feel some warmth."* (Appel-Opper, 2019, p. 34)

A more pernicious process involves the challenge of everyday racism and the enduring intergenerational trauma/pain of historical racism which powerfully impacts the therapeutic relationship. (The excess mortality in black, Asian and minority ethnic – BAME – communities resulting from COVID-19, plus high-profile reports of police brutality such as the brutal George Floyd killing in the US, highlight the systematic oppression, structural inequality and racism still embedded in our culture.)

Whether a therapist/supervisor identifies as black, white or as a person of colour, says McKenzie-Mavinga (2016, p. 6), 'there is a need for a less inhibited dialogue ... about black issues and the impact of racism on therapeutic practice'. She notes the prevalence of subconscious white privilege and the myth that a focus on 'cultural sensitivity' has eradicated racism.

She shares her own problematic experience of therapy/supervision with white professionals where there seemed no possibility to explore issues around racism and internalised racism.

> I have had three experiences of long-term therapy and clinical supervision with white women. In all three of these situations, it took me at least a year to begin talking about my experiences of being black, my heritage, experiences in care and racism. I was never encouraged to explore my parental history, my interracial heritage or early experiences of racism, so I stayed in the present with my everyday life whilst building a dossier of the lack of attention to anything I said about being a black person. I became enraged by the attitude of these white professionals who were engaged to support my journey. On reflection, it is now clear that they had neither experience nor appropriate training to assist me with these matters. When eventually I expressed my accumulating rage, my therapist and primary supervisor acknowledged their naivety ... My therapist said she did not have a white experience, and I felt that her attitude became that of anger towards me for provoking this insight. My supervisor seemed to give up ... we did not have the opportunity to work through this phase of the fear and guilt evoked by their recognition trauma. (McKenzie-Mavinga, 2016, p. 83)

McKenzie-Mavinga's research finds that the vast majority of therapy practice is designated by white people for white people and that training programmes do not do enough to develop tools to work sensitively with white privilege, racial abuse experiences and race-based trauma. She argues for the need to tackle the silences (around the way that black trainees/therapists play down their identities, while white practitioners are blind to institutional racism), calling for a 'black empathic approach' rooted in empathy (see Box 5.5).

Somatic interventions

There are numerous interventions to choose from when it comes to engaging the body (both our client's and our own) during therapy. Beginning

Box 5.5 Case example: culturally empathic therapy

Nazia, aged 30, initially feared that her therapist might be prejudiced against her Islamic background. (Her grandfather had immigrated to Britain following the Partition of India and Pakistan in 1947 and her family had a long experience of such prejudice.) The focus of therapy, instead, was on her depression, low self-esteem and how she was being bullied in her work as a university librarian. While she was a strong, capable professional woman, she felt unable (and unentitled) to fight back.

Eventually, her therapist persuaded her to speak about her cultural background more by showing non-judgemental curiosity and openness. Nazia lived in a small house near the university with her husband, a gentle scholarly man who also worked at the university. She spoke positively about him and their arranged marriage, but his long working hours meant she was often home, alone and lonely. Her family and in-laws had begun to press her to start a family and she found it hard to explain that she had neither the energy nor resources to become a mother.

It took nearly a year of weekly therapy before Nazia was able to share that the anniversary of her sister's death was approaching. She had died, it transpired, in what seemed to be an unproven honour killing six years earlier. Since then, Nazia had carried layers of profound grief, guilt and shame that she hadn't done more to protect her sister or challenge her community that condoned this violence.

Nazia experienced her therapist as empathic, calm, consistent, and able to listen and empathise without criticising her – morally or culturally. Instead, her therapist acknowledged, and was compassionate about, the different internal and external pressures that weighed so heavily upon her. Nazia learned to feel and express her grief after the therapist openly showed her own tearing up. Once Nazia even wept in her therapist's arms. Eventually, she proved able to challenge her guilt directly (when 'it' was put onto an empty chair) and she began to realise that some of her shame involved an intergenerational trauma carried in her body. They engaged body work and Focusing, which increased Nazia's awareness and integration.

As Nazia became more aware of her own needs, she began to express them more openly with her husband. Together they took the decision to move to Canada, where they both secured good jobs. She continued her therapy online for a few months and, two years after her therapy ended, Nazia emailed her therapist, sharing her delight at birthing twin boys.

with the work by Reich in the 1920s, the twentieth century saw an explosion of body energy and somatic therapies: bioenergetics (Lowen), biodynamic psychotherapy (Boyesen), Hakomi (Kurtz), biosynthesis (Boadella) and Rolfing (Rolf). Many of these neo-Reichian techniques involved hands on (e.g. deep tissue massage), discharge and cathartic work.

In the last thirty years, neuroscientific insights (Damasio, Schore) have shed light on the body's crucial role in emotional well-being and trauma. Various therapies have emerged, among them Somatic Trauma Therapy (Rothschild), Somatic Experiencing (Levine) and EMDR (Shapiro). Contemporary body therapists frequently combine techniques by drawing on gentle mindfulness practice (Kabat-Zinn) and/or felt-sense Focusing (Gendlin).

This chapter cannot do justice to such an array of practices but the categories described below (see Figure 5.1) serve as a taster:

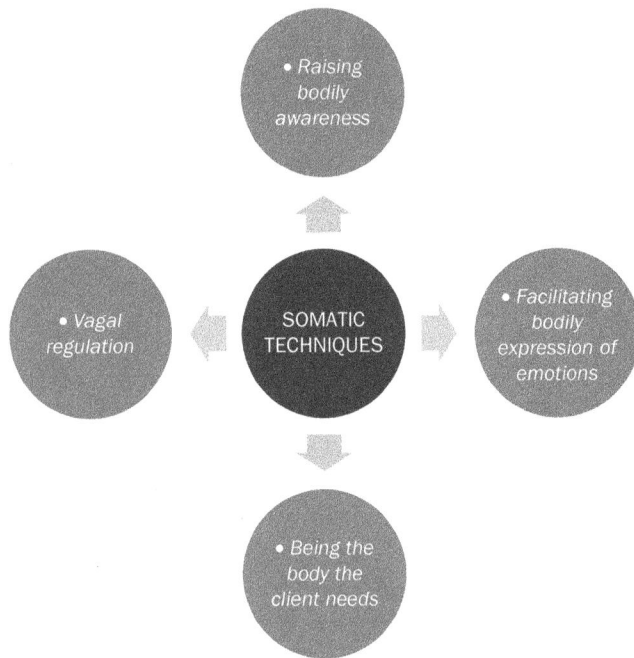

Figure 5.1 Somatic interventions

Raising body awareness

We attempt to raise a client's bodily awareness to help them become aware of themselves, their process/needs, by asking them to tune into their body:

- How does your body feel (e.g. tired, tense, relaxed, alert, holding, pained ...)?

- What might it be saying ('I'm anxious' or 'I don't want to be here' or 'I'm interested' ...)?
- What size and shape do you feel?
- How does your body move (e.g. flowingly, cumbersomely, stiffly ...)?
- Are you especially conscious of any particular parts of your body?
- Are there any parts you feel disconnected from?
- I'm noticing that the expression on your face seems at odds with your words. What is happening for you?

One way of increasing bodily awareness (in both the client and ourself) is by doing a 'body scan'. This involves closing one's eyes and then systematically and slowly running through each part of the body, paying attention to the way each area feels. Perhaps starting with their feet, the individual slowly moves upwards, taking in the abdomen, back, arms, head, and so forth. When combined with recognising tension areas and tensing/relaxing different muscle groups progressively to release stress in the body, the scan offers a platform for relaxation techniques.

> *Step 1*: Start by inviting the client to adopt a relaxed and comfortable position (seated or lying down).
>
> *Step 2*: Encourage them to become aware of their breath, noticing its rhythm and the sensation of breathing in and expelling. (If breathing is laboured, the client may first need to learn to breathe slowly, gently and deeply, into the lower part of their lungs).
>
> *Step 3*: Guide the client to attend to each part of the body in turn and to be aware of how it is feeling – e.g. 'Notice how your feet are planted on the ground' or 'Notice the sensation of pressing against the chair'.
>
> *Step 4*: Guide the client to any parts of the body that are feeling particularly heavy, sore, tingling or uncomfortable, noting also parts where they don't feel any sensation at all.

(Try the full 30-minute guided narrative by the founder of *Mindfulness-Based Stress Reduction* by Jon Kabat-Zinn: www.youtube.com/watch?v=15q-N-_kkrU&feature=emb_title)

Having identified particular bodily issues, interventions can target the specific area as Joyce and Sills show in some work with breath and body position:

> His breathing was shallow; his posture was rigid and tense. His relational support was also low and he had no real friends. After some negotiation, the counsellor decided to prioritize focusing on increasing the support of body process. She suggested that he experiment with different types of breath and body position as they talked. Alex soon found that when he allowed himself to breathe freely and sit relaxed and supported by the

chair he felt much more free to express himself and felt more confident with the counsellor. She noticed that Alex's voice became quieter when he lost energy and was able to use this as a guide to alert him when he was losing touch with his energetic support. (Joyce and Sills, 2018, p. 88)

Facilitating bodily expression of emotion

We help clients use their bodies to express and explore emotions in all sorts of ways, including through us modelling the process.

If a client tunes into their body saying something like, 'I feel hollow inside' or 'my stomach is churning' or 'I feel a pain in my chest, where my heart is', they are ready to explore what the body is saying in its wisdom about what it needs (see the case study with Gillian, below). At that point, we can use the connection with the felt-sense to explore what the person is needing or how it shifts with imagining the needs being met.

The work of dance movement therapists offers us additional techniques. For instance, they use bodily 'mirroring' (where the therapist helps to find ways to experience the client's feelings by embodying and reflecting back particular expressive movements) or 'bodily exaggeration' (where little movements are enlarged to express feelings more fully). Another technique is to invite the client to engage some storytelling in the form of embodied narratives or movement. While there has been little research thus far on the effectiveness of dance therapy, a few significant studies indicate that there is a therapeutic value in movement (see Box 5.6) and there are many wonderful case study accounts of dance therapy (e.g. Levy, 1995).

In Box 5.7 Joanne Ablack (2000) discusses her work as a black mixed-heritage woman who works with black women clients to explore their

---

Box 5.6 Research: value of dance movement therapy

Karkou et al. (2019) conducted a systematic review of studies that aimed to explore the effectiveness in the use of dance movement therapy (DMT) with people with depression. They offer a qualitative narrative synthesis and meta-analyses. Of 817 studies reviewed, only eight studies were identified as meeting their inclusion criteria, confirming the paucity of high-quality studies available. A total of 351 people with depression (mild to severe) participated, 192 of whom attended DMT groups while receiving treatment as usual (TAU) and 159 received TAU only. Overall findings suggest there was a decrease in depression scores in favour of DMT groups in all studies. The authors conclude that DMT is an effective intervention in the treatment of adults with depression.

> ## Box 5.7 Case example: working through the racial body
>
> One of the things my trauma clients have taught me is that the rage is literally unbearable. If we as Black people walked around feeling the rage engendered by our/her history, the world could not hold us. Yet, we need to find some way to come to terms with the rage or it will consume us. If I carry somatic trauma, be it through violence, abuse, torture and/or deprivation and add that to the cauldron of existing as a Black person in this society, it is volcanic. But the volcano is not allowed, so I turn it in on myself or act it out destructively. The area of exploration with my clients is their internal world of violence, mayhem, and murder. Many of my trauma clients have told me that the only way they could hold onto some semblance of sanity was to imagine killing others or themselves ... I sometimes get them to draw the different 'voices' in the dialogue of rage; to find body postures and phrases; to move/dance/walk their rage and their fear of their rage. Rage is not easy for anybody; it is particularly difficult for those of us who have experienced the stereotyping of the least expression of our anger, usually in the classic criticism 'you're so aggressive' ... The question the therapist needs to be asking (internally/externally) is, if this is what is showing, what may be hidden AND if the client shows this to me, what is it that they want me to understand about what it is like to be them? (Ablack, 2000)

traumatic somatic history. She recommends using the body to explore and express emotions, specifically to 'find body postures' and 'to move/dance/walk their rage'.

Being the body the client needs

Sometimes we are called upon to embody our presence in response to clients' needs. Just being a stable benign body who is 'there' may be enough. But some clients may need to be touched or held to repair what was missing for them developmentally. Some might need us to be the 'tuning fork'; others a 'sponge', a 'witness', a 'battering ram', a 'truth sayer', and so on.

In the following passage, a client expresses why working online during the Coronavirus pandemic didn't suit her because she needed the actual co-regulating, caring physical presence of her therapist:

> For me, the 'being' is what's held everything together, it's what underpins everything we've done. It's where the repair has been able to slowly sketch out a shape, and even more slowly start to fill it in.

> Safety – always key for me – and what a novelty of this being taken seriously – safety emerging from [therapist's] ... predictability, solidity. Care, compassion, kindness. Constancy.
>
> It's been her physical presence. Availability. Week after week, even when I was unable to consciously respond, she was there, dependable, consistent, empathic. Understanding ...
>
> The enormous importance of her embodied presence. Co-regulation that I don't feel in the same way over FaceTime. It feels less safe.
>
> Touch. Availability to touch. Safely. Responding. And even without actual touching, simply her presence. Feeling her beside me close, oh how I've liked that.

Working in a relational psychodynamic way, Orbach argues the case for attending carefully to our counter-transferential bodily responses – bringing the bodies of both client and therapist into relationship. She offers an illustrative case study of her own alarming response, which she understood as revealing her client's need to have her be a stable body who could safely receive and contain his desperate, destructive impulses:

> Rob was a 48-year-old man ... A barrister who was required to perform in front of juries and judges, he could only get himself going on a case if he found a love or sexual interest ... The sexual interest took the weight of his anxiety which became transformed into pursuit and sexual performance anxiety ... He frequented call-girls, picked up prostitutes for dangerous car rendezvous around a red-light district and engaged in consensual sex so close to the edge that it took a great deal on my part to be curious rather than frightened ...
>
> I found myself one day in a perfectly ordinary session suddenly fearful that Rob would rape me ... I became rigid, started to sweat, cursed myself for not having an alarm alert in my room ... I was stunned at the level of brutality and the visual acuity of a scene of bodily fluids, teeth and fight coursing through my body ...
>
> I took the savagery I experienced as a clue to his terror and his search for another body, for a body that could respond, a body that didn't collapse, a body that could meet his body ... The patient needs to destroy the object and the analyst needs to survive the destruction ... I was required to ... remain stable, rooted in my own body in order for there to be a body in the room for him. He could only put together a body for himself via a violent encounter with another and yet on-the-edge and dangerous sex failed for him because he had to hold the boundary. (Orbach, 2003, pp. 4–6)

Vagal regulation

In neuroscience, the vagus nerve is understood to be the main component of the parasympathetic nervous system through its overseer role of numerous significant bodily functions (e.g. control of the immune response, digestion, heart rate and mood). Polyvagal theory (Porges, 2011) hypothesises that the dorsal branch of the vagus nerve shuts down the body moving us into dissociation or immobilisation while the ventral branch dampens the body's flight/fight sympathetic nervous system responses. Regulating bodily responses can ease emotional states. Both clients and therapists can benefit from becoming aware of how our brain/body automatically reacts to threat or safety, and then by learning techniques of self-stabilisation.

Dana highlights how neurobiology is woven into the therapeutic relationship. Recognising implications of therapeutic use of self, she asserts that we are 'responsible for being a regulated and regulating presence for … clients' (Dana, 2020, p. 3). She argues for the benefits of therapist self-regulation as our clients' sense when we are not regulated. When we are in our ventral vagus state, we connect with self and others and feel both alert and compassionate. Clients, she says, will struggle to engage the therapeutic process without predicable co-regulation.

Similarly, Schwartz (2015) offers some useful practical advice to indirectly stimulate our vagus nerve to relieve hyper-aroused or closed-down nervous system states (see Box 5.8). In particular, she recommends vagus interventions to help keep our immune systems in check and to release helpful hormones and enzymes such as acetylcholine and oxytocin to reduce inflammation and increase relaxation. These techniques can help teach client and therapist to both self-regulate and engage in self-care.

Box 5.8 Practical application: somatic psychology

- **Humming:** The vagus nerve passes through by the vocal cords and the inner ear and the vibrations of humming is a free and easy way to influence your nervous system states. Simply pick your favorite tune and you're ready to go. Or if yoga fits your lifestyle, you can 'OM' your way to wellbeing. Notice and enjoy the sensations in your chest, throat, and head.
- **Conscious Breathing:** The breath is one of the fastest ways to influence our nervous system states. The aim is to move the belly and diaphragm with the breath and to slow down your breathing. Vagus nerve stimulation occurs when the breath is slowed from our typical 10–14 breaths per minute to 5–7 breaths per minute. You can achieve this by counting the inhalation to 5, hold briefly, and exhale to a count of 10. You can

further stimulate the vagus nerve by creating a slight constriction at the back of the throat and creating an 'hhh'. Breathe like you are trying to fog a mirror to create the feeling in the throat but inhale and exhale out of the nose sound (in yoga this is called Ujjayi pranayam).

- **Valsalva Maneuver:** This complicated name refers to a process of attempting to exhale against a closed airway. You can do this by keeping your mouth closed and pinching your nose while trying to breathe out. This increases the pressure inside of your chest cavity increasing vagal tone.
- **Diving Reflex:** Considered a first rate vagus nerve stimulation technique, splashing cold water on your face from your lips to your scalp line stimulates the diving reflex. You can also achieve the nervous system cooling effects by placing ice cubes in a ziplock and holding the ice against your face and a brief hold of your breath. The diving reflex slows your heart rate, increases blood flow to your brain, reduces anger and relaxes your body. An additional technique that stimulates the diving reflex is to submerge your tongue in liquid. Drink and hold lukewarm water in your mouth sensing the water with your tongue.
- **Connection:** Reach out for relationship. Healthy connections to others, whether this occurs in person, over the phone, or even via texts or social media in our modern world, can initiate regulation of our body and mind. Relationships can evoke the spirit of playfulness and creativity or can relax us into a trusting bond into another. Perhaps you engage in a lighthearted texting exchange with a friend. If you are in proximity with another you can try relationship expert, David Snarch's simple, yet powerful exercise called 'hugging until relaxed.' The instructions are to simply 'stand on your own two feet, place your arms around your partner, focus on yourself, and to quiet yourself down, way down.'

Source: Schwartz, 2015. Included by kind permission of the author.

Case study

I had been seeing Gillian (aged 28) weekly for a couple of months. She had come for help with anxiety and panic attacks, specifically relating to swimming in deep water …

One session she mentioned her uncle … His presence had brightened the family home one summer when she was about 10 years old. He took on the responsibility of reading to her at night and tucking her in. Gillian described his attentions as making her 'feel special'. She started to say something more and then went quiet …

The silence between us stretched out. Gillian seemed frozen in a *no-where land* as she gazed sightlessly out of the window and I felt her withdrawal. I tried to reach out by asking what was happening to her. She replied that she didn't know and just felt 'empty'. At that point I, too, lost my words and joined her in feeling blank …

I sensed a large blockage in my throat … Was this mine or did it belong somehow to Gillian's experience? Could it be that my body was vibrating to something occurring between us? …

I shared with Gillian my sense that my throat felt blocked and how I was feeling the opposite of her emptiness, being choked up with unshed tears. She turned to me in surprise saying that her throat too was feeling like it had a 'fist-size blob in it' …

I invited Gillian to focus on her throat sensation, utilising the technique of *Focusing* (Gendlin, 1996). 'What might your blob throat be saying?' I asked …

'Get out … I don't want it', she eventually whispered. She tried to clear her throat and then said, 'It's not, it's not … c … c … coming out'. She started to get tearful and began to look visibly anxious. 'I don't want to speak anymore. Stop this'. (Gendlin, 1996)

At this point I did not know whether she was still talking from her throat or expressing her own desire to not explore further or pleading with me to stop her pain somehow …

It took two more sessions for her story of being sexually molested to emerge more fully. Together, we came to understand Gillian's sense of her *blobby* throat as partly representing the *re-membered* experience of the oral sex and partly her own fearful pushing down of her desperate emotions relating to that unspeakable experience (Finlay, 2015, pp. 347–8).

Critical reflections

Whenever I quiet the persistent chatter of words within my head, I find this silent or wordless dance always already going on – this improvised duet between my animal body and the fluid, breathing landscape *that it inhabits*. (Abram, 1996, p. 53)

It is impossible to separate our bodies from who we are and what we do. The body is the vehicle for doing, being, and becoming … We use our bodies often before we think about it, in every moment; we perceive the world and relate to others through our bodies. Our body is our openness to the world (Merleau-Ponty, 1962). Body, self and world intertwine in the way that our bodies are relationally and culturally situated.

This chapter has emphasised that 'being embodied' is not simply about being attentive to non-verbal behaviour. Yes, we can observe clients and help facilitate client's bodily awareness. But 'being embodied' is also about our embodied use of self. We need to be attentive to what may be happening (for the client and within the relationship) when we start feeling sleepy, tearful or experience unexpected bodily shifts or tensions. It's about being reflexive and actively using our bodies in interventions.

It's about exploring our embodied inter-subjective relationship – that somatic duet lying beneath and between verbal interaction where significant implicit meanings arise in a 'more-than-verbal' way (Todres, 2007). The body is a sensor (detector of meaning) which helps us interpret clients' experiences. If we're alert to both bodily metacommunications and our own felt sense, we can get crucial cues to inform our therapeutic decision-making (Finlay, 2014).

I find it curious that so much of counselling/psychotherapy seems to be focused on a verbal ('talking therapy') level, while the body in all its complexity is relegated to a secondary, separate status. I believe it is an ethical-professional obligation to find a way to bring the body (whether of client or therapist) holistically into our work. Engaging bodily, we help the client to own more of their fuller being-in-the-world.

I worry about the explosion of counselling via robot apps or set protocols. Such formulaic approaches to therapy can never tap into the intersubjective meanings that spark and hover about the relational body. We put so much store in the words people use and seem to value words as truth. Yet words can so easily mislead, deflect or camouflage. The inadvertent messages conveyed by bodily responses may offer a better window on or entry point to the truth.

Our bodies are the home of our being and every experience, emotion, thought, interaction. Even when we're dissociated from our bodies – or disembodied (in the case of online work) – we are still embodying those states; bodily disconnection (or the absence of a bodily presence) itself carries important meaning.

The body holds untapped wisdom. We just need to find ways to release it.

Discussion questions

1. Evaluate how your embodied being changes with different clients.
2. Identify the ways your culture and cultural assumptions (related to your ethnicity, family heritage and class) may impact on therapy.
3. Think about the extent you identify with the following different modes of therapeutic bodily being: the 'trusted-healer body', 'scientist-professional body,' 'sexual body', 'vulnerable body' and 'mother body'. Which mode do you identify with most strongly? Are there other metaphorical bodies you identify with more strongly?

Resources

Book: Bessel van der Kolk's best-selling classic *The Body Keeps the Score: Mind, Brain and Body in the Transformation of Trauma* explains the science/theory of trauma and its treatment while drawing on touching human stories.

Journal: *International Body Psychotherapy Journal* (online) includes a wealth of clinical and research articles which can be downloaded for free. Available at: www.ibpj.org/archive.php

Website: Babette Rothschild's somatic therapy website contains many valuable references and resources. Available at: www.somatictraumatherapy.com/

Video: Eugene Gendlin explains Focusing. Available at: www.youtube.com/watch?v=j7PEC5Mh5FY and www.youtube.com/watch?v=zmL4zjVi8Dk

Video: Deb Dana offers an accessible and warmly compassionate introduction to polyvagal work in: *A Polyvagal Approach to COVID-19*. Available at: www.youtube.com/watch?v=T2QtVThBK28

SIX

BEING AT A DISTANCE

The fascinating aspect of computer-mediated therapy is that the degree of presence can be regulated. (Suler, 2000)

In 2020, the world of psychotherapy found itself hugely impacted by the Coronavirus pandemic. The ensuing global public health crisis did more than amplify global anxiety, grief and trauma affecting clients and therapists alike; it also forced a radical shift into online working (Simpson et al., 2020).

For better or worse, this abrupt expansion of our clinical environment was transformational. While some therapists found it difficult – even impossible – to shift to online work, others embraced this new way of working and the opportunities it created. For therapists already familiar with online working, the transition was reasonably seamless and they found creative ways of engaging relationally with the medium. Others viewed the move to online work as an unavoidable concession to the times and it remained an uncomfortable, problematic way of working.

Client responses were similarly varied. Many were initially reluctant to go online but then felt forced to compromise. While some appreciated or, at least managed, the transition, for others it remained an uncomfortable, challenging, diminished, diminishing medium.

Despite the divided nature of responses, many therapists now offer a blended practice where the degree of contact is decided on a client-by-client basis. In an early survey conducted by the UKCP in the summer of 2020, only 8 per cent of the 210 psychotherapist respondents intended to return to in-person only contact (Niblock, 2020).

This chapter contemplates the ways our therapeutic use of self has been changed or even compromised by this shift to remote working. It explores the possibilities opened up by this shift, in particular the question of how we can work safely and creatively in relational, embodied, attuned ways despite a mediating screen. It starts by outlining the opportunities and costs of remote work and pinpoints pragmatic ways of creating safe spaces for remote work. Then it goes deeper to explore the nature of therapeutic holding through technology and ways of negotiating distance and intimacy online while highlighting practical considerations for working with video-conference platforms and the latest research. The chapter concludes, as usual, with a case study, reflections and questions.

The use of the phrase working 'at a distance' encompasses all remote, digital, online work, along with the different technologies we can employ: telephoning, texting, emailing, messaging (for example, via WhatsApp) and video conferencing via platforms such as Zoom, Microsoft Teams, Whereby. com, and Facetime/Skype.[1]

Opportunities and costs of remote work

Each of the points highlighted in Table 6.1 are discussed briefly below.

Costs

The basic problem with remote work is that it is remote. One of my clients once described the experience as 'doing therapy through two panes of glass'. The screen can become a distancing barrier between therapist and client (though the discomforts of the screen may feel less intrusive than, say, wearing masks for in-person work). The fact that both parties might see their own face on screen injects additional self-consciousness.

For both therapist and client, not being able to fully see and 'feel' the Other can be disorientating and it may involve multiple losses. When a client yearns for the safety of co-embodied relationality, the absence of the therapist's presence may be experienced as painful abandonment. The shift to online work can also involve other potentially painful losses, including the loss of a familiar safe, special therapy room and routine. It's too easy to feel ungrounded or even to lose one's own sense of self or relationship with so many losses.

Table 6.1   Costs and opportunities of remote work

Costs of remote work	Opportunities of remote work
The screen as a barrier	New openings
Multiple losses	Creative possibilities
Access obstacles	Multi-media options
Extra ethical engagement needed	Practical benefits
Technical failures/stresses	Equalising opportunity

In the following passage, one client expresses what the loss of her therapist during the Coronavirus lockdown meant to her:

> One week she was there, then she wasn't. Our therapy room also disappeared overnight. The loss felt so acute, so traumatic, I was devastated. I just wanted to withdraw. My therapist kept trying to contact me offering online therapy, but I couldn't go there. We tried it once, but it was horrible. It felt worse seeing her as a facsimile than not seeing her.
>
> Somewhere deep-down I really believed she had gone or died, even though I knew this was illogical. When we did eventually meet again, it was both confusing and wonderful. Slowly I made the link to my history of my being put in an institution as a baby and losing a mother I never had …

Remote access can itself be an obstacle, one with the potential to stir feelings of shame or inferiority. Unequal skills or technological access could make the therapist seem more privileged, which can negatively fuel the power dimension. It is important not to assume that clients have access to appropriate technology or online space. Not everyone can afford a computer or smartphone, and many people do not have sufficient privacy in their homes if they live with others. For example, if a client is in an abusive relationship, teletherapy may put them at risk: they may be overheard or the forum being used may be monitored by the abuser.

It's also worth remembering that BAME people in the UK experience greater poverty and deprivation so are less likely to have access to digital equipment/Wi-Fi (British Psychological Society, 2020) (though, conversely the lessening of travel and childcare costs may make online therapy more accessible). BAME groups were disproportionately affected by COVID-19 (Public Health England, 2020), highlighting inequalities in protection/risk, privilege/deprivation and power. Restrictions in lockdown affected people in poverty disproportionately and their limited access to digital equipment/Wi-Fi made remote therapy challenging.

From our perspective as therapists, the inability to see our client's entire bodily way of being removes crucial non-verbal cues about their mental state – cues we would normally process. How thoroughly can we make our risk assessment? Is it still possible to sense and attune to our client? Can they still 'feel' us?

In addition, the therapist's ability to be a 'host' who holds safe boundaries is compromised when the therapy room has moved into the client's environment, with its lurking threats of interruption or distraction. Extra care needs to be taken to safeguard ethical boundaries, particularly those relating to confidentiality and ensuring a safe physical space (Finlay, 2019; see Box 6.1).

The inevitable disruptions triggered by technical failures also need consideration. Glitches occur through problematic internet connections, frozen

---

Box 6.1 Research: online work

Stoll et al. (2020) carried out a literature search via three databases (PubMed, PsycINFO, Web of Science) to review the main ethical arguments for and against different forms of online psychotherapy. Findings across 249 publications identified five key benefits: 1) increased access to psychotherapy and service availability and flexibility; 2) therapy benefits and enhanced communication; 3) advantages related to specific client characteristics (e.g. remote location); 4) convenience, satisfaction, acceptance and increased demand; and 5) economic advantages. The top five ethical arguments against engagement in online psychotherapy were: 1) privacy, confidentiality, and security issues; 2) therapist competence and need for special training; 3) communication issues specific to technology; 4) research gaps; and 5) emergency issues. The researchers stress the importance of careful assessment and informing clients about risks and benefits.

Simpson et al. (2020) offer a literature review acknowledging significant challenges for therapists trying to adapt to therapy online. However, they cite research showing that the more 'neutral' videotherapy space can prove a powerful pathway for clients to experience intimacy, connection, collaboration, creativity and self-expression.

---

screens, echoes, distorted sounds and lack of technical competence (on the part of therapist and/or client). Internet strength, weather and other external variables also play their part. A sense of humour is necessary at these times: one of my clients jokingly maintains that loss of contact occurs on FaceTime whenever she experiences the work as too intense and part of her feels relieved to dissociate (Finlay, 2019).

Despite the multiple challenges involved, remote work is not necessarily a substandard, potentially problematic alternative to in-person therapy (Mitchell, 2020). Some therapists and clients welcome its added benefits.

Opportunities

New openings are created by online work: we can see intimate aspects of the client's life and home that we are not normally privileged to see. Clients may choose to share the things in their everyday environment that are particularly meaningful for them: a special picture, say, or a view from the window. Other creative opportunities come with the technology: I know of a couples/family therapist who occasionally mutes one person's microphone to ensure everyone gets a chance to speak!

E-therapy also offers intriguing creative possibilities, says Tosone (2013). Further, psychoeducational groups, coaching and many everyday mental health resources (including information websites, self-help programs and online community supports) are available – and continually evolving. Cognitive-behavioural therapists, for instance, may find therapy Apps, structured online protocols and automated interventions to be helpful tools while asynchronous text-type communications may be useful when therapy is focused on developing personal and reflective narratives as in some psychoanalytic therapies and bibliotherapies.

It is also worth considering how online work can be used to supplement in-person work – for instance, by alternating online and in-person meetings. At its most radical, it can be employed in a committed way by drawing fully on different multimedia possibilities. One therapist I know offered email therapy to a client who lacked a safe private space to talk. The contract was for both to sit for their work hour as planned and dialogue in real time via text. While this was a compromise, the client valued the therapist's holding and flexibility. (Of course, writing down private material could feel more anxiety provoking for another person where confidentiality is of particular concern.)

There are also practical benefits (Simpson et al., 2020). Remote work is highly flexible. The forced shift in its direction has proved a boon for people unable to access therapy easily, perhaps because they live in remote locations, lack convenient transport or have limited mobility as a result of age or disability. Clients may lack the time, financial resources or freedom to travel to therapy sessions. Therapists, too, may find themselves making savings (both time and money) by working at home and not having to commute.

Many clients may feel more comfortable in the familiar setting of their home or office where they face no possibility of being seen by others or encountering strangers in the therapy reception area. Both clients and therapists who are inclined towards agoraphobia or who prefer more solitary ways of being, may actually favour working at a distance because it feels safer and less stressful.

Suddenly, too, a global network of therapists becomes accessible. This can also involve financial savings: while a therapist in the USA may charge $500 per hour, one in the Philippines may require only $25 for a consultation of similar length. In addition, appointment times will be subject to fewer constraints.

Cyberspace is an equaliser, an arena where everyone has equal access to online information and resources, and equal opportunities to express themselves, argues Suler (2000). This, he suggests, offers therapists the opportunity to move beyond 'transference-determined' ways of being, where the therapist acts as a powerful authority figure to embark on the more broadly conceived role of 'psychotherapeutic consultant'. This perspective potentially challenges the notion of therapist-as-expert; it invites the client to be an active, knowledgeable participant in their own healing.

It is useful to consider the specifics of each situation. Which virtual medium (or not) might best suit a particular client? Suler (2000) advises trying to achieve the best fit between people and technology. For example, the initial use of text-based, asynchronous (or even automated programs) communications for those who have social phobias, interpersonal anxiety or intimacy issues may be helpful. Recognising that both phone and online platforms change our perceptions of others, Russell (2020) explains that she herself prefers using the phone as she is able to move her eyes and body around more fluidly and naturally while talking. Interestingly, she makes the point that moving around helps to cement memory. (Russell points out that it's easy to forget what took place online as we sit more statically.)

In summary, online work opens up a range of new possibilities. With a little ingenuity, we can still engage in embodied activities online such as chair-work, mindfulness and art-related therapy. It's about being creative within an established, safe and comfortable online workspace – the topic of the next section.

Creating safe spaces for remote work

There are extra risks involved with online work, so it's important to pay attention to creating a safe space – and this matters for both client and therapist.

The issue of safety/risk is all the more vital given 'the barrage of ubiquitous connecting made possible by our always on [and] always on us connection devices' (Essig, 2019), eroding space for silent reflection. For example, during the 2020 Coronavirus lockdowns, our various technical devices brought work into our private spaces. Many of us found ourselves almost continuously online, whether for work or socialising purposes, and 'Zoom fatigue' became a lurking threat (Russell, 2020).

The first requirement for online work is to attend to the therapist's space: the place where we, as therapists, reach out to clients. Here we need to invest the same degree of attention and awareness as when creating a hospitable physical space. One option is to place ourselves in the familiar therapy room, conducting online therapy from there. But if that's not possible, we need to re-create a welcoming, confidential space elsewhere: perhaps in an office room at home. Ideally, this should have a neutral background setting and perhaps a 'white noise machine' outside the room to mask any sounds. Some therapists offer softening touches: an indoor plant or a vase of flowers in the background can convey messages of peace, care and beauty while also giving the client something to focus on (Schwartz, 2020).

Attention then needs to be given to the client's space as part of any risk assessment. Do they have a safe, private space for remote work? Are they able to speak freely or are family members nearby? Might they get interrupted? Are they comfortably seated? Sometimes clients say they feel strange when therapy takes place in rooms that have other associations. (I know that both therapists and clients feel challenged when they become aware that sessions are taking place in a bedroom.) It's important to recognise that the therapist is no longer able to take full responsibility for maintaining a safe space; the potential for outside distractions and intrusions at the client's end can impair feelings of trust and safety (Russell, 2020).

Having organised a suitable physical environment, we then need to attend to the emotional environment. Trust can be promoted by replicating features of in-person therapy – for example, ensuring that the client has a box of tissues and a drink at hand.

A formal risk assessment may prove trickier to do online and we need to be extra mindful of the security and confidentiality of the online space. If we are working in ways where we can't properly see the client, we are more reliant on what they tell us, so need to ask more questions. Beyond these kinds of considerations, we should recognise that some clients are simply less suited to online work, particularly if they lack the appropriate technical equipment, skills and/or privacy, or are simply not in a suitable psychological state – for example, clients caught up in a crisis.

It is particularly important to attend to routines that enable transitions into and out of therapy. Some clients can find it disorientating to make sudden transitions away from their everyday life, followed by equally abrupt returns to it. It can be hard – for both clients and therapists – to go from one self-state to another: for example, from being a busy family member and capable worker, to being a vulnerable client. Clients might be advised to give themselves five minutes' quiet time both before and after the session. If that can't happen, then extra time for regrounding and review needs to be made within the session (see Box 6.2). The therapist, too, needs to take extra time before and after the session to reflect and recalibrate (Russell, 2020).

Having carved out a safe place, it's then important to attend to being as comfortable and as present as possible. Your own ease with online working is essential; lots of practice and supervision re: online working may be needed before you engage clients (see Box 6.3).

Therapeutic holding through technology

The story in Box 6.4 alerts us to the challenge of 'connecting' and 'holding' a therapeutic process remotely. When we work virtually, our contact boundary is the screen/phone. The screen/phone is both mediator and threshold and part of the relationship. Given the priority we place on the

---

Box 6.2 Practical application: warm-ups and wind-downs to ease transitions

To 'warm up', it can be useful to have a 'check in' about what's happening with the client's life. During the Coronavirus lockdown, for example, my therapy sessions would typically start with a few minutes of reviewing the latest news about the pandemic and how clients were managing.

Some therapists engage a regular and explicit routine of engaging some grounding mindfulness techniques, such as starting sessions with a body scan or slow breathing as technique to arrive bodily into the 'here-and-now' (Schwartz, 2020).

Similar routines can be engaged in the last few minutes of the session to 'wind down'. It can work well to engage routines that involve stepping back to review the session – for example, highlighting 'one thing you are taking away with you today' or agreeing to continue the exploration in the next session. Fixing the next appointment and/or chatting more normally about the day ahead can also be helpful.

Box 6.3 Practical application: technical tips and tricks for online work

1. Be familiar with the particular videoconferencing platform (VOIP – voice-over internet protocol) you are using. Make sure you have played with it thoroughly, so that you feel comfortable/grounded and in a position to troubleshoot or advise your client if they have technological difficulties.
2. Recognise that online working is tiring, intense and requires a lot of concentration. I recommend having at least 30 minutes between clients. It helps to take regular breaks and move around physically. Both therapist and client may choose to have a mid-session break and/or vary the length of time of the appointment. For example, instead of an hour-long session once a fortnight, it might be beneficial to negotiate a weekly half-hour session.
3. Check your camera angles with a view to what your client will see. It can help, for instance, to raise the laptop/tablet so that the camera is at eye-level. Also, having an overly close large head to interact with can be both distracting and can overwhelm activating flight/fight responses (Russell, 2020).
4. Check your (and the client's) internet speeds. It may help to turn off all other online functions. For instance, the close presence of a teenager

streaming or playing an online game could severely mess with your internet signal.

5. Before beginning a session with the client, set out a back-up plan in case the technology fails. For instance, have alternative equipment available. To improve the sound quality, for instance, you might use headphones, change platforms or use a mobile phone on speaker while muting the online microphone.

6. Attend to eye contact. Clients need to feel you are looking at them, so try to look into the camera, rather than at the screen. Note that sitting further away helps give the impression of eye contact and has the advantage of allowing the client to see more of your body particularly relevant if you're doing body work.

7. Turn-taking needs to be more deliberate online. This means that we need to be more explicit and careful, making sure the client is equally on board. It's advisable to avoid the encouraging noises we often make in in-person therapy (like 'Uh, huh') as they interfere with speech clarity. Instead, use non-verbal signals such as nodding. Keep (hand) gestures to a minimum as they can be distracting.

8. Be attentive to the possibility of interruptions (including turning off notification/alert noises on devices). Therapists and client alike may be tempted to check text messages during the session, disrupting presence, trust and connection (Russell, 2020).

9. Consider adjusting your time boundaries to compensate for any technological failures (simultaneously holding clear boundaries) – something to negotiate on a client-to-client basis.

therapeutic relationship, it follows that we need to manage what is happening at that interface. Client, therapist and what is happening between, all need attention.

The insertion of additional elements (such as screens) requires the therapist to adapt actively and employ themselves therapeutically in subtly different ways compared to in-person therapy. For one thing, in the absence of fuller bodily cues, we need to train our senses to pick up the client's process and experience in different ways. For example, we might pick up on the client's sighs and other non-verbal communications or ask the client more directly to report what is happening to their body. Similarly, we might cultivate extra awareness of our own bodily countertransference. These points feature in the research by Mitchell (2020), who interviewed several experienced therapists about their videoconferencing therapy experiences (see Box 6.5).

Box 6.4 Case example: client's experience of unsafe online holding

When I agreed to a Skype session with Laura, a 19-year-old girl who sought help for panic attacks, she was very appreciative ... At the agreed time we 'met' on Skype, Laura was in an empty room within the university. When I enquired as to whether this was a private space she reassured me that it was. As she spoke, I was struck by the worried look on her face ... She said she was worried about her exams and her long-standing anxiety about not being popular with friends. She then recounted a long story about another student in her halls of residence who was feeling very anxious because someone had broken into her room. Laura now also felt unsafe and could not sleep at night ... She emphasised how no one could be trusted these days ...

As I listened to Laura I was aware of how difficult it was to feel engaged with her. She was expressing anxiety which no doubt was partly connected to the imminent exams but here was also a sense that our exchange was unfolding in a space that did not feel safe ... For Laura at least, at an unconscious level, [Skype] was experienced as a breach in the safety of our relationship. (Lemma, 2017, pp. 81–2)

Box 6.5 Research: therapists' experience of videoconferencing therapy

Mitchell (2020) conducted semi-structured interviews with six integrative psychotherapists about their experience of using videoconferencing for psychotherapy. Thematic Analysis revealed four themes: 'Seen and Hidden', 'Intimacy and Distance', 'Open to Connect' and 'Similar but Different Worlds'. Mitchell's findings suggest that similarities and differences exist between in-person and online work and that the latter is 'much more than second best'. While the absence of bodily contact does impose limitations, therapists can certainly experience relational depth and multi-level contact with their clients via videoconferencing. Participants discussed how a working alliance and reparative, counter-transferential processes can still be experienced via this medium:

> I remember thinking, 'I can really feel the child in you right now' and they were like a hundred miles away and it's like wow! I can really feel that part of them with me even though we were communicating through a screen. (Boris)

It's something intangible when you've got that connection. It doesn't matter if it's in person or online – you still get that felt sense of 'oomph' that's a tough week or wow that's exciting. (Deborah)

I think what's amazing is that [the way] you embody countertransference is perfectly good online; so even if you can't see the body you can still feel the knot in the stomach. (Claire)

We need to be mindful of how we are vibrating and resonating to/with the client via the technology. We are involved in the client's experience, so it makes sense to include ourselves in any reckoning. Take, for instance, the situation where a client is dissociated or shuts down during a Zoom therapy session. What is going on? Is this the client's habitual response to their environment? Or are they responding to the specifics of this particular environment (their situation or what they are observing of the therapist)?

The convenience of working remotely enables more off-the-cuff sessions, along with more frequent encounters. For instance, during the 2020 lockdown when some of my clients and supervisees were struggling with anxiety and isolation, we decided to meet more often for half an hour rather than the usual hour. While there was less time to explore things in depth, the extra meetings offered an important holding function and made the work more current.

Another option at our disposal (irrespective of whether therapy is in-person or online) is using technology to communicate with clients between sessions. By this means we can 'hold' a client and maintain relational connection (Finlay, 2019). However, texting or emailing between sessions can also confuse or violate therapy boundaries, thereby compromising the normal therapeutic frame.

Therapists differ over whether having textual exchanges (texting, email, WhatsApp, and so on) between sessions is viewed as useful or damaging. Some argue that 'no texting' boundaries between sessions ensure both parties are properly present when they have contact. Others might allow clients to text on such matters as appointments and payment or to pass on small bits of information or news. It is advisable to agree the use of additional communications in the initial contract.

Some therapists might go further and allow texting or emailing exchanges between client and therapist as part of a wider therapeutic strategy. For instance, a therapist might encourage a client to email once between sessions as a way to encourage that client to hold the therapist in mind. The symbolic psychic/physical link to the therapist may prove powerful for those clients who are insecurely or ambivalently attached to the therapist. In my own practice, for instance, I might send an occasional email to let the client know I'm thinking of them. However, I avoid texting as it is too easy to respond impulsively without being properly grounded and present. If a client contacts me out of the blue because they are in crisis or need something from me, I prefer to offer an actual (boundaried) session rather than make do with off-the-cuff exchanges (Finlay, 2019).

However, in some cases therapists actively choose to communicate with clients by writing (paper or digital). When engaged in a relationally responsive way, written communication can prove therapeutic. Lamprecht (2013), for example, recommends the spontaneous, contact-full writing of letters to clients, outside of (paid, contracted) sessions. With specific reference to mobile phone use, Innocente (2015) explains how therapist–client texting can be used to expand the holding therapy environment. She gives an example of doing therapy via texting:

> Although Matt was in his home experiencing an emotional crisis, his fear, anger, and abandonment did not remain contained inside him. He composed his text message ... His crisis travelled several miles through a mobile operating system until it found its way to my house, where it arrived as an uninvited visitor requiring my immediate attention. Whether I liked it or not, the clinical holding environment had expanded. ... By holding him, literally in the palm of my hand, and metaphorically with my willingness to be with him through his crisis and meet him where he was in a virtual holding environment – a powerful reparative relational experience occurred that had a significant therapeutic impact. (Innocente, 2015, pp. 83–4)

Negotiating distance and intimacy

Whether we're meeting a client in person or remotely, our way of being sensitive and caring is likely to be similar. What is subtly different is the way we negotiate and manage the different opportunities for both intimacy and distance.

While remote working involves extra distance by definition, the space can – paradoxically – feel more intimate (Simpson et al., 2020). As the quotation from Innocente above shows, clients can hold therapists close and be 'held' themselves. Conversely, the client can 'put' their therapist a long way away, increasing the distance between. The point here is that clients have more choice about their proximity to the therapist than they would normally with in person work. The therapist can remind the client of this and together they can decide their mutual preferences for degrees of proximity. (This could make a useful check-in exercise to be engaged at the start of online therapy.)

Beyond negotiating physical proximity, the emotional side of distance-intimacy must be navigated. Research (e.g. D'Arcy et al., 2015) suggests that when people feel more comfortable or relaxed in their home space, their way of being online can feel more casual and less threatening and emotionally arousing. For example, if the client routinely Skypes with friends and family, then Skyping with a therapist may feel comfortably natural, though personal and professional boundaries could get blurred.

The converse is also true. Clients can feel that the therapist isn't truly present or isn't properly seeing them, particularly if camera angles distort eye contact. Clients may feel self-conscious about being on video and become derailed by checking their own image. Equally, the therapist may spend too much time checking *their* image, leaving the client feeling insufficiently attended to.

The net result of all these experiences – both being more casual and feeling more self-conscious – is that clients (and therapists) can disclose, regress or act out more than they would face-to-face. This process has been identified in the tech literature as the 'disinhibition effect'. The disinhibition effect is usually seen when there is an absence of in-person cues – for example, when work is conducted by phone or by textual means). This encourages some people to be impulsive and act out unproductively. Work with a client may go deeper, or it may become more superficial. This alerts us to the need to work out an optimum way of relating with each client.

Six interacting factors create this online disinhibition effect, Suler (2004) argues: dissociative anonymity, invisibility, asynchronicity, solipsistic introjection, dissociative imagination and minimisation of authority. He argues that rather than thinking of disinhibition as revealing of an underlying 'true self', we might be better advised to conceptualise it as a shift to a within self-structure constellation, involving clusters of cognition/affect that differ when in face-to-face encounters.

It's important to understand the potential effects (and lost opportunities?) of disinhibition for both client and therapist, and to recognise the need to regulate emotions or titrate the intensity/intimacy of the therapy experience. Here, Schwartz (2015) advances the benefits of vagal work (to reduce inflammation, improve the immune system and engender feelings of relaxation) and offers guidelines for co-regulation including employing the use of conscious breathing and reaching out for healthy connections to others.

Case study

Zara, a single 40-year-old corporate lawyer, began long-term weekly therapy three years ago. She struggled with a binge-eating disorder, low-grade depression and carefully concealed self-harming behaviours. While attractive and successful on the surface, she suffered from chronic shame and a sense that she could never be 'good enough'. Throughout her life she engaged well-hidden self-harming behaviours.

Zara's Anglo-Indian mother, whom she adored, died when she was eight years old. She was then brought up by a rather distant, dismissive father and a succession of nannies. Her father was a senior executive in an international corporation, travelling extensively. Despite her materially privileged life (including an exclusive boarding school), Zara was a lonely, withdrawn child. She never formed close relationships yet excelled at school and learned to please others, winning many accolades over the years.

When the Coronavirus lockdown occurred, Zara's therapist wrote saying that until further notice their in-person work would be suspended in favour of online work. Zara somehow heard this message as 'therapy was ending' and her therapist 'no longer wanted to see her'. The therapist – concerned about the silence from Zara – followed up her email and clarified that she was proposing they videoconference for the foreseeable future. Initially, Zara felt self-conscious about being filmed and was reluctant to engage videoconferencing. While she used her computer competently for word processing, she was less familiar with videoconferencing platforms. The therapist offered Zara the possibility of phone therapy, but asked if Zara would be prepared to experiment with a mixture of phone and Zoom for a session. The aim of the session was to 'play with' the technology so as to get Zara used to what was required. That extra hand-holding proved useful and Zara soon felt more comfortable with videoconferencing, a skill which also enabled her to conduct her own corporate work more effectively.

The focus of the online therapy during lockdown was Zara's intense isolation, given she lived alone. (The corporation she worked with had asked her to work from home – something she was able to do easily as her role mostly involved legal documents and using the phone.) What quickly became clear was that Zara's childhood traumas, involving profound loss, isolation, feelings of abandonment and worthlessness, were 'triggered'. The sudden and dramatic changes to her life prompted by lockdown, in particular the loss of contact with people, intensified Zara's grief. She experienced flashbacks, and her sleep and eating practices became more disturbed.

Until now Zara had resisted exploring her childhood in therapy, in particular the grief of losing her mother. Previously she declared that she didn't remember much and what she did remember was having a reasonably good time at boarding school. Now, the shame and loss she felt on being suddenly 'abandoned' by her employer and her therapist seemed to lay bare her childhood trauma, and this became the focus of her therapy.

In one significant session, Zara was showing her therapist, via video-link, ornaments and pictures on display in her living room. When Zara showed off a beautiful antique Kashmiri carpet, her therapist recognised that it had special significance. It was the one item she had inherited from her mother and it had been passed down through generations of her Indian family. Zara revealed that the rug brought her real comfort. Sometimes when she couldn't sleep at night, she would bring her pillows downstairs so that she could lie on it.

The therapist wondered if Zara would be prepared to do her therapy sitting on the rug. Zara liked that idea and, sitting on the floor, she became aware of how young she felt. Together they recognised her Child-part was present and the therapist gently welcomed 'her' into their therapy space.

Zara's Child-part found it difficult to express herself verbally, so her therapist suggested they tried artwork. Over a series of sessions Zara used felt-tip pens to create a series of paintings of her mother and herself. She would spend part of the session drawing on the rug with her 'laptop therapist' lying on the floor next to her. Then the two of them talked together about the drawings.

Later in the therapy Zara began to explore some intergenerational grief. She recognised her mother's grief at leaving her home in India to come to Britain. Slowly the fuller story of Zara's layers of loss emerged. By facing her grief, paradoxically Zara gained comfort from feeling closer to her mother.

Critical reflections

Although therapy at a distance is still evolving, all the evidence suggests that it is far from being a substandard compromise. It is best seen as a space where therapists use themselves and the relationship in similar and different ways (compared with in-person work). Research confirms that deep, relational work *is* possible when working remotely, but the process needs to be consciously and deliberately managed. It's important to remember that virtual connections involve different ethics, rules, routines, opportunities and risks. Therapy at a distance works better for some than for others.

As therapists who are committed to the use of self in our work with clients, we need to consider how our preferences, values and theoretical commitments might map onto distance working – or not. Those embracing relational and developmental approaches may be challenged by not being present to the full sensory-embodied interpersonal encounter.

How exactly we elect to work remotely partly depends on our clients' preferences. I tend to let the client select their preferred video platforms. Some clients may need extra time to acclimatise to online working. Others may reject it entirely, particularly those who gain comfort from the therapist's actual physical presence/touch, or who lack appropriate access, or who find it difficult to cope with the intrusive, frustrating, occasionally shaming elements of the technology.

My personal experience of videoconferencing therapy and supervision has generally been positive. It works surprisingly well for me and a significant proportion of my practice remains online. Even so, it has involved much compromise for me and for my clients. I still grieve the loss of some clients who couldn't make the switch during the pandemic. Those who persevered online found that our work deepened with new possibilities for intimacy. Could that be connected, I wonder, to the fact that when working online I put extra effort into holding the therapy space? Or is it that some clients feel safer in their own space and one-step removed with online activity?

I own my positive bias in the way I've selectively presented online work in this chapter. I remain all too aware that online work is experienced by many as aversive and disturbing, for therapists and clients alike. Distance working can only work if it is responsive to the individual client's therapeutic needs. We need further conversations on how to creatively manage our online therapeutic use of self. The topic of creativity is discussed further in the next chapter.

Discussion questions

1. Thinking about your experience of online work, identify the opportunities, challenges and costs of remote working.
2. How might you ease the transition for clients into – and out of – online meeting?
3. Discuss ways in which therapeutic boundaries should be negotiated with online therapy as distinct from in-person work.

Resources

Book: *The Digital Age on the Couch: Psychoanalytic Practice and New Media* by Alessandra Lemma. A deep, scholarly exploration of psychoanalytic practice and new media with some nice illustrations.

Book: *Theory and Practice of Online Therapy: Internet-delivered Interventions for Individuals, Groups, Families, and Organizations*, edited by Haim Weinberg and Arnon Ronick. There's something for everyone in this volume given its wide-ranging discussions of theory and practice.

Website: https://acto-org.uk/ Association for Counselling & Therapy Online (ACTO). Umbrella organisation in the UK for therapists who practise online offer a directory of trained online practitioners, training, information, blogs. See their competencies at: https://acto-org.uk/acto-recommended-competences-for-counselling-and-psychotherapy-online/

Website: BACP guidance for online work: www.bacp.co.uk/media/2162/bacp-working-online-supplementary-guidance-gpia047.pdf. See also their Telephone and E-Counselling Training Curriculum which provides information and minimum training standards: www.bacp.co.uk/media/2046/bacp-telephone-ecounselling-training-curriculum.pdf

Powerpoint: www.bacp.co.uk/media/8610/naomi-moller-andreas-vossler-presentation.pdf Created by Naomi Moller and Andreas Vossler, this powerpoint offers a nice summary about the experience, practice, research and training re: online therapy.

Note

1. Of the numerous online platforms and forms of video-conferencing software around, some are more secure than others. *Zoom, Teams, VSee* and *Doxy.me* are all recommended for therapeutic work. Experts advise using platforms that are suitable for therapy and handling sensitive private information (beyond ensuring that online methods are end-to-end encrypted). Some comply with HIPAA (US insurance oversight body) standards, which make them highly secure. Free products may well pass on your data (including your contacts list) as well as your clients' data. However, even HIPAA said *Skype* was acceptable during the unusual conditions imposed by the Coronavirus pandemic.

SEVEN

BEING CREATIVE

The flow of therapy should be spontaneous, forever following unanticipated riverbeds; it is grotesquely distorted by being packaged into a formula that enables inexperienced, inadequately trained therapists (or computers) to deliver a uniform course of therapy. (Yalom, 2001, p. 34)

Creativity can be defined as the use of original ideas and imagination to create something new. Applied to therapy, creativity comes into play when we go beyond the formality of protocols and rules to a place of imagination, play and intuition. This is the artistry of therapy, the subtle process that dances in the mysterious 'between' of the therapy relationship. Being creative is about knowing your therapist self-as-an-artist and your therapy work as artistry. It's about the curiosity, passion, permissiveness, vitality, absurdity, joy, courage and sheer heart and soul that can animate our work. I say 'can' because some therapists fall into being unduly mechanical in their work, stultifying the dynamic growth-enhancing potential of therapy.

In the therapy context, creativity involves more than using therapy techniques that draw on art, drama, writing or other cultural forms. 'When we are artists and our work is artful,' says Mitchell (2016, p. xiii), 'we give ourselves and our clients permission to let doubt and anxiety and inspiration be part of the process of change.'

Creativity emerges both in the doing of therapy and in our way of being. This chapter starts by taking a look at these two dimensions. Four creative processes – those of flow, permission-giving, experimenting and taking risks, and playfulness – are then discussed. Ways to engage creativity practically are explored, highlighting the manner in which it emerges out of the therapy relationship. The chapter concludes, as usual, with a case study, reflections and questions.

Creative doing

Creative doing includes applying art-related therapies[1] such as drama therapy, art therapy, music therapy, dance and movement therapy, and play therapy. In addition to offering modes of emotional/embodied expression and exploration, creative activities such as painting or dancing can themselves have calming, grounding, integrating effects for both client and therapist.

Here are the words of a practitioner (nurse and academic) who, back in the 1980s found a way out of her eating disorder through writing a journal and painting (see Figure 7.1). In 2020 she wrote an autobiographical piece to explain her healing journey through arts:

> Art, images, and colouring exceeded my speechlessness and I began to re-story my life. Journaling allowed me to learn to write out and then articulate my distress; it has been a long-term process. Art surpassed the sense that "no one would believe me if I really told them how I felt about myself and in relation to adverse events". (Kuhnke, 2020, p. 91)

Figure 7.1   80 lbs and Thinking (reprinted by kind permission of Janet Kuhnke)

In a subsequent paper, Janet Kuhnke (2021) describes using journaling and art (sculpture and gardening) reflexively once more to find a way to cope with the trauma of the Coronavirus pandemic (see Box 7.1 and Figure 7.2).

Some skill and inventiveness are required when selecting a creative strategy for a specific client (or, indeed, for ourselves as therapists). Many factors enter into the choice of activity: the specific interests of the client involved and degree of motivation, the therapist's own skills and interests,

---

Box 7.1 Case example: coping with COVID

Creating art outside was my outlet. The fresh air relieved the tension from viewing the large image of the Coronavirus that dominates the news ... Dad and I talked on the phone, we joked about my COVID art. He too was a collector of old bottles and glass, appreciated my journey to the dumps and digging metal from the earth.

In time, old steel plowshares and iron teeth from an old hay mower, were painted red and bolted together to become the legs of my next art form. I call it *'mutation'*. In my need to not be at the laptop, present on e-conference calls and phone calls, I sought comfort in the sacred stillness of the bush ... I scoured the earth. I walked the hills and valleys near the streams for strewn iron, copper, and glass ...

In May, reflexive practice and art created were my mainstay. My new and growing garden space was my place to push-back against the harshness of COVID times. It became my place of inspiration ... I engaged in journaling with regularity. At work, I methodically prepared to teach and research using technology. At times it was overwhelming, yet possible. I had this sense of that COVID would not prevail. Then I got the phone call.

> Today, my Dad passed in intensive care. The new pacemaker could not keep him going. Alone for seven days. He died alone, no family by his side. COVID would not allow us to be with him. None of his children or wife of 66 years were called, until he died. In death, the health care team called. I am furious. I cannot fly to be with my siblings and Mom. COVID rules. I cannot go. COVID prevails, harsh, demanding and in control. COVID is in control of my grieving. My pen remains my friend. (*Research Journal*, May 23, 2020)

In response I journaled, tears pouring, I wrote to my sister and friend "nothing in my 37 years of nursing prepared me for the loss of my Dad, nothing" (*private communication*, May 23, 2020) ... In time, my husband encourages me to plant a clematis and I create a trellis in honour of my Dad. Two lilacs now grace the driveway and the corner of my flower garden in Dad's memory. I hike away from everyone seeking to offer me comfort. I hear the crashing stream; the sounds of the moving water overwhelm my pain ... The water washes over my tears and brings a calming, coolness and comfort. Solace is slow to arrive. (Kuhnke, 2021, p. 19)

---

the resources available and the aims of therapy. Once a choice is made, it's about finding an inviting way of presenting it to the client, opening a space for creative process (see Box 7.2).

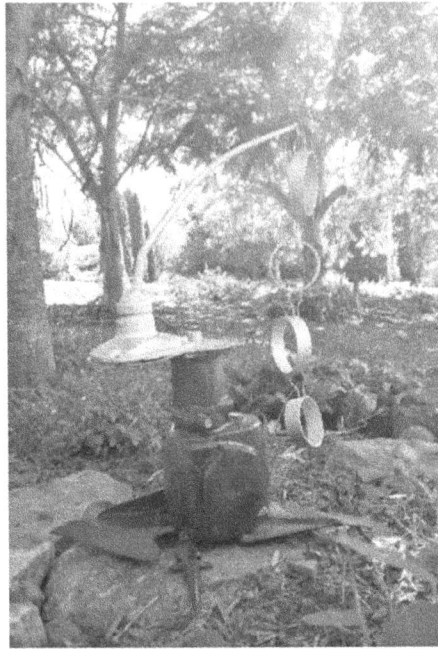

Figure 7.2   Mutation (reprinted by kind permission of Janet Kuhnke)

Box 7.2 Practical application: ideas for creative activities

The following are a few ideas for creative activities using different media that can be easily applied in different contexts.

- **Sociogram sculpt with toys/figurines** Invite the client to choose figures (or objects) to represent different parts of themselves which they position in a pattern to represent the relationship between parts. After the client has completed their 'sculpt', explore the meanings of each figure. Invite them to take a photograph of it so the sculpt can be returned to or revised in future sessions.
- **Life mapping through art** Take a large piece of paper and invite the client to sketch a winding road which represents their life journey. Using stickers, colour markers, etc., the client then notes significant life events (at different ages) which have taken place along the way.
- **Life mapping through music** Ask the client to note significant songs/ music they've connected with through their life and explore what the music meant to them.

- **Body mapping** Ask the client to draw a rough outline of their body, then fill in the outline using crayons of different colours to represent where/how emotions are felt in different parts of the body or how they see their body.
- **Moving the body** Invite the client to try out different poses or movements and explore the bodily experience. The client could compare their habitual postures/movements with contrasting ones.
- **Writing 'unfinished business'** Invite the client to write a message on a postcard (that will not be sent) to a person in their life with whom there is some unfinished business. Prompting questions such as 'What do you want them to know?' or 'What do you *really* want to say to them?' can be helpful.
- **Art therapy** In a group context, invite each member of a group to paint a rough line down the centre of a piece of the paper. Then ask each participant to (roughly) paint two symbolic representations of themselves: how they see themselves now on one side of the line and, on the other, how they would represent themselves in 'five years' time'. Give everyone 20 minutes to do their pictures before sharing the results with the group as a whole.
- **Drama therapy as part of family work** To help a family member understand another member's perspective, they could be invited to swop chairs in a role reversal and speak as if they are the other person.
- **Empty chair** Imaginatively place a person with whom the client has 'unfinished business' on an empty chair and encourage them to dialogue. (This might also be done in imagination if a client feels too silly talking to a chair.)
- **Guided fantasy** The client is invited to visualise a scene (from the past or future or in fantasy) and then to imagine a positive unfolding or a healing connection being made.

Once a client gets going in their creative activity, it's important to explore what it means to them (what exactly are they trying to express?) and to witness the process, rather than judge the end-product (Shallcross, 2011).

When creative activities are used as part of counselling/psychotherapy, clients usually spend some time engaged in them before stepping back to talk about the experience. It's important to allow sufficient time for both aspects: the creative process itself and the follow-up discussion on the meanings of what has emerged out of it.

Creative being

Being creative involves an attitude of open, playful spontaneity. Our creativity comes into play when we improvise, react, respond and adapt to the individual client; when we truly open ourselves in the moment to whatever is happening. It could mean spontaneously following up with a particular activity/experiment or pursuing a particular intuition or image. It could involve doing something extra in therapy – for instance, where a client seems to need a bit of extra holding, maybe offering an extra phone call through the week or suggesting a shift in the contracted way of working.

We need this to maintain energy and freshness in our efforts to inject new life into clients and help them break loose from their stuck, self-defeating patterns (Kottler, 2017). A playful attitude also helps therapists stay curious and engaged; it offers protection against burnout and empathy fatigue.

Creativity is unleashed in various ways. It happens when we start sessions in more unknowing places – for example, when we resist the temptation to arrive already armed with advice, agendas and techniques. It happens when we strive to be reflexive – for instance, when we catch ourselves falling into habitual phrases or ways of being – indicators that we may be on auto-pilot. It arises, too, when we are prepared to let go of 'rules', think outside the box, experiment and flow with the process.

Being creative is about resisting the routinised, mechanical use of techniques, protocols or work patterns. It means engaging a non-judgemental permission-giving attitude (within an atmosphere of support and safety) of being-with the other. This sets the foundation for novel responses and creative shifts. The aim is to tune into our felt sense, going beyond words to find space for awareness, insight and connection to emerge:

> In our therapy work we are often guided by interpretive hunches, gut feelings, images and bodily impulses. When attending to our clients, we use all our five senses, together with other embodied, intuitive senses ... Such 'receivings' are the foundation of our clinical intuition and act as creative touchstones for inspirational transformation. (Finlay, 2016a, p. 88)

Creative processes

A 'new therapy' should be created for each patient, insists Yalom (2001), one tailored to their needs. In addition to eschewing standard recipes, we're invited to:

- go with the flow;
- be permission-giving;
- experiment and take risks;
- be playfully spontaneous.

Flow

The concept of 'flow' is important in the creative process. Csikszentmihalyi (1992) identified flow as the intrinsically rewarding experience that occurs when people are absorbed, even enraptured, in the moment of doing an activity. He cites a dancer's description of how it feels when a performance is flowing: their concentration is complete yet they are not consciously controlling and thinking about their performance.

Applied to therapy, flow enters when we encourage clients to act spontaneously and accept whatever comes. When a client sets out to paint a picture, for instance, the goal is free expression rather than the creation of a nice picture; the client should not worry about the results or what 'people might think' (Finlay, 2004). Therapy receives an injection of freedom, enabling clients to find different ways of being (see Box 7.2).

When therapists are in the flow, we are spontaneous, intuitive and narrowly focused on what is emerging. We can lose a sense of time or later may not even remember exactly what occurred (Kottler, 2017).

Permission giving

Being creative involves giving ourselves and clients permission to experiment – to be alive to possibilities, prepared to get things 'wrong'. This involves the therapist giving clients space to be themselves, feel their feelings, speak their truth. However, it can be challenging for some clients to receive such an invitation, as the following dialogue shows:

> 'Phillip, I experience you talking to me in an apparently unconcerned and indifferent manner, but at the same time you look very sad, is that right?'
>
> Phillip looks surprised, alarmed even, and tears up. Choking on his words he apologizes while attempting to sound unaffected, 'Sorry, I didn't realise I was appearing so emotional.'
>
> Phillip's resistance to his feelings touches me and I remark that it must be difficult to be in contact with his feelings and at the same time try and hold everything together.
>
> Phillip replies, tearfully attempting and failing to appear unaffected, 'Sorry I am not used to showing myself like this, I'm … sorry … I'll be ok in a minute.'
>
> I reply as a challenge to obvious introjects, 'Why do you think you have to apologise?', 'Isn't it ok to feel what you feel, Phillip?'
>
> Phillip looks at me with what appears a range of conflicting emotions, anger, bewilderment, vulnerability and hope, and remarks rather confusedly, 'Not in my family … a man doesn't show his feelings … It's not ok … is it[?]'. (Evans and Gilbert, 2005, pp. 87–8)

To help the client freely express and explore, the therapist needs to communicate a permission-giving stance. This is shown in the example in Box 7.3, where the therapist encourages an adult client to 'play' with toys

---

Box 7.3 Case example: sand-play

She noted that she was a small, scared bunny trying to hide behind a shrub ... Her husband was the fierce lion standing on top of the mountain, able to see whatever she was doing wherever she went. Even her children were depicted by small animals cowering in fear ...

[Over the next few months, the client periodically returned to the sand tray]

It was as if she was using it to acknowledge the progress she was making toward her goals and to make tangible her progress for her own sense of forward movement ... The main images had shifted dramatically from her first session with the sand. Here, she had her husband represented as a smaller lion standing beside the mountain – no longer did she feel that she was under his predator's gaze. The client chose to represent herself with an elephant because she had grown to see herself as a stronger player in her relationship with her husband ...

Creative expression often serves as the pathway for unearthing feelings that were previously hidden beneath the surface, Degges-White says. "The arts, in brief, make the unconscious conscious. They bring light to the darker recesses of our psyches. Moreover, they do it in a nonthreatening way in which we frequently reveal hidden sides of ourselves [through] metaphors or visual representations rather than through a stereotypic, psychoanalytic talk-therapy way." (Shallcross, 2011)

---

in a sand tray, using the figures symbolically and imaginatively to articulate her current concerns non-verbally. Here, Degges-White (reported by Shallcross, 2011) evaluates her work with a 42-year-old female client who was struggling with her husband's controlling behaviour. Degges-White invited her to express her 'world' by the use of figurines and a sand tray.

Experimenting and taking risks

One of the ingredients of being creative is being prepared to let go of safe known routes and go 'off-piste' (see Box 7.4).

Boundaries first need to be established and respected, but when the situation requires it, we must be willing to be flexible, creative and individualised in the therapy we offer (Yalom, 2001, p. 177). Carlson, an Adlerian therapist, describes his creative approach with Frank, a severely depressed man whose eight-year-old son had been killed by a bus in front of their

Box 7.4 Case example: spontaneous creative intervention

In the following quotation, a client describes a moment in therapy when her therapist spontaneously and unexpectedly suggested they leave the therapy room to go to play on some swings in the park opposite.

> I was feeling very young and lost, and she suggested I speak from one of the girls – I remember talking about singing on the swing when I was about six, and knowing I was alone and unhappy, and also knowing that everyone else would think I was happy.
>
> She suddenly asked me if I would like to go for a walk, and, surprised, I agreed.
>
> We walked through some woods. It was cool and shady, sunlight filtering through the trees, and very peaceful. As we walked, I felt very safe, and cared for, as if she was holding my hand. We got to a swing, and she invited me to sit on it. We sat together, and swung gently, quietly. It was a time of real connection, no longer being alone, togetherness. It was magical.

home (Kottler and Carlson, 2009). All therapy/treatments seemed to fail until Frank eventually suffered a life-threatening heart attack. Carlson's creative solution was to meet Frank at his house at 7 o'clock every morning so that they could go walking together (their long-term goal was to run a marathon, which they eventually did). Carlson describes his doubts about loosening professional boundaries and his fears that the exercise might precipitate another heart attack. But by letting go of the conventional approach to therapy, he found a radical new way to enact his caring, compassion and hope for Frank, which paid dividends.

Playful spontaneity

Playfulness involves lightness, warmth and humour. It manifests when the therapist offers smiling, gently teasing, contactful responses, when we don't take ourselves too seriously. As such, it can be a much-needed antidote to shame and other highly intense emotions.

DeYoung has highlighted the role of relationally validating connections based in 'right-brain-to-right-brain' communication when working with clients who experience chronic shame. She draws on Hughes's anacronym PACE (playfulness, acceptance, curiosity, empathy).

For shame-ridden clients, our open, playful stance becomes, over time, deep reassurance that they can't mess up with us. From the very beginning of therapy, playfulness is an invitation for them to open up their thoughts and feelings to new possibilities, to welcome spontaneity and surprise. We can hope that eventually playfulness becomes a mode of being they can claim for their own, having experienced that their own right-brain emotional processes are trustworthy and good to share with others. In the context of a playful stance, acceptance is radical ... There are no judgements from us that some feelings are better than others, no pressure from us that clients feel or think differently. (DeYoung, 2015, p. 83)

There is value in the therapist spontaneously sharing intuitions, even if these may at first seem odd or not particularly relevant. For example, a therapist might come out with 'I've got this sudden weird but vivid image of xxxx. I'm not quite sure how it's relevant but does it evoke something for you?' (see Box 7.5).

Box 7.5 Case example: 'flowing' with metaphor

Alex noted that she felt her brain was 'shrunk' when in the company of others ...

I found myself blurting out "You're a vacuum-packed person!" We were both taken aback by these unbidden words. They stood oddly in contrast to Alex's way of being, which was gentle, loving and warm ... The phrase was not one I had ever thought about or used before. I worried that Alex might have experienced the image as derogatory and dismissive. However, she took it well, noting the humour in both the image and my own consternation about using it.

Together we wondered what could have prompted this metaphor. It began to make sense when we recognised how Alex, when in the presence of others, felt sucked dry, without air, and made to shrink ... I asked if the image brought any associations to mind. Suddenly Alex gave an exclamation: she made a link with a storybook she had created in words and pictures with her granddaughter just a couple of days before:

A little girl was very attached to her small suitcase ... called Lexa. They went everywhere together. One day, the little girl was going to go with her family on an aeroplane and she desperately wanted Lexa to go with her. But the girl's mother said Lexa had to stay behind as she was too big to take on the plane. The little girl was very upset. To comfort her child the mother tried to be helpful, saying that they would measure Lexa and if she was the right size and could fit on the plane, the two friends could travel together. As Lexa was being measured, she sucked herself in. She sucked more and more, making herself as small as possible. It worked! ...[2]

I playfully shared an interpretation with Alex that Lexa symbolically represented Little Alex who was so desperate not to be left behind or abandoned that she made herself fit the plane (representing family demands, society's expectations). It seems that Alex has to disappear in order to attend to the requirements of others. (Finlay, 2015, pp. 343–4)

Case study

Brenda was 23, living with her family and pursuing her Master's degree. She was deeply depressed. Before coming to me she had been in verbal therapy but was totally frustrated. I saw her for three years in individual and group sessions. Brenda felt physically frozen and was petrified to do even the simplest movements ...

Since movement was too provocative for her, I suggested that we start with drawing. She welcomed this option and chose the size paper she wanted and the colors she wanted. I encouraged her to just enjoy the use of color and allow her hand to move freely on the page, not worrying about the results. What occurred was exciting to witness. Her previously rigid body became animated and expressive ...

One day, at Brenda's suggestion, she and I painted a mural that included a group of kids playing baseball. On paper we playfully pretended to throw the ball by painting a ball in motion and similarly, batted the ball and ran the bases, using large sweeping lines on the page. Drawing became an animated experience that grew, gradually lifting more and more off the page. There were expressions of joy, laughter, competition and self-assertion.

Since this experience became a drawing in motion, I suggested that we act out the mural together using the studio as our baseball field. Brenda was willing. To warm up, we began to throw an imaginary ball back and forth and then began to bat the imaginary ball. We tagged each other, yelled a lot, and generally had a great time. I had never seen Brenda so animated and fun-loving. Her previously very soft, childlike voice became deep, almost husky, and her passive defensive demeanour became assertive and playfully tenacious. She bullied me around and I fought back. When we finished, Brenda was still laughing. She said, "I haven't had this much fun since I was a child. I loved to play ball. I was a good athlete. I loved playing football with the boys. When I reached puberty, my parents stopped me from all of the activities that I loved."

Brenda's family was orthodox. They became more and more religious as she grew up and less and less tolerant of their daughter's behavior. This attitude paralyzed Brenda psychologically and physically …

Brenda's masculine, tomboy energy, the part she kept secret, even from herself, had become the enemy … When Brenda denied the part of her that loved sports and drawing, she … lost access to the joyful, playful, and assertive aspects of her personality. Brenda emerged in our individual and group sessions as an extremely fun loving and warm young woman, caring and empathic to others. All of this was released when she got in touch with and was helped to enjoy and love her lost tomboy self. (Levy, 2014, pp. 10–12)

Critical reflection

While some therapists regularly inject creativity into their work, others stay with practised, known routines. Perhaps one of the unexpected benefits of the Coronavirus pandemic is that it disrupted our practice, pushing us to adapt creatively and do therapy in different ways. One therapist I know fell into 'walking therapy' (talking while walking); it proved a successful eco-therapy intervention – one that he intended to retain.

It takes courage to be spontaneous and honest in our interventions and responses. But such therapeutic uses of self also, paradoxically, need to be offered in disciplined, mindful, relational ways towards cultivating spontaneity and emotional honesty in the client (Barsness, 2017).

Perhaps the most important message for our therapeutic use of self is to stop thinking of techniques as something we do *to* the client and instead place our trust in the relational process (Mitchell, 2016). In this sense, creative activities work best when both therapist and client open to being creative together. As Winnicott (1971, p. 38) says, 'Psychotherapy has to do with two people playing together.'

Creative moments can't be forced but the flow of healing connection that comes with them is probably at the core of why I am a therapist. I like it when warm, contactful, creative playfulness enters the room. It is often what breathes life into the client and animates the therapy. It's also a great antidote to shame and the intensity of self-absorption which so often accompanies therapy journeys. Playfulness and shared moments of humour bring healing, lightness and the release of tension. 'Creativity … adds a dimension of vitality and positivity to what can be an otherwise somewhat painful and almost tedious process' (Blatner, 2003).

Of course, creative playfulness needs to be engaged sensitively, at the right time, in an attuned, authentic way. Jokes often miss their mark and are misunderstood. Humour doesn't always translate across cultures or different class and age groups; much depends on the relational context, and how well attuned the therapist is to the client's own sense of playfulness (Blevins, 2010). Further, open invitations to 'play' may be experienced as shaming and threatening. It helps to introduce creative activities tentatively, as one possibility that, perhaps, can be first modelled by the therapist.

I like Maslow's take from his essay on 'Creativity in self-actualizing people':

> When you are creative, you are more self-accepting than average, less afraid of your own thoughts, and less afraid of being laughed at or disapproved of. You can let yourself be flooded by emotion and you waste less time and energy protecting yourself. (Maslow, 1959, p. 59, cited in Mitchell, 2016, p. 11)

My favoured way of engaging creativity is to invoke imagery and metaphor. Perhaps the most significant metaphor I regularly return to is the idea of working with different 'selves' – the topic of the next chapter.

Discussion questions

1. To what extent is there a place for humour in therapy?
2. Describe how to present creative activities/experiments in non-shaming, inviting ways.
3. How might we inject creativity into therapy which follows prescribed protocols in an effort to get the 'best of both worlds'?

Resources

Book: *A Therapeutic Treasure Box for Working with Children and Adolescents with Developmental Trauma* by Karen Treisman. In-depth exploration of trauma-informed creative work with young people including lots of examples, tips, techniques and worksheets.

Book: *Dibs: In Search of Self* by Virginia Axline. One of my old favourites telling the story of a boy's play therapy, showing a Rogerian play therapist in action.

Book: *Dance and Other Expressive Art Therapies*, edited by Fran Levy, offers a fascinating compilation of case studies and theory about work with different groups 'when words are not enough'.

Website: Blog post: Working outside the box by Lynne Shallcross, *Counseling Today*, offers some nice ideas. Available at: https://ct.counseling.org/2011/02/working-outside-the-box/#

Website: 100 art therapy exercises reproduced by Shelley Klammer – e.g. to encourage the expression/exploration of emotion, offers a comprehensive resource. Available at: https://intuitivecreativity.typepad.com/expressiveartinspirations/100-art-therapy-exercises.html

Notes

1. In the UK, drama therapy, art therapy and music therapy are considered professions in their own right and practitioners must be registered with the Health and Care Professions Council (HCPC). Other talking therapists draw on their techniques, however. Gestalt therapists, for instance, commonly use drama therapy techniques of improvisation, role-play, enactments, etc.
2. I have taken the liberty to paraphrase Alex's original story; I remain aware that it doesn't do it justice.

EIGHT

BEING-WITH PARTS OF SELF

Unacknowledged voices in the memories and histories of therapists and clients, together with the accumulated residual trace of others ... make for cacophonous conversational spaces, full of sedimented trauma and bereavement and populated with ghost voices. (Speedy, 2016, p. 274)

When clients enter the therapy space, they bring along many parts of themselves: not only their social 'selves' (their roles and relationships – mother, son, wife, brother, friend, colleague), but also 'selves' from different points in their life history. They arrive with conflicting, ambivalent emotions. While the client may feel one thing – for example, a need to be seen or a longing to be connected, another part of them may feel the opposite. On top of this, the client also brings along internalised significant others, perhaps in the form of the remembered voice of a critical parent or the soothing presence of a loving grandparent.

And exactly the same is true of us. Our therapist's Being is subtly layered with 'ghosts, traces, sediments, and accomplices' (Speedy, 2016, p. 268).

With multiple 'people' in the therapy room, it's a thickly populated encounter (DeYoung, 2003). The critical question at stake is 'Who is talking to whom?!' Our work then can be seen as therapeutically using our fullest selves to enable understanding of, and dialogue with, the various parts.

This process is the focus in this chapter. The first section introduces the theory and practice of 'parts of self' work. Then sections on working with clients' parts and working with therapists' parts recognise parts-work as profoundly relational: both external and internal relationships are implicated. The chapter ends with the usual case study, reflections and questions.

'Parts of self'

Theorising multiplicity of self

Many of us routinely refer to different metaphorical 'selves' within us. We talk about our 'Inner Critic', for example, or our 'Caring Parent' or 'Stroppy Adolescent'. Writing about his own numerous 'subpersonalities' (among them 'Big Eggo', 'Jean Starry', 'Black Dwarf' and 'Behemoth'), Rowan (2006) cautions against fixing their number, given they emerge, shift and fade with time (see Box 8.1).

Sometimes it can feel like different parts are at war with each other (such as the conflict between the 'Studious' part of self that wants to study and the 'Party Girl' who just wants to have fun). For some people, the splits within are more extreme and can become profoundly disturbing – for instance, when a person's suicidal/acting out part takes over in self-destructive ways or when an individual embodies different personas in dissociative ways without conscious memory of their actions (as in dissociative identity disorder).

There are myriad ways to conceptualise parts of self. Jung, for instance, wrote extensively about universal ancestral figures, symbols and images which he saw as deriving from the collective unconscious and presenting themselves in cultural myths and narratives as well as our dreams, fantasies and delusions. He noted four key archetypes: Persona (our mask), Shadow (source of our creative/destructive potential) and Anima/Animus (the image of our biological sex) and Self (the unifying part). Since Jung, the work of elaborating these archetypes has continued: hence, for example, the more recent additions of Hero, Rebel, Magician, Trickster ... (see Figure 8.1).

Applying such motifs to our use of self, we might recognise how sometimes we wear a professional cloak (Persona) to hide our woundedness (Shadow); or how we strive to be a Healer-Sage for our clients; or how we are transferentially pulled into being an 'Earth Mother'. We also engage

Box 8.1 Practical application: identifying your parts

1. Who are your primary selves that drive your 'psychological car'?
2. How have these selves helped you? What rewards have they earned? What dangers have they avoided?
3. Are there ways in which these selves have changed over time?
4. Can you foresee a time when some selves might not work so well in the future?
5. If you were to introduce a bit of a disowned part into your life, what effect might that have? (adapted from Stone, 2005)

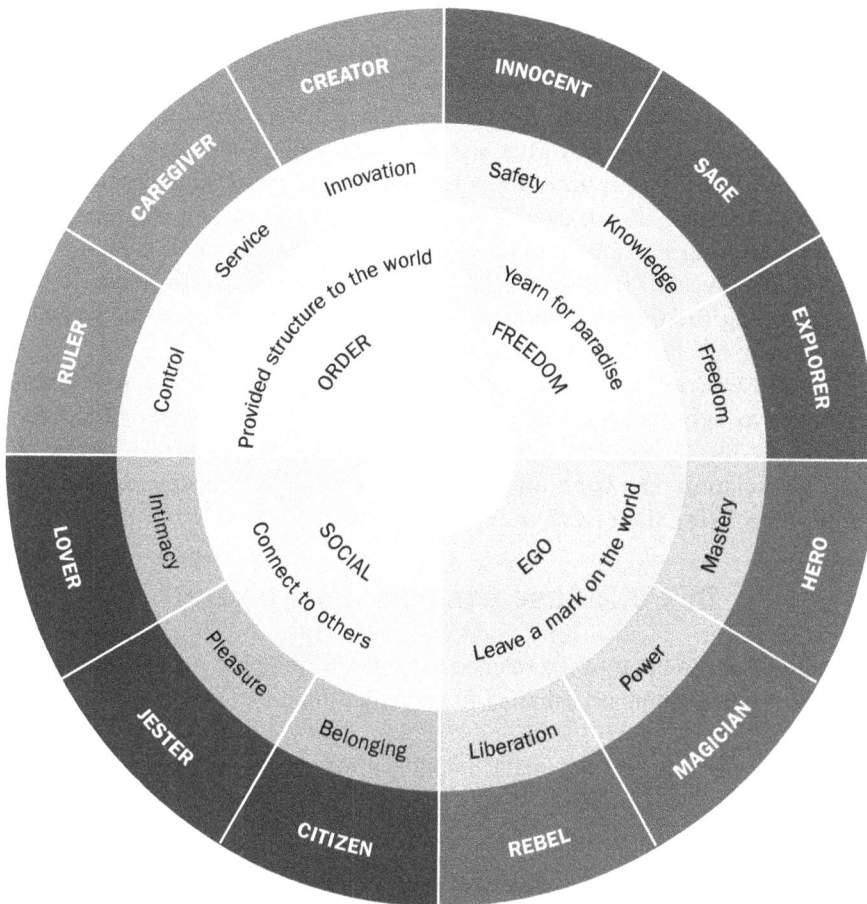

Figure 8.1   Archetypes (adapted from Jung, 1921)

clients' archetypes – for instance, when we try to activate their 'Warrior' or work with their 'Addict'.

Whether people have parts that function like multiple 'selves' (subjectivities, subpersonalities) is contested and understood differently across theoretical perspectives and counselling/psychotherapy subcultures (see Rowan, 1990; Rowan and Cooper, 1999, Cooper et al, 2004). While traditional humanistic theory champions the idea of a private, unique, authentic, core Self, current postmodern or person centred and experiential therapy theory frequently acknowledges a plurality of selves – existential, gestalt and transpersonal variants celebrate plurality and dialogical polyphony, where selves are seen to emerge through dialogue. Psychoanalytic theory accepts each person as being psychologically fragmented, made up of unconsciously introjected parts of others. Social constructionist and post-structural approaches view multiple selves as distributed across contexts emerging out of different social relationships. For instance, narrative therapists see selves as constructed through dialogue and the stories we tell ourselves.

In the psychotherapeutic field of trauma work, again, there are different perspectives. Most, however, seem to subscribe to the idea that people who have a history of trauma show evidence of internal fragmentation (e.g. splitting or dissociation), even if they present as whole on the surface or are not suffering from actual dissociative identity disorder. The metaphorical use of 'selves' to represent parts-of-self in therapy can be a useful way of containing the fragmentation and exploring problematic aspects (which may or may not be owned).

The illustration in Box 8.2 presents a dialogue with a client who seems to have two 'selves'; each way of being has a function that helps the client to navigate life. The psychotherapist Ernesto Spinelli chooses to see the client's dissociation on a continuum between normal and extreme dissociation rather than fixing them with a diagnostic label.

Box 8.2 Case example: dual person?

I pointed out to her that she seemed somehow different to the Jennifer with whom I had become accustomed to engaging in dialogue.

> 'That's because it's not really Jennifer whom you're talking to!' she giggled.
> 'Who am I talking to then?' I asked, revealing my surprise.
> 'Well …' she said hesitantly, 'in a way, you're still talking to Jennifer, but when I'm like this, I prefer to think of myself as Susie.'

My shock must have been as obvious to Susie as it was to me. My persistent reminder to my students to 'always to be open to the unexpected' reverberating all too loudly, I mumbled:

> 'Ah … So, I guess it's better for me to address you as Susie then. Would you prefer that?'
> 'It sounds strange,' answered Susie.
> 'How's that?'
> 'Well,' Susie confessed, 'You're the first person that I told about me being here at times. It's been a secret up till now.'

Somehow, in spite of my astonishment, I found that I was both moved by Susie's faith in me and optimistic about this new twist in my relationship with Jennifer.

'I'm touched and grateful that you felt yourself to be trusting enough towards me to let me in on your secret,' I said …

As she said her goodbyes, I witnessed for the first time the 'transformation' from Susie to Jennifer. It was an amazing sight to behold. The changes reflected in her posture, her facial expressions, her breathing were subtle, yet evident. Within seconds, I was back in the presence of Jennifer. As soon as she saw me, she flushed, then turned her eyes away from mine.

That action suggested to me that Jennifer knew that I knew her secret …

'Jennifer,' I said, measuring my words with care, 'before we say anything else, I want you to know that I'm not going to push you to explain what just happened. If you don't want to say anything, or refer back to it ever again, I promise I'll respect that.'

Still avoiding looking at me, Jennifer began to cry. I made no attempt to disturb her. Eventually, she wiped her eyes and said,

'You're the first person to know about Susie.' (Spinelli, 1997, pp. 149–50, 152)

Working with multiplicity in practice

Multiplicity is worked with differently across psychotherapeutic theories including:[1]

1. Internal family systems (IFS) (Schwartz, 2001) – see Box 8.3.
2. Transactional analysis (TA) and ego state theory (Berne, 1961; Watkins and Watkins, 1997) – see Box 8.4.
3. Structural Integration Theory (van der Hart et al., 2006).
4. Gestalt parts work.
5. Jungian archetypal work.

In practice, these models get reworked and integrated in different ways. Examples include the 'parts and sensorimotor exploration' (Ogden and Fisher, 2015); 'Internalized Parent Interview' (McNeel, 1976; Erskine and Trautmann (2003); and the psycho–spiritual 'Voice dialogue' process (Stone and Stone, 1989).

In my own practice, I draw on these different theories in various ways responding to moments when clients seem to embody different self-states – an experience that can feel as if different people have come into the room. For instance, I had a client who was an experienced, capable counsellor. As we explored her historical trauma, she regressed in front of my eyes. Her posture, movements, facial expression, voice, all changed subtly as she morphed between assured professional and shamed, terrified child.

Box 8.3 Practical application: IFS theory

Richard (Dick) Schwartz developed Internal Family Systems (IFS) based on the hypothesis that the mind is made up of multiple parts and that, underlying them, is a person's core Self. A person's parts can take on extreme roles or subpersonalities. Each has its own embodied perspective, feelings, interests and memories, like members of a family. While some parts may act in problematic dysfunctional ways, they have positive intent. IFS aims to heal these wounded parts and restore mental balance.

IFS proposes three general types of parts:

- *Exiles* represent psychological trauma (e.g. from childhood). Exiles may become disowned or isolated from the other parts that polarise the system.
- *Managers* have protective roles and try to prevent Exile's pain from coming into awareness by being controlling (evaluating, striving, care-taking).
- *Firefighters* are also protectors in diverting attention away from the Exile's hurt and shame (perhaps through over-working or impulsive, problematic behaviour like bingeing, substance use or violence).

NB: Managers and Firefighters can be in conflict with each other (resulting in stuckness or chaos internally). The aim is to help the Protectors trust the Self to take control and lead the system in more harmonious ways.

In general, I find that working with clients on the relationship between their Big (Adult) and Little (Child) 'selves' helps them voice their ambivalent, dissociated and fragmented self-experience. This work also highlights the relevance of having a positive, validating relationship with oneself (see Box 8.4) where a more resilient part stands at a distance from pained parts – which is particularly useful when working with rage or shame. Clients gain the insight that, while there may be a part of self that is vulnerable, there is also a part that is grounded and resourceful (Finlay, 2016b).

Working with client's 'parts'

When doing parts-work, it's important to value and acknowledge each part of the person; every part has a role to play. It makes sense to give each a voice towards witnessing the client as a whole.

Box 8.4 Case example: working with 'Little' and 'Big' parts

Marnie was required to visit with her father (from whom she had learned to keep a good distance) for a family funeral. Marnie expressed her understandable anxiety about this upcoming visit and we explored the terror arising in Marnie's Child ego. Together we came up with a strategy (Adult–Adult problem-solving) whereby she would leave 'Little Marnie' with me for a 'holiday' while 'Adult Marnie' went to stay with her father and attend the funeral alone. The thought that I was continuing to protect and hold her in mind felt enormously powerful and nurturing to her and proved something of an epiphany. That 'Little Marnie' was safely cared for elsewhere felt freeing to Marnie, allowing a more capable, balanced, resourceful 'Adult Marnie' to 'take over' when relating to her father. Importantly she learned to view her father less with terror and rage and more with compassion. When an Adult, she could see a sad, ill, old, alcoholic father shaped by his own toxic, traumatic childhood. This bile-full, aggressive man was her father – one who was never going to give the love and appreciation she craved.

Thereafter Marnie was more able to actively care for her own Child part. By doing so, she understood that she was growing a new choice-full, balanced, compassionate and nurturing Adult side. She saw that she had begun to internalise a version of both her mother and myself, which offered a counterbalance to her internalised father.

The latter stage of therapy focused on reinforcing this new integration. 'New Marnie' ... knew those shamed and shaming parts of herself, while never likely to completely disappear, were mostly contained and could be managed better. ... I saw 'Little Marnie' less often ... There was less need to mother Little Marnie now as New Marnie seemed to have this calmly in hand. Instead, our work focused on being curious about, and celebrating, the emergence of, 'New Marnie'. (Finlay, 2016c, pp. 79–80)

The goal is to raise awareness in the Adult self and enable that part to dialogue with, and care for, more vulnerable parts (which may carry disowned traumatic memories). Along the way, the client might begin to differentiate trauma parts which live in the 'there-and-then' from the healthier 'here-and-now' parts, thereby recognising that they have different skills, motivations and embodied experiences of the world.

Trauma resolution comes first from recognising and valuing disowned parts, giving them a voice and dialoguing with them. An example from TA theory is the 'bull's-eye' transaction[2] where all ego states feel talked to – e.g.:

Therapist: No wonder you decided it isn't safe to voice your opinions!
Client: ['Parent' hears, 'My therapist seems to think this understandable.'
'Adult' hears, 'Ah, there's a reason for this!'
'Child' hears, 'At last! Someone gets that I don't feel safe.']
(Frettingham, 2020, personal communication)

After that, it's about helping the client to recognise that they now have other choices and the possibility of using new resources to cope with challenges. Use of self here involves the therapist offering a transitional space to nudge the client away from old protective script-led patterns towards new ways of relating (Erskine et al., 1999).

Different therapy models specify different processes and protocols for interventions (see, for example, Schwartz, 2001; Ogden and Fisher, 2015). While they prioritise different aspects, all agree that the key steps involve:

- establishing safety and boundaries;
- working with the parts;
- repairing and integrating.

Establishing safety and boundaries

There are three tasks here:

- **Introducing the client to parts work** This involves informed consent and discussion of basic trauma theory, especially the notion that parts of self can be in conflict or disowned. With IFS, for instance, work with Exiles does not occur until the client has obtained 'permission' from the Protectors.
- **Resourcing the adult self to feel safe, steady, grounded and ready to work** (This stage may include use of techniques such as 'anchoring' or teaching of grounding/relaxation/mindfulness exercises.) Clients need to have an adequate window of tolerance – e.g. they should be able to stay with an emotion without becoming dysregulated or dissociated. Initially, it might only be possible to evolve awareness of the parts; direct work with past trauma may need to come later.
- **Opening a hospitable space for hidden parts to enter** Here, for example, the therapist unambiguously conveys their acceptance of darker, potentially violent or shame-ridden, woundedness as well as resourceful helpers (Box 8.5). 'Therapists should be listening intently for the "voices" of the different parts' (Fisher, 2017, p. 116).

Box 8.5 Practical application: inviting a 'self' to emerge

A client explains how she met a new part in therapy.

> I was talking to my therapist about this argument with my mother where she was shouting at me and I was silenced and made to feel stupid as usual. My therapist drew my attention to my hand that was shaped in a fist; I was rocking it slowly. He invited me to 'make the movement bigger and stronger'.
>
> It became a strong fist that was ready to fight. My therapist invited me to put some voice and movement to match my arm. I raised my arm upwards gave a war cry.
>
> My therapist encouraged me to move around and embody it further. Soon my 'Indian Chief' emerged. He was strong and fearless; my Defender and Guardian.
>
> From that one session, something shifted inside. I'm now able to call on that part of me to speak up for myself.

Working with the parts

There are numerous ways to work with parts. Here are few instances.

Meeting the different parts and perhaps giving each a name (e.g. 'People Pleaser', 'Warrior'), raises awareness of the particular needs and bodily experience of individual parts. 'It seems like there are two very different ways of being that are operating in you. There's the x you, and the y you. Would you be okay with us talking separately to these ways of being to see if this might help clarify some of the conflict that you are describing?'

Acknowledging that competing parts can reduce defensiveness and shame (Yalom, 2001). 'There seems to be a part of you who wants to withdraw from contact with me; yet I also see a part which wants to connect with me.' Or, 'You've spoken about wanting to give up and take your life, but the part of you who wants to live and find a way through has come into therapy today. Can we speak to that part?'

Exploring the origin and motives of different parts. Asking 'Whose disparaging voice is that?' or 'Who are you really angry with?' can be revealing.

Giving disowned parts a voice. Explore the feelings, perspective, and experience of each part: How old are they? What do they feel/think? What did they need then and what might they need now? What is their bodily arousal level and window of tolerance? Sometimes the therapist might say they will carry and 'hold' a part (e.g. hope or anger) until the client is ready to accept it.

Confronting the traumatic memory and working through it by witnessing how it was for that part who experienced it. The therapist might recognise the context and the lack of choices at the time of the trauma. 'Of course that young girl who looked after her mentally ill mother and siblings didn't feel she had a right to her own life. She was busy attending to others.' Or, 'It seems this was the way you protected yourself previously in order to survive. You have other options now.'

Enabling dialogue between parts – e.g. 'Could you ask that part why she is so scared?' or 'How could your adult part help keep your child part safe?' or 'What does your part that wants to enjoy intimate relationships want to say to the protective part of you that closed down so you never got hurt again?'[3]

Recognising the pull to revert to 'old' parts when 'scripts' are being challenged. When a person is trying to change, the parts of self that are terrified of being seen, abandoned or damaged get triggered, which may result in self-destructive behaviours. In systems theory when one part does something different, other parts try to bring it back to normal functioning (to avoid disturbing the equilibrium).

Repairing and integrating

The final stage of integration can be enabled by (see Figure 8.2):

- Opening the space for 'corrective emotional experience' and repair of the missing experience by fulfilling developmental needs. For example, 'I see that part of you. He is sad and lonely and feels no one hears him.' Or, 'If I had been there, I would have wanted to protect you – like a tiger with her cub.' Alternatively, it can be powerful to invite the client to offer their own self-care: 'Imagine you holding that baby lovingly.'
- Appreciating the protective role played by parts within a creative defensive structure and the possibility of self-sabotage given how the 'Protector' part may start frantically trying to reset the status quo to return to safe and familiar patterns.
- Reinforcing the 'Co-ordinator' part. This is the healthy, balanced, self-aware part also called 'Integrating Adult' in TA (Finlay, 2016c) and 'Aware Ego' in Voice Dialogue (Stone and Stone, 1989). Encourage its awareness that it can 'care for' vulnerable and younger parts and can make new choices (see Box 8.6).

- Enabling the befriending of parts by helping the client to be curious/interested instead of dismissive or reactive. It's about accepting, and collaborating with, our different parts. It starts with asking about each part's experience, fears and what it needs (Fisher, 2017).
- Reducing the volume of the 'Internal Critic'. Understand its origins yet also challenge it, particularly where it acts as a 'child abuser' (Stone and Stone, 1993).
- Encouraging self-respect, self-compassion and self-acceptance of the client's *whole* self (as opposed to reinforcing splits) counteracting shame.

Highlighting the role of respect and compassion when working with chronic shame and multiple parts of self, DeYoung offers a relational psychotherapeutic formulation:

> Bringing shame to light often illuminates a needy part of self who is despised by a tough, independent part of self. Listening respectfully to both parts and helping each to find compassion for what drives the other brings better balance and harmony to the whole self system ... Parts of self can find space to speak the unspeakable about need, longing, and humiliation, and in their speaking and being heard, integration happens. Often a time of working with 'parts' comes and goes in therapy, and later clients look back with fond nostalgia on parts they once encountered as 'other' but that are now just everyday aspects of the self they know. (DeYoung, 2015, pp. 132–3)

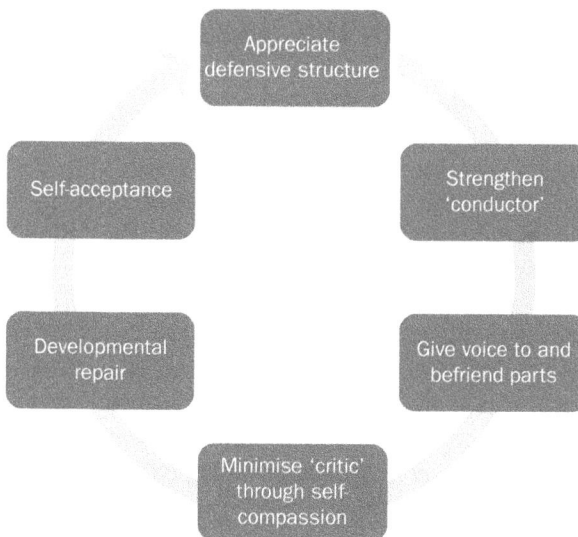

Figure 8.2   Repairing processes and integrating cycle

Box 8.6 Practical application: nurturing the 'Integrating Adult'

Transactional analytic psychotherapy often aims to 'strengthen the Adult': to develop a thinking, analytical part of Self that can manage overwhelming, problematic emotions. More profoundly, we can nurture the client's Integrating Adult – the cohesive, 'grown-up' part of our thinking-feeling-experiencing Self in the here-and-now, free of contaminations from old Parent and Child scripts.

Four ways to foster the process of enabling the Integrating Adult are:

1. Raising the client's awareness of their needs and relational patterns: 'What part of you is talking now?' or 'How are you experiencing this in your body?' or 'What does that mean to you?'
2. Exploring and enjoying the client's Adult – e.g. by having a humorous or intellectual exchanges. The therapist needs to be in Adult too (rather than perhaps being a nurturing/controlling Parent which elicits the client's Child), revelling in mutually nourishing Adult-to-Adult transactions.
3. Engaging relationally and compassionately with different parts of self. Working strategically to help clients be in contact with parts of self (rather than disown) helps to strengthen their sense of identity.
4. Helping the client reconnect with, and reclaim, their wider family/cultural heritage. Is there space for the client to own any positive aspects, both of their legacy and of their current social location? (Finlay, 2016c)

Working with the therapist's parts

Parts work is fundamentally a relational endeavour: both external and internal relationships are at stake. Not only do we work relationally with client's parts, we have our own internal relational landscape of parts to deal with. The issue is an ethical one: how to manage our relationship with our self/selves towards therapeutically being-with clients. The following quotation from a therapist sums up the challenge:

> The most challenging part of doing therapy is not the client work; it's the juggling of all my different parts which get activated by clients. Of course, my *Professional* part is always around, and it mixes with my various counter-transferential responses, such as being a *Nurturing Mother* or when I feel the urge to be *Rescuer* or *Persecutor* when pulled by a client who stuck in a drama triangle as a 'Victim'.
>
> There are those *Vulnerable* parts that feel rage, anxiety, shame, jealousy ... They want to be seen and yearn to share my own problems with clients in return.

My *Internal Critic* constantly confronts me: 'he' questions and undermines me, whispers to me that I'm a "fraud", that "they'll find me out". I start to feel exposed and incompetent and end up overworking. Then *Burnt-Out* appears: She's sucked dry, bored, and irritated with the endless repetition ...

When I feel myself fragmenting into these different parts, I try to pull my wise *Internal Supervisor* to the fore. She pushes me to take responsibility to hand over my different parts to my supervisor. Last week I took some rage that I've been feeling towards a self-absorbed client who was blind to her child's needs. I knew it was my *Child* part who was howling in the background against her own narcissistic mother. But in allowing my supervisor to hold my process, I was able to step back and see how my client too was raging with her unmet needs. My rage, I saw, was arising both in my *Child* and counter-transferentially in my *Adult*. My supervisor's *Compassion* also helped me access my own and I could then contact my *Self-care Coach* and return once more to my *Professional Self*. *Burnt-Out*, at this point, disappeared. She only arrived to remind me I needed support.

One question therapists confront is the extent to which our own 'parts' should be allowed a voice in the therapeutic space. How much should/ might we self-disclose to clients? Yalom (2001) distinguishes between here-and-now disclosures and ones that spring from the therapist's personal history; while the former are recommended as 'grist for the mill', the latter are discouraged. For instance, while it might be reasonable for the therapist to share with the client something that has arisen in the moment ('I'm noticing that there is a part of me that is feeling some anger in response to your story. I'm wondering if that might be something you're feeling?'). If that therapist was then to share details of their own Child rage, that would cross a boundary and wouldn't be in the client's interest.

Reinkraut makes this point with regard to disclosing his sexuality:

I am a gay man. It matters to me as a political and moral act to be out. That said, in my work with my clients I believe I have an obligation to place my clinical responsibilities to my clients ahead of my personal moral commitments. I make self-disclosures to my clients only when I believe they are in the service of the therapeutic work and when they do not compromise my sphere of privacy. (Reinkraut, 2008, p. 20)

The disclosure of parts thus involves complicated negotiations between our professional and personal parts when with clients. That we have potentially contradictory pulls shows the importance of being reflexive about our process in order to ensure an ethical focus on the client's needs. That our vulnerable parts require a compassionate, constructive eye rather than a dismissive/disowning one further underlines the importance of therapist self-care and supervision (Williamson, 2013, p. 104).

Case study

The following case illustration has been condensed from Fisher (2017) who offers narratives around healing fragmented selves of trauma survivors using a blend of IFS with sensorimotor and mindfulness-based therapy. Empathy and compassion are modelled and combined with (left-brain) psychoeducation.

> Carla came to therapy in a highly activated state, having just had to take a leave of absence at work. As she described the past year of her life, it became clear that she had functioned highly for so long because her normal life self was supported by two trauma-related parts, one afraid of failure and one equally determined to succeed. This team drove her to develop a successful professional career and long-term relationship with her partner, but, I explained, 'It was held together with rubber bands and chewing gum.' Then her partner had an affair; she was mugged at knife-point ...; and her father died, activating the trauma-related parts ...' No wonder you have been feeling 'not yourself'. Your parts staged a coup d'etat ... These emotions that have been overwhelming you belong to very young distressed parts.
>
> At the next session, as Carla made connections between her reaction to the affair and a childhood spent parenting her mother and soothing her father to ensure her safety, I translated her narrative into the language of parts: 'So that little girl was all on her own – with no one to help her take care of her mother or protect her from her father – she had to grow up very fast, didn't she?' Carla responded immediately ... 'She did – she couldn't afford to feel lonely and scared – she had to take care of herself because no one else was going to ...' That's how it felt when I found out Amelia was cheating on me. I felt all alone again.' ...
>
> I added: 'Remember: a betrayal would be deeply distressing for any adult, but on top of that, it triggered the worst fears of your younger parts ... They fear being abandoned more than they fear attack.'
>
> Carla: 'True, but even though the little girl was heartbroken, I put up a wall with Amelia – 'you can't hurt me any more because I am not really connected to you.'
>
> Me: 'That sounds like a bodyguard part' ...
>
> A week later, Carla was back with good news: 'I've been thinking a lot about the little girl ... and crying a lot for her ... Before, I was so focused on my career that I never thought of what she had been through and how lonely she was ... I've been taking good care of the little girl this week ... and the wall is softening a little ... The wall wants me to know that it doesn't trust me yet to protect her.' (Fisher, 2017, pp. 194–6)

Critical reflections

While the idea of parts of self is largely accepted in therapeutic fields, there is debate about the existence of multiple 'selves' and whether engaging them is a positive therapeutic way forward.

Guidelines issued by the International Society for the Study of Trauma and Dissociation (ISSTD, 2011) advise engaging with all parts of a person's personality in a non-judgemental, affirming way. In this way, therapists offer a 'unifying gaze' and act as a kind of 'relational bridge' – one that supports the client to relate to disowned memories or dissociated parts of themselves (Finlay, 2019). However, it is recommended that therapists continue to hold in mind that they are working with *one* client; they should avoid colluding with dissociation by encouraging unnecessary elaborations or strengthening the autonomy of 'alters' (Spring, 2010). Here, the therapist holds on to the whole which, in turn, may help the client begin to accept and embrace those less disowned parts.

In my own relational integrative practice (Finlay, 2016a) I work somatically and existentially with longer term clients. Parts-work figures regularly as we explore past trauma. The theory makes sense to me as it mirrors my internal landscape and therapeutic journey: I see parts in myself and perhaps that sensitises me to see them in others.

I appreciate the way that working with parts calls forth an integrating, self-compassionate, creative energy. It's rewarding to see calm spaciousness replace inner cacophony (Schwartz, 2001). When a new part comes forward (is recognised by my client or myself), the moment of insight can resemble an inspirational epiphany. With awareness comes the possibility of greater choice. The client becomes aware of the possibility of change, of escaping from old ways of responding or doing things, of turning down the volume on persistent choruses of strident voices.

But for all my curiosity and excitement about this way of working, I remain aware of the perils of over-using parts work. I wouldn't want to impose this metaphorical device on clients, particularly if the idea of having multiple 'selves' doesn't resonate with their experience. Wonderful work can be done without any reference to parts. Forcing symbolic fragmentation of self into parts may even be contraindicated, especially when such an approach is applied automatically or mechanically. It's better to wait until the moment in therapy when we strongly sense the presence of different parts, eager or ready to speak. While there is a time and a place to work with 'parts', the same applies to staying with the 'whole'.

There is also an ethical imperative for us to be reflexively aware of which parts of us may become triggered when we're engaged in parts work. Since we all carry traces of a Wounded Healer part, we must take care not to act out from damaged places (by smothering another, rescuing, indulging ourselves, being needy, being abusive, being self-destructive, and so on). This aspect of our work is taken up in the next chapter.

Discussion questions

1. Does the idea of 'multiple selves' resonate for you? Are you able to identify parts of yourself?
2. Which parts of you regularly surface in your therapy work? Are there certain parts that get triggered by particular parts in clients?
3. 'Doing parts work is like doing family therapy on the inside.' Explain this statement with examples.

Resources

Book: *Parts Psychology* by Jay Noricks. Compelling narratives of parts work trauma-based therapy where 'parts' are normalised as part of healthy development.

Book: *Healing the Fragmented Selves of Trauma Survivors* by Janina Fisher. Core text offering detailed exploration of the theory and practice of parts work.

Book: *The Plural Self: Multiplicity in Everyday Life* by John Rowan and Mick Cooper is a scholarly, clearly written edited volume that unpacks theory, research and practice around working with multiplicity.

Website: Carolyn Spring's videos, resources and courses for working with trauma and about dissociative identity disorder. Available at: www.carolynspring.com/ (linked also to an older site full of stories/resources around working with 'selves': www.pods-online.org.uk/ – Positive Outcomes for Dissociative Survivors).

Video lecture: Richard Schwartz explains Internal Family Systems work. Available at: www.youtube.com/watch?v=Ym8o762U7uc

---

Notes

1. There are similarities between the different models of parts work although their terms and concepts differ. The 'Adult' and 'Child' of TA can be likened to the 'adult' and 'inner child' many other models talk about. The 'Parent' of the functional model in TA mirrors the psycho-analytic 'super-ego' in linking to parental or societal values and there is even some resemblance to some versions of IFS's 'Protector'. Note that the capital initial of the ego states in TA distinguish them from normal uses of parent/adult/child.

2. This is also sometimes called a 'duplex transaction' (Berne, 1961), where the therapist talks simultaneously to the client's Child and Adult ego states. Strictly speaking a duplex transaction traditionally refers to the hidden psychological transaction within an overt one between two people's ego states.

3. In Voice Dialogue method, the parts are not invited to dialogue with each other – the emphasis is on curiosity, not change.

NINE

BEING A WOUNDED HEALER

Our woundedness is our vulnerability, which is our key to opening the flow of healing to others, and back again to ourselves. We recognize both its power and its risks. (Stone, 2008, p. 49)

The archetype of the wounded healer, which comes from Greek mythology, is representative of those therapists who are able to use their wounds effectively in the service of helping others. Jung was one of the first to write about its relevance to therapy:

> We could say, without too much exaggeration, that a good half of every treatment that probes at all deeply consists in the doctor's examining himself, for only what he can put right in himself can he hope to put right in the patient [...] it is his own hurt that gives the measure of his power to heal. This, and nothing else, is the meaning of the Greek myth of the wounded physician. (Jung, [1954] 2014, p. 116)

It is the recognition of our imperfections, limitations and potential for our feelings to get hurt which grants us the humanity and humility that allows us to empathise with our clients and work in their service (Adams, 2014). Hycner similarly argues that 'it is the very nature of one's own difficulties which sensitizes the therapist to the vulnerability of the other' ([1991] 1993, p. 12). He calls on therapists to 'incessantly struggle to bring [their] ... woundedness into play in the therapy' ([1991] 1993, p. 13).

Our woundedness can both help and hinder therapy, however. This chapter focuses on *how* we can bring our woundedness into play while keeping our client's interest to the fore. The first section considers the nature of therapist woundedness. The following two sections examine (respectively) how therapists' wounds help and hinder therapy. The fourth section focuses on the challenge of managing our wounds: the practical steps we can take to contain our own wounds rather than project them or dissociate from them. The chapter ends with a case study of a wounded therapist giving voice to her experience, followed by critical reflections and questions.

Therapist woundedness

All of us have experienced pain, adversity, grief, suffering – it's what makes us human. In the world of therapy, many eminent theorists and practitioners, from Sigmund Freud and Carl Jung to contemporary writers such as Irvin Yalom and Marsha Linehan, have documented their personal struggles with mental health issues.

It's likely also that most of us have been touched at some time by serious mental or physical illness or disability (be it our own or that suffered by family members) and perhaps even by trauma/abuse. In this sense, we all have sore spots which can be considered our woundedness. Anecdotal and empirical evidence (see Box 9.1) suggests that these wounds were what probably propelled us into the therapy field in the first place, perhaps in the hope of being healed psychically (Farber, 2017; Sussman, 2007).

Even if we've been lucky enough to have escaped largely intact from painful life experiences, we remain open to being wounded by our work with clients. Beyond the relentlessness of our daily exposure to clients' pain, the self-denial and secrecy integral to therapy, and the relative isolation of our work, also take their toll.

A social worker quoted by Sussman describes the challenge:

Box 9.1 Research: therapist woundedness

Barr carried out quantitative (using descriptive and inferential statistics) and qualitative (thematic analysis, with a grounded theory approach) research using online questionnaires on why people become therapists and whether wounded people were more likely to be attracted to enter the profession. Psychological wounds were defined as 'the effect of one or more traumatic events that had significant emotional impact on you' (p. 1). Of the 253 participants who responded, 73.9 per cent believed their wounding experience(s) had led them to pursue a career in counselling or psychotherapy. Although no significant differences were found regarding the ethnicity, age and theoretical approach of wounded healers, sex clearly mattered: women were found to report their wounding experiences significantly more than men. (Barr, 2006)

> Being used as an instrument who is smashed against the wall ... kicked, reviled ... Just the enormous range of emotions I get subjected to on a daily basis in my body, mind, soul. And the cumulative effect over the years of being the container for all that intense emotion ... I can't think of a more masochistic profession. To deny one's own needs, to contain the other person's. *Especially* when most likely, one's been used like that one's whole life in some way, or you wouldn't be doing it in the first place. (Sussman, 1992, pp. 183–4, cited in Farber, 2017, p. 38)

Just because we've been 'wounded', however, doesn't automatically make us 'healers'. If wounds have not been processed sufficiently and mostly healed, there is a risk they will contaminate the field and impact negatively on the client (Jackson, 2001; Gelso and Hayes, 2007).

The distinction between 'the wounded healer' and 'the impaired professional' (Jackson, 2001) is relevant here. With the former, the therapist has actively worked on (reflexively processed) their wounds, enabling the wounds – and experience of recovery – to be used as potential openings to empathy and connection. But when the therapist is an impaired professional, wounds are unprocessed and leak out in damaging ways. The wounded can become someone who wounds.

It's probably realistic to place ourselves along a continuum where we may be more or less impaired at any point in time. As Sussman (1995), Adams (2014) and Farber (2017) have pointed out in their various compilations of therapists' accounts of their woundedness, the myth of the fully healed, untroubled therapist needs robust challenge.

One problem we confront is the ambiguity around the degree of healing/ recovery we need to have experienced to practise responsibly (Zerubavel and Wright, 2012). That remains moot and is probably at the heart of many conversations to do with ethical practice that take place during supervision. A range of considerations enter the picture here, including the institution we may be working in and the wider cultural expectations surrounding what is expected from professionals – for example, to what extent are self-disclosure or blurred boundaries accepted?

The first step is to identify the nature of our woundedness. Where does it spring from? Does it come from our own history? Or is it part of life's challenges in the present – perhaps specifically something to do with our current client work? We then need to reflexively examine how this woundedness comes into play, in both helpful and hindering ways (see Box 9.2).

When our woundedness helps

There are three significant ways in which a therapist's wounds can be beneficial to therapy: empathy, hope and healing.

Box 9.2 Practical application:
being (physically) wounded

Ingham discusses the challenges of being a physically disabled counselling psychologist in training. A discourse analysis of extracts from her own reflexive journal highlights subtly discriminatory therapy/training environment (perpetuating societal negativity) where physical disability is insufficiently understood by peers/colleagues, let alone clients. Ingham gives examples of things people have said, including 'I don't consider you to be physically disabled'. For her, this indicates that person's belief that:

> to be physically disabled was something so negative as to be almost unthinkable; wretched and to be pitied ... She ... was bestowing the generous 'gift' of mercy, or looking the other way, to justify the existence of the friendship. (Ingham, 2018, p. 39)

Ingham saw that reflexively developing her own understanding of the relational implications of her 'wounded' physicality would be an important step to promoting deeper relationships with both colleagues and clients.
    She makes the important point that the responsibility for raising awareness should not just rest with the disabled trainee:

> Any institutional lack of awareness of the needs and experiences of individuals with physical disabilities whilst training in the profession allows for negative attitudes and stereotypes pervading society to subtly permeate the training environment, and therefore to continue on to negatively affect service provision and therapeutic relationships. It also places extra demands on the physically disabled trainee to negotiate their way through an environment that could be experienced as alienating and subtly oppressive, despite being one that purports to define itself by its ability to be self-aware and accepting of all. (Ingham, 2018, p. 31)

First, our own vulnerability reinforces our capacity for empathy with clients (regarding sensitivity towards, and compassion for, *their* vulnerability). Awareness of our wounds helps us connect with clients and offers a useful internal reference point for understanding their pain (Hayes, 2002).

If we are to be an understanding relational home for a traumatized person, we must tolerate, even draw upon, our own existential vulnerabilities so that we can dwell unflinchingly with his or her unbearable and recurring emotional pain. (Stolorow, 2014, p. 135).

The therapist's empathy will not be seen as authentic unless it comes from 'a heart wounded by … suffering', argues Nouwen (1972, p. xiv). This doesn't mean, however, that we need to share exactly the same wounds as our clients to appreciate pain. A therapist may not have had the experience of going through specific experiences: suffering a significant bereavement, for example, or having a miscarriage, or enduring chronic pain, or being sexually abused. However, they may have experienced a similar but different trauma, loss or challenge which enhances their empathy.

Second, a therapist's own experience of recovery and resilience can inspire confidence and hope. 'Therapists who are themselves survivors can perhaps give the greatest gift of all – a living demonstration of hope' (Bond, 2020, p. 284). As Samuelson says (2017, p. 184): 'I am a wounded healer. I use the discoveries from my own healing process to guide others on their paths.' Many organisations make practical use of this wisdom. Alcoholics Anonymous and Hearing Voices networks, for instance, deploy practitioners who themselves have struggled with the same issues. Hearing first-hand how struggles were resolved, even if the therapist's particular history is different, can help clients see how to move forward and survive. Here, a therapist might admit that they, too, have to battle their own shame demons, even if the source of shame differs from the client's; a therapist with a sibling who abuses substances may have extra insight into the nature of that struggle; a therapist with a disability may have empathic understanding of a client's chronic health issues.

Third, the therapy itself can be healing for both therapist and client (Gelso and Hayes, 2007). In those special moments of deep, relational connection, we get nourishment and can be inspired by our clients' creativity and resilience; we can learn from their healing. How could we not be touched and impacted, and even changed, by the painful, extraordinary, challenging, intimate, heart-and-soul stories we hear? These gifts 'find our tender, vulnerable spots', says Kottler (2018, p. 132), and they bring 'attention to our own unfinished work'.

Two eminent therapists reinforce this point:

> Carl Rogers owns that he became a therapist to relieve his own longing for intimacy:

> I recognize how much I need to care deeply for another and to receive that kind of caring in return. I can say openly what I have always recognized dimly: that my deep involvement in psychotherapy was a cautious way of meeting this need for intimacy without risking too much of my person. (Rogers, 1980, p. 84)

> Irvin Yalom writes of taking a break from his practice to write, only to find himself depressed:

I grew depressed, restless and finally arranged to treat two patients – more for my sake than theirs. Who was the patient and who the therapist? I was more troubled than they and, I think, benefited more than they from our work together. (Yalom and Elkin, 1974)

When our woundedness hinders

It is immensely challenging to witness and hold people's pain and trauma, day in, day out, and do so without becoming overwhelmed. Feelings of powerlessness and hopelessness can result in therapists becoming desensitised or even burnt out. Even the best intentioned therapists can, in the face of clients' relentless, self-destructive stuck processes, get ground down, sucked dry and vicariously traumatised. In such circumstances, therapy can go seriously off-piste; care can morph into something darker that edges towards an abuse of power.

We pay a price for involving ourselves with our clients and allowing them to matter to us (Wosket, 2017). Lurking anxiety or anger can be acted out in bullying, manipulative, seductive or persecuting ways.

In the course of our work we are likely to hear about many acts of human wickedness and depravity, and to witness the open wounds and scars that these inflict. We cannot help but feel contaminated by such experiences and will, at some level, feel angry with our clients for soiling us (Wosket, 2017, p. 206).

In addition to holding our clients' pain, we also have to contain our own vulnerabilities, insecurities, script limitations and the narcissistic needs stemming from our own histories. Many of us battle with 'impostor syndrome' (see Box 9.3). Those piercing arrows of self-doubt and shame about our accomplishments/entitlements, together with our fear of being exposed as frauds, can impair our professional performance and contribute to burnout (Bravata et al., 2020).

Thériault and Gazzola (2008) interviewed twelve experienced therapists to investigate therapists' feelings of incompetence. Their emerging grounded theory suggests that most therapists routinely have low-level (containable) self-doubt, questioning whether they are 'right' or 'effective'. Self-doubt stemming from personal historical wounds remains challenging, however, because of their continuing potency and the attached threat of potentially regressing to previous levels of vulnerability. Interestingly, clinical experience was not found to be a helpful buffer as self-expectations tend to be raised with experience, making the therapists more vulnerable to feelings of incompetence.

Thériault and Gazzola (2010) then followed up this research with novice therapists and found that feelings of incompetence were a familiar and ongoing aspect of their lives, and this experience was complex; the

> ## Box 9.3 Practical application: seven steps towards managing 'impostor syndrome'
>
> 1. Lower impossible standards of perfection – be human.
> 2. Focus on your particular strengths/qualities/abilities.
> 3. Work actively to take in positive feedback.
> 4. Stop comparing yourself to others, assuming their superiority.
> 5. Share your insecurities with good friends/mentors who support, respect and challenge you.
> 6. Take stock of who you are. Own the historical origins of your shame, achievements and way of being.
> 7. Pursue what you really care about, what feels like meaningful choices and achievements, rather than seeing them as simply a means to gain more credentials or plaudits.

intensity of feelings depended, in part, on the source of these feelings. The authors discuss the importance of attuning to this complexity in supervision. Becoming more directive – a common response to supervisees' uncertainty – may not be the most helpful response (see Box 9.3).

Sussman offers a brutally honest look at the deluded hopes and covert aims that motivated his becoming a therapist:

> I hoped to be admired and idolized ... I hoped to make up for the damage I believe I had inflicted on my family as a child ... I hoped to transcend my own aggression and destructiveness ... I hoped to escape my own problems by focusing on those of other people ... I hoped to achieve a deep level of intimacy within a safe context ... I hoped to meet my own dependency needs vicariously by attending to those of my patients ... I believed that I might become free of limitations. (Sussman, 1992, pp. 16–22)

By recognising how he sometimes subverts client work to meet his own needs, Kottler (2017) similarly owns up to his own shadow side with remarkable candour. For him, the bigger worry perhaps are those times when he is *not* aware of meeting his own needs at the client's expense.

Inevitably, our darker stuff leaks into our work from time to time. This happens when the wounds are too great, or when a therapist hasn't sufficiently acknowledged and worked on their own demons. The result is that therapist's wounds can get acted out in therapy and professional boundaries can get eroded.

Client safety is compromised when boundaries are too loose or too tight. It gets compromised when the therapist over-discloses, thereby shifting attention away from the client, or holds too much (smothers and infantilises), or is too distant, judging or withholding, or is unable to be sufficiently present. Of course, the list of mis-steps we might make is endless. We all make 'mistakes' – it's part of the process. The key is to try to catch those errors, repair any ruptures and manage the wounds. Both therapist and client may then learn and grow.

It's best to view our mistakes with curiosity and compassion, rather than beating ourselves up in a context of shame and guilt. Many so-called mistakes arise out of therapists' genuine care, concern and compassion. Trying to do our best, we may have fallen into the trap of working too hard, of trying too much.

In addition, therapists have an understandable need to feel helpful/needed; we yearn to be appreciated. Or perhaps therapists are working too hard in order to combat their own feelings of anxiety or shame stemming from unrealistic (impossible?) professional hopes and ideals. It's more than likely that the 'mistake' or rupture has arisen out of a relational process to which both client and therapist are contributing. Reflexively exploring underlying dynamics more deeply will help enrich the work and strengthen the awareness/choices of both therapist and client (see Box 9.4).

Box 9.4 Practical application: processing 'mistakes' in supervision

In my work as a supervisor, one of the most common 'mistakes' I see is when the therapist works too hard, is over-protective and/or tries to be too helpful. They may have fallen into being a 'Rescuer', which threatens professional boundaries and compromises the therapist's safe, consistent frame. It is then important to explore what is going on. Why has the 'Rescuer' in the therapist been activated? It's likely that any rescuing is done out of a genuine desire to help but there is probably more going on ...

Perhaps the answer lies in the therapist's own wounded history. Perhaps they have learned to care for others (maybe to ensure the safety of their environment), which means they find it hard to attend to themselves? Perhaps caring for others is the way they care for themselves? Or is the rescuing a way to feel needed and appreciated? Could being overly-protective be the way the therapist manages their own anxiety?

It's also possible that the source of any rescuing is located in the therapist–client relationship. For example, the therapist may have been pulled into a confluence with the client's idealisation of them. Taking on the fantasy of being 'Saviour' or 'Sage' can itself be a defence which distances the therapist from their own (and their client's) feeling of vulnerability and

> powerlessness. Or might the client be replaying – re-enacting – some 'drama triangle' dynamics? By pulling the therapist in to 'rescue' them, they may be playing out longstanding 'Victim' or 'Persecutor' roles.
>
> Once therapist and supervisor have come to a deeper (and more compassionate) understanding of what may be going on, appropriate steps can be taken. For instance, the therapist might come to recognise that 'rescuing' is ultimately unhelpful when they see the drama triangle dynamics more clearly.
>
> The point is to note the value of processing the 'mistake' rather than getting caught up in the shame of having made one.

Managing our woundedness

There are three routes to managing our woundedness:

- awareness;
- processing;
- self-care.

Awareness

It is an ethical priority to have sufficient robustness, emotional literacy and containment to avoid loading clients with distress accumulated from our own past experience. Heron (2001, p. 12) notes that we must ensure that our disturbance does not 'drive and distort' our interventions. It's not going to work if we try to be Sorcerer, Sage, Shaman and/or Saviour (Sussman, 1995). Our work is not about 'rescuing' or 'persecuting' our clients. Nor should we allow ourselves the status of being a 'victim': whether to feelings of being overwhelmed, or of abandonment, or of being invaded/attacked.

Instead, our work requires us to face our strengths and limitations. Once we can do so – once we can hold our own – we offer clients a safer space.

From my own experience, I know that if I lack the necessary support for the difficult work I do, particularly when such work connects with unresolved issues of my own, there is a danger of my using therapy (out of awareness) with a client to act out (or get the client to act out for me).

In the following story, the author recognises her own history, and this helps her to be more present and to tune into her client more empathetically. By being aware of her woundedness, she is enabled to manage it and do more than simply survive as a therapist.

> Marjolaine is a woman in her 40s ... She tells me her story without any hesitation and with a self-confidence that does not correspond to the

horror she seems to be describing. She replaced her sexually frigid mother as a sexual partner to her father in her early adolescence until well in her 20s ... There are many meetings with her during which I feel totally useless, helpless, where I feel bored, and during which I withdraw in a passivity that seems totally acceptable to Marjolaine, but feeling guilty and ashamed of not contributing more, of being so "out of touch" and in a disjunctive posture with her without her conscious awareness.

In this monologue from Marjolaine, ... It is difficult for me to stay present – I find myself in dissociative states – or I struggle silently with shame and guilt over my aversive reactions to Marjolaine ... This is familiar to me: I would feel empty, passive, bored in my original family; and later, also, when things were that silent and were hidden behind appearances of happiness. I knew how to accommodate myself and to stay "correct."

... Would you be surprised if I told you that it is by recognizing myself in this painful repetition that sustains me and permits me to do better than survive? (Richard, 2012, pp. 133–5)

The first step to managing wounds, then, is to be aware of the shadow cast by our own scars, motivations and needs. I like Gibertoni's words (2013, p. 50) when she writes of having 'thought of myself as a container, sometimes with leaks, holes or cracks in need of repair, a pot with a cover that does not do its job very well'. The point is to know where the leaks, holes and cracks are. Are there moments when we find ourselves gratifying our own needs before those of the client? Therapists who lack awareness – or don't take sufficient care to try to be reflexive about their behaviour – can inadvertently fall into unhealthy enactments or ruptures. Even worse, they risk abusing their power.

Once we have developed our awareness, we confront the ethical challenge of monitoring and containing our wounded process. This is to avoid projecting it unhealthily on to others, sublimating it or dissociating from it (which results in dissociating from our client's pain as well as our own). Part of the challenge involves managing our counter-transferences so that we don't become shredded by reminders of our own fragility or traumas. We need to find ways to avoid vicarious traumatisation. For instance, if we find ourselves being over-protective in our anxiety for a client, it can help to remind ourselves of the need to respect the client's own choices and resources, and to maintain consistent (safe) therapeutic boundaries.

Processing

Once we have an awareness of our wounds, we have a chance of ensuring that these don't overwhelm the therapy. We then need to process them by identifying the precise nature of each wound and how it influences our way of being. This, in turn, impacts on both client and therapy (see Box 9.5).

Box 9.5 Practical application: uncomfortable questions

In his book *The Secrets of Exceptional Counselors*, Kottler suggests that it is useful to separate out the client and therapist issues that may be 'getting in the way'. He recommends reflexively asking oneself the following 'uncomfortable questions':

- What am I doing to create or exacerbate the problems?
- Who does the client remind me of that is blocking my ability to see him or her as he or she is?
- What personal issues of mine are being triggered by our interaction together?
- How am I acting out my impatience with the client's lack of apparent progress?
- What expectations am I demanding of this client that he or she is unable to unwilling to meet?
- What needs of mine are not being met, especially those related to recognition, approval and feeling competent?
  (Kottler, 2018, p. 76)

Adams (2014) interviewed many practitioners who admitted that their work acted as a 'buffer' against personal pain. Several of the therapists owned how the grief in their own lives helped them to be sensitive to others' grief. At the same time, offering therapy to others helped grieving therapists to gain some distance from their own pain. But each life situation needed to be negotiated individually.

Part of facing our process involves recognising our limitations and the effects of any shame or problematic scripts. If we become overwhelmed by our emotional process/history to the extent that we are unable to be present to another's, then we need to step back. There was a time when I had some stressful, sleepless nights caring for a family member who had had a life-threatening medical procedure. Initially, I was going to 'soldier on' with my work regardless. Thankfully, my internal supervisor interceded and alerted me to the fact that I was not in a fit condition to work. It was the nudge I needed to cancel my appointments for the week and engage in some serious self-care. It was only when I stopped work that I realised that traumatic memories from my past had been triggered, adding to my stress and my script response of soldiering on.

The relational dimension needs to be factored in here, too. In situations where therapists feel overwhelmed, they may project their dependence and neediness onto clients, perhaps infantalising them in the process. In turn, clients may become overly dependent on, or uncritically admiring of, their therapist. In another situation, a client might be expecting to be criticised or abandoned by their therapist. Somehow, through projective identification, the therapist might get caught up in persecutory relational dynamics and inadvertently fall into being critical/abandoning. In all these situations it is vital for therapists to monitor and contain their process (Finlay, 2019).

Cuseglio (2019) offers a powerful portrait of himself as a wounded healer who analyses – and works through – some challenging countertransference. He gives the example of his year-long work with Luke, a disturbed, destructive 15-year-old whose family history contained repeated instances of suicide on both parents' sides. Months after the forced ending of his therapy with Luke, the therapist kept thinking of the boy. He recognised he was still concerned that Luke had felt abandoned by the ending. One night, Cuseglio had a vivid dream which he then processed. He eventually recognised his need to 'rescue' the boy with whom he identified. He became aware of how his omnipotent healer fantasy had stopped him seeing that his woundedness had also allowed him to offer some healing to Luke in the form of being a listening, non-judgemental presence.

> My inability to protect Luke from self-injury and multiple suicide attempts caused me to feel incompetent during the treatment. With each call from Ruth [mother] detailing another failed suicide attempt, I experienced another lash of the whip. I punished myself. Based on the dream's content, Beck (1967) would categorize it as 'masochistic dream', expressing themes of physical attack and punishment. In reality, I felt partly responsible for Luke's behavior. I erroneously believed that if I gave him something more, something better, then he would have stopped acting on his rage. Luke's image in the dream is my shadow self, an unacceptable representation of me, which I in turn projected on to him ... I was a slave to the notion of rescue, but also a sadistic master who beat myself mercilessly when I could not provide it. (Cuseglio, 2019)

Self-care

Having processed one's woundedness, it's important to engage in nourishing, compassionate self-care and to get some extra support (perhaps through supervision). Given our human vulnerability, it is an ethical imperative as well as a professional priority to be reflexive about our processes and make active use of supportive opportunities. Therapy, CPD, formal and peer supervision – all offer precious moments to be witnessed, held and healed ourselves (Finlay, 2019; see Box 9.5).

Self-care involves first recognising signs of shame, tiredness, overwhelm, compassion fatigue and/or vicarious traumatisation. Here it can help to recognise the difference between 'burnout', which can be eased by having a

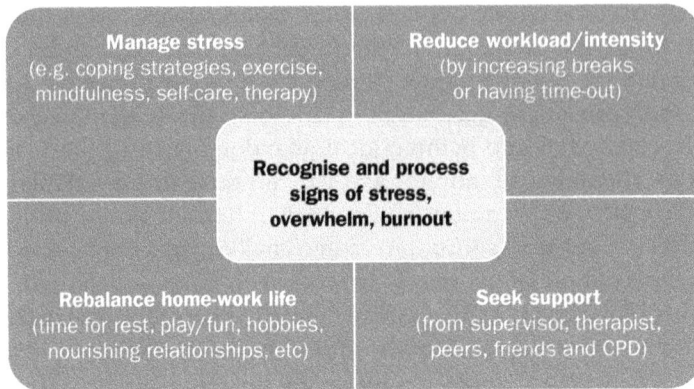

Figure 9.1   Managing stress, overwhelm and/or burnout

break, and 'vicarious trauma', which lingers for a much longer period (Branson, 2019; Smith 2021). By identifying our vulnerability, we can take action to reduce or rebalance our workload, manage the stress and seek support (physical, emotional, social, spiritual) towards rebuilding our resilience (see Figure 9.1).

In line with all the authors mentioned in this chapter, I would add that we can enhance our healing process by sharing our personal stories (see, for instance, Smith, 2021). It's perhaps time for us all to be more open about our vulnerabilities. Then we can explore our wounds more deeply, helping us clarify when our wounds may help our work, and when they may have a hindering or negative impact. Sharing our woundedness also strengthens our ability to give each other support.

Therapy Today currently publishes a regular column where members are invited to answer the question: 'How do you care for yourself?' Many examples of hobbies and helpful strategies have been discussed. One important message is that what works for self-care varies strongly from one individual to another (British Association for Counselling and Psychotherapy, 2018).

Case study

I work with refugees and asylum seekers. When I first found myself in this field, I realised I had a gift. This was how I can 'make a difference', I thought to myself. But it's harrowing work and every Monday morning I wonder how much longer I can keep going. I wake up each morning feeling sick about the day to come; I go to bed each night dreading the nightmares that I know will come.

I can never fully know the trauma my clients have endured and somehow survived. But at the same time, I do know something of what's involved.

For I myself am a migrant. Twenty years ago, I left my homeland to go to university. Then I got married, had two children and became a naturalised citizen of my new country.

Perhaps you'll be surprised to learn that I've never returned to my place of origin. Leaving my 'home' for good has indeed left a deep scar, one that will never heal. I live with profound grief for what I have lost. Yet the thought of returning home is even more traumatic. For my decision to leave my country was all about escape: making my escape from my family and my former life.

Through therapy I've also managed to pull myself out of some of the layers of intergenerational trauma (to do with the brutality of war, lost and divided families, and poverty).

Why would I go back? It is enough that from time to time I am terror-ised and tortured in my dreams. Sometimes I wake up screaming, bathed in sweat, having palpitations. I tell myself that this is vicarious traumatisa-tion, that it's fallout from the challenging work I do. Yet I know that at such moments I'm also back in my childhood, trapped and desperate for escape. I have to remind myself that I am safe now in my new country, even if I will never fully belong here.

These wounds I carry into my counselling practice. As my clients tell me of the horrors they have fled, of the acute loneliness and shame of their life in exile, I know something of their experience. This understanding nour-ishes my therapy; it expresses itself in the empathy and compassion I lavish on my clients. They, of course, don't know my story, but they sense I am a kindred spirit, and, on better days, we heal together.

Sometimes when the shared pain gets too overwhelming and excruciat-ing, I have to cut off. I know that place of vicarious trauma and burnout when I feel rage and want to shout at my client to shut up. I'm ashamed that I sometimes envy clients for the families and community they still have around them. Once more I am reminded of my loss, of how I've disowned parts of myself to survive.

Maybe I should go back to my homeland. Maybe I should face my demons. Maybe this is how I will finally feel whole.

Maybe I should, because – unlike my clients – I can. (Anonymous)

Critical reflections

All of us carry some wounds, whether from current pain or past trauma. It's part of the human experience (Nouwen, 1972). 'There is no therapist and no person immune to the inherent tragedies of existence', says Yalom (2001, p. 8).

I get inspired by reading autobiographical accounts of therapists who disclose their woundedness openly and find ways to grow through trau-matic experiences (see, for example, the research by Cvetovac and Adame

(2017) who analysed key themes within eleven first-person published narratives written by psychotherapists who have struggled with their mental health). Describing her relationship with her own trauma as a Holocaust survivor-turned-psychologist, Edith Eger talks about healing as 'discovery' rather than 'recovery'. Importantly, her trauma experience enabled her to be more attentive to her clients' existential challenges. She explains how her trauma was 'a well I could draw on, a deep source of understanding and intuition about my patients, their pain, and the path to healing' (Eger, 2017, p. 239).

I like the way Norcross and Karpiak describe our woundedness as inspiring our 'best selves'. They quote from the great nineteenth-century novel *The Mill on the Floss* (1860, p. 527), written by George Eliot (the pen name adopted by Mary Ann Evans):

> Our best selves have weathered adversities, confronted life, and struggled with its vicissitudes ... Our best selves emerge, ... "from a life vivid and intense enough to have created a wide fellow-feeling with all that is human." (Norcross and Karpiak, 2017, p. 73)

While it is not necessary to have experienced a particular pain to properly empathise with a client's specific suffering, I would say that we need to be open to our humanness. When we see vulnerability in ourselves, we're more likely to be sensitised to the same in others; then we can truly connect. At that point, the 'magic' of therapy can enter.

Our challenge is to do enough personal work to allow us the self-awareness to use our wounds (and healing) in the service of our clients, rather than acting out from that sore place and becoming that impaired or wounded–wounding healer. It's also about knowing when to step back and get extra support when we judge we are not sufficiently grounded to work ethically.

It's often tricky to strike a balance between accepting our vulnerability and protecting ourselves from further wounds. We need to be able to recognise that we're in danger of becoming impaired and need to care for ourselves.

Constant monitoring is required; all of us are works-in-progress. Even Rogers has admitted to struggling with this balance: 'I have always been better at caring for and looking after others than I have been in caring for myself. But in these later years I made progress' (1995, p. 80).

Self-care and supervision should be our constant companions. Just as we work hard with clients to tailor treatments to their specific needs, we should do the same for ourselves. I appreciate the statement put out by the American Counseling Association's (ACA) Taskforce on Counselor Impairment: '[u]ltimately the care that counselors provide others will only be as good as the care they provide themselves' (ACA, n.d., para. 9).

And once we learn to manage our woundedness, we will be able to better connect and 'provide the balm of compassion and understanding to others who have sustained emotional wounds' (Sussman, 1995, p. 24). There is humble pleasure to be found in nurturing another's growth.

Discussion questions

1. Does your woundedness (stemming from current pain or past trauma) help or hinder your client work?
2. Take one 'mistake' you have made in therapy and process it more fully. Think about the ways in which your own history/vulnerability may have contributed, and also what might have been happening relationally.
3. What self-care do you need to ensure that your woundedness does not impinge negatively on the therapy?

Resources

Book: *On Being a Therapist* by Jeffrey Kottler. Classic text about therapists' use of self and their vulnerabilities (see the latest 5th edition).

Book: *Staring at the Sun* by Irvin Yalom. Compassionate, personal, professional and scholarly exploration of existential anxiety and fear of death.

Book: *The Myth of the Untroubled Therapist* by Marie Adams. Forty research narratives of how therapists managed strife in their personal life (bereavement, divorce, being ill, etc.).

Academic paper: The dilemma of the wounded healer by Noga Zerubavel and Margaret O'Dougherty Wright. *Psychotherapy*, 49 (4): 482–91.

Blog: The wounded healer psychotherapist by Sharon Farber posted October 2016 on *Psychology Today* provides a brief but compelling narrative of wounded healer processes. Available at: www.psychologytoday.com/gb/blog/the-mind-body-connection/201610/the-wounded-healer-psychotherapist.

TEN

RELATIONAL THERAPEUTIC BEING

Perhaps the most important ingredient in our therapeutic being is for the therapist to be "present as a person meeting the person of the other." (Yontef, 1993, p. 24)

All the chapters in this book have emphasised two points about the therapeutic use of self: being relational and being present as a human being. While we might sometimes engage 'therapist first' (instrumental use of skills/techniques), our humanness remains the basis for relating and it is both our strength and vulnerability. In this concluding chapter, I would like to re-emphasise these points, highlighting how use of self is fundamentally an ethical undertaking and part of living in a social–relational world.

Beyond professional, ethical guidelines which talk about 'duty of care', 'respect', 'therapist integrity', 'informed consent', 'holding of boundaries', and so on, our use of self involves a certain spaciousness. We strive to create safe therapeutic openings where the client can feel affirmed, supported, resourced, empathised with and challenged to grow. But the sheer messiness, uncertainty and complexity of practice mean there are no clear-cut recipes. Rarely can we plan our work in advance.

Our therapeutic way of being depends on many factors: the context, our theoretical model, clients' needs and the nature of the relationships we co-create with clients. In this final chapter, where I offer some reflections on being human, being-in-relationship and social being, I invite you to reflect critically on your practice, preferences and values in general. The chapter concludes with the usual case study, questions and reflections.

Being human

A healing relationship would seem to require psychotherapists ... to engage with their clients as a multifaceted human being ... The principles they embody are universal and timeless: a deep respect for clients – for all humanity; and *a willingness to engage as simply one human being to another*. (Cooper, 2007, p. 17; italics are my emphasis)

In the passage below, Mandić (an existential therapist) describes his use of self during therapy with clients. His compassion and sense of his client's needs and vulnerabilities emerge from being a human being like her:

> I sense that she is a little shy and unsure of herself. Neither one of us is very sure about what might happen next. I feel a twinge of sadness mingled with familiarity – this is how I experience many moments like this – and I give a reassuring smile, as if to acknowledge her unease. Her eyes manage to hold my smile, before then looking down and away. Her gentleness almost overwhelms me, and a film of wetness starts to feel itself form over my eyes ...
>
> I have no props, I can only be, rather than do, anything, and a wish to understand her, to be some-*one* for her. I have no desire to absorb her to be me, or to take her over, but to simply meet her as herself ... I want to be the planter of seeds of possibility for her, long after she has finished seeing me. Her life is not broken, not bad, or wrong, it just needs the nutrients to make that seed take root. And I sense it all only through being a human being, just like her. (Mandić, 2016, pp. 111–12)

As we sit, day after day, listening to people's stories of pain, conflict, struggle and trauma, we cannot help being affected. At times, we can get drawn into the client's dramas and processes, perhaps unwittingly finding ourselves embodying unfamiliar ways of being (as when we are pulled into projective identification or counter-transference). At other times we can feel swamped and overwhelmed. Our client's pain haunts us, rendering us raw and vulnerable. We are human, after all.

In a vivid portrayal of the world of the therapist, Kottler (1917, p. 11) advises us to 'leave behind some of our amor and defences' even as we enter into 'mortal combat' where sparks can fly leaving 'third degree burns' and where there is 'nowhere to seek shelter': Given our shared humanness, there will be moments when we can feel utterly stuck – when, filled with self-doubt, we question whether we have anything at all to offer our clients. At other times clients touch our human vulnerabilities and we momentarily disconnect from the therapy in progress. Just like our clients, we are works-in-progress. And, we, too, can receive healing from our clients in turn.

Madison captures some of the contradictions that form an inevitable part of our experience as therapists:

> At times I can be didactic and preachy with clients ... My client and I collude in forgetting that this is my first life too. What do I know?
>
> Outside the consulting room I am not always so wise. I can lose my soft-spoken, reflective stance and be as reactive and unreasonable as the next person ...
>
> I am coming to the realization that some of the most significant and poignant moments in therapy are not really about the content of the discussion. Not really about behavior change or unravelling the past. In fact, in a sense, they are not really about the client's trouble at all. In the deepest moments of therapy I am freed by my client and my client is freed by me. (Madison, 2009)

Research supports the view that being humble and having some self-doubt are among the hallmarks of a good therapist (Nissen-Lie, 2020). Studies show, for instance, that therapists who score more highly on professional self-doubt tend to receive more positive ratings from clients re: the therapeutic alliance and outcomes. A willingness to listen, learn and be reflexive (rather than rush to conclusions, address clients from a position of superiority or even blame them for their plight) is central to good practice.

Research also suggests that therapists need to engage in self-care and treat themselves in a kind, forgiving manner. Good self-care in this context involves:

- cultivating self-compassion (Germer, 2021);
- holding healthy work–life balance and boundaries;
- regularly engaging leisure (exercise, hobbies, creativity, playful escapism);
- ensuring regular, supportive, nourishing connections with others;
- taking 'mistakes' and vulnerabilities to supervision/therapy.

Supervision is crucially important for ongoing support. The supervisor can help remind us about the need for self-care and help us recognise how problematic stuckness/ruptures may be rooted in the relational process rather than in our inadequacy as therapists.

Research also shows that significant events or breakthroughs in therapy are often preceded by relational tensions between therapist and client (Safran et al., 2001; Ardito and Rabellino, 2011). It's inevitable that at times therapists will make mistakes or misattune. What matters more than anything else is how effectively these are handled:

The good news is that when therapists are good at detecting ruptures in the therapeutic alliance and have the skills to work with them therapeutically, it can end up being one of the most valuable things that happen during the treatment. (Safran, 2018)

An example from my own experience illustrates this point. I remember struggling through a passage of rupture-repair sessions with a client after I had misattuned in one session and then somehow forgot our appointment the following week. Feeling abandoned, and with her shame history triggered, she scathingly declared she could never trust me again. Of course, I felt my own share of shame and regret (and still feel it 30 years later!), and I needed extra support from my supervisor (my internal supervisor wasn't quite up to the job). She reminded me to encourage my client to express her hurt/rage about how I had 'betrayed' her (just as every significant adult in her life had done). She also reminded me that I was resilient and needed to show this to my client by communicating that our relationship didn't have to be destroyed and that my client finding a way to be angry with me was actually a sign of progress. It took a few weeks where I felt distinctly beaten up (by my client and myself), but my supervisor's affirming, containing, compassionate advice eventually bore fruit.

Research by Nissen-Lie et al. (2017) found that therapists who reported comparatively high levels of self-doubt in their work were more effective in alleviating client distress *if* they had a strong sense of their identity (self-affiliation) and tried to be kind to themselves outside of work. These researchers summarise their findings in the shape of a handy take-home message: 'Love yourself as a person, doubt yourself as a therapist' (see Box 10.1).

Box 10.1 Practical application: therapist self-doubt and personal self-care

Nissen-Lie et al. (2017) summarise key messages for practitioners arising from their research findings:

- Therapists who doubt themselves therapeutically but have a high degree of self-affiliation as a person is most fruitful; less professional self-doubt with high positive self-affiliation or exaggerated self-confidence is not.
- Coping well and constructively involves dealing actively with clinical problems and that includes exercising reflexive control, seeking consultation/supervision and collaborating with the patient to problem-solve.
- Less change in patients is associated with therapist tendencies to avoid problems, withdraw from therapeutic engagement or act out frustrations in the therapeutic relationship.

Being-in-relationship

It's the relationship that heals, the relationship that heals, the relationship that heals. (Yalom, 1989, p. 91)

The preceding chapters have foregrounded different facets of our therapeutic use of self but threaded throughout is the relationship we nurture with clients. Ideally, we offer a compassionate space for clients to be witnessed and mirrored, enabling them to find a voice and make sense of their lives. We are contactfully present, responding to clients' relational needs. At the same time, we are teacher, facilitator, guide and catalyst. We walk along beside them as they explore their past and present, and find new life pathways. Throughout every session, we have choices to make about how precisely to be with each client depending on what is in the client's interests and the nature of the collaborative relationship.

Exploring these ideas further, this section highlights the significance of:

- emergent being-with;
- nurturing the relationship;
- attending to relational needs.

Emergent being-with

We do not use ourselves in any pre-set way. Rather, our being emerges in relationship with another. With one client I might be gentle, with another challenging. With one I might be robustly present, with another I might contain myself to allow more space for the client to emerge. With one I might be directive and offer techniques, with another, it might just be important to hold the space in silence to enable the client to internally process our dialogue or simply to allow them to *be*. The key here is to tune into (attune) to the client's affect, rhythm, cognitive style, level of development and relational needs (Erskine et al., 1999; Erskine, 2021).

Our way of being shifts according to cultural context and the theoretical approach we're adopting, but mostly, our being is best co-created in the immediacy of the relational encounter. Over the years, I've asked many clients what they found helpful in their therapy. Rarely do they talk about techniques or what they've learned or things the therapist has done. Mostly, the person will say things like, for example, they felt 'listened to', 'supported and held', 'fully seen', 'accepted, not critically judged' or 'I had a space to be me'.

As Yalom's 'professional rosary', quoted above, affirms, it's all about the relationship (see Box 10.2).

When it comes to how our relationship with clients unfolds and is understood, much depends on the therapeutic approach we adopt and the nature of the work we are doing. Here the 'teacher–student' type of relationship

Box 10.2 Research: therapist relational qualities

Goldstein (2020) interviewed seven women diagnosed with borderline personality disorder (BPD) about their experience of interpersonal therapy. Phenomenological and narrative analysis revealed that the participants sought therapists who demonstrated caring and kindness, and who joined them in their experiences through a deep form of listening and validation. These conditions were necessary but not adequate for the development of a healing alliance. Participants also favoured clinicians who maintained a collaborative approach, balancing strength with flexibility, and who were willing to address conflicts and tensions head-on. Therapist neutrality, withholding and inactivity were experienced as aversive, and participants expressed a desire for explicit evidence of clinician humanity.

central to psychoeducational and CBT approaches can be contrasted with the traditional analytic 'blank screen' transferential focus. Contemporary relational-dialogical approaches increasingly place the focus on the relationship rather than on the individual client. How we bring this relational dimension into therapy varies according to perspective and context (Paul and Charura, 2015). A key debate revolves around the extent to which we emphasise the here-and-now *inter*subjective relationship, rather than the *intra*subjective one, where past developmental relationships are accessed transferentially.

Petruska Clarkson (2003) identifies five different types of relationship available for constructive use of self across *all* therapeutic approaches:

a. **Working alliance** – the part of the relationship enabling therapist and client to work together, even when the client experiences a desire to disengage;

b. **transference/countertransference** relationship – the experience of unconscious processes (needs, fears) entering/obtruding into the partnership;

c. **developmentally needed/reparative** relationship – the intentional provision by the therapist of a corrective/replenishing interaction in cases where a client's original parenting was deficient or problematic (abusive, overprotective);

d. **person-to-person** relationship – the core dialogic (rather than object) relationship;

e. **transpersonal** relationship – the more mysterious, spiritual elements arising in the healing.

Clarkson emphasises that at any one moment in counselling/psychotherapy, depending on the task at the moment, one of these relationships comes to the fore while the others recede. She argues that, rather than 'stages', these are overlapping states that map loosely onto theoretical frameworks. For example, 2 and 3 are more explicitly used in psychoanalytic and relational integrative work, whereas 4 is associated especially with humanistic encounters. While transpersonal moments arise across the board, they are explicitly engaged in various humanistic, systemic and mindfulness approaches. Although all five types are potentially present in any therapeutic encounter, the alliance is usually the necessary starting point of all therapy (see the next section for examples of how all these types of relationship are enacted in practice).

Nurturing the relationship

The therapeutic relationship develops through the therapist's active involvement, for instance, in ways we are present, and acknowledge, validate and normalise the client's experience (Erskine et al., 1999). The quotations below from Erskine (2021, p. 17) show this involvement:

> At times my eyes have filled with tears or I have felt a protective anger when I hear about the neglect or abuse my clients suffered in their young lives. Presence requires one to be emotionally moved and yet stay responsive.

When I respectfully make a normalising comment, I am challenging the client's 'something's-wrong-with-me' perspective and inviting the client to experiment with a new perspective that honours his or her archaic attempts at resolution of conflicts.

In the dialogue below, a therapist acknowledges the client's experience bringing her process to light and they begin to consider how their therapeutic relationship could evolve:

> **Client:** I wish I could just be 'me' instead of bending over backwards to please others. All my step-children love me as I'm there for them 24/7. I love and care for them, kiss their hurts better, help with homework, provide career planning advice. I perform 'perfect step-mother'.
>
> **Therapist:** I'm hearing that you work incredibly hard to attend to everyone's needs.
>
> **Client:** Constantly.
>
> **Therapist:** What would happen if you didn't?
>
> **Client:** (Client thinks and then in a quiet voice reluctantly admits her fear.) They'd reject me and my husband would leave me. If I'm no value to them, they'd go elsewhere. At least this way I manage to be part of a proper family.

Therapist: A proper family which you didn't have in your childhood? (Client nods sadly; therapist pauses to give the client space to hear the acknowledgement.) And what about your needs beyond being part of a family?

Client: I dunno.

Therapist: Really? My hunch is that you do know what you're yearning for but daren't let yourself go there. I think you give others the care you wish someone would give you.

Client: (Starts to cry.) You're right. But I'm not ever going to get the love I'm wanting so it's better not to want and need.

Therapist: So you shut down and don't let others see these parts that are wanting to be loved and appreciated? I think you learned that strategy early in your life. (Pause as the client takes in this important insight.) I really want to meet these hidden parts of you. (Said in a compassionate tone.) I think they deserve some TLC even if they don't quite agree. Maybe that is something of what I can offer here?

Attending to relational needs

The relationship is nurtured over time as we attune and respond to clients' developmental and relational needs, while both holding and challenging their process. Erskine (2021; Erskine et al., 1999) has identified at least eight primary relational needs we work with in therapy:

- security-in-relationship;
- validation, affirmation and significance within a relationship;
- acceptance by a stable, dependable and protective other person;
- mutuality and companionship that provide confirmation of personal experience;
- self-definition;
- the need to have an impact on another person;
- the need to have the other initiate;
- the need to express love (see Box 10.3).

The relevance of these relational needs in therapy are that clients can be helped to become aware of their relationship patterns. The attuned therapist and client together can work on these issues. For a client who lacks supportive/protective people around them, it may help if the therapist shows support/protectiveness, for instance. For a client who feels invisible to others, unable to impact their environment, it could be therapeutically effective for the therapist to take opportunities to let the client know that the therapist is impacted by what the client says and does. With a client who is cut off from different parts of themselves, a therapist might attune to these and model contactful presence while validating those parts.

Box 10.3 Research: developing the Relational Needs Satisfaction Scale

Žvelc et al. (2020) developed and evaluated a scale for measuring the satisfaction of relational needs based on the work of Erskine and colleagues (1999). The scale assesses five areas of relational need: authenticity, support/protection, having an impact, shared experience and initiative from the other. Satisfaction of relational needs was found to be positively correlated with secure attachment, self-compassion, higher life satisfaction and well-being. The authors propose that their Relational Needs Satisfaction Scale (RNSS) can be used in counselling/psychotherapy and research to assess relational needs and evaluate progress in therapy.

We address these needs through our sustained, compassionate, attuned presence, as well as by engaging in relational enquiry about the qualities of our relationship as it evolves. Erskine (2021) suggests asking explicitly about the client's experience of the therapist's tone of voice, or what it is like when a therapist reacts a certain way or draws attention to the client's behaviour. In another version of relational enquiry, Spinelli (2015) explicitly invites clients to recognise similarities and differences between the here-and-now therapy relationship and what happens outside in 'real' life. Through such phenomenological relational enquiry, the client becomes more aware of their needs and more choiceful about their actions, while taking in the relational nourishment being offered (Finlay, forthcoming).

Understanding that a client's sense of self, agency, competence and esteem arises through relationships and being able to impact the environment, has significant consequences for our therapeutic use of self. For instance, we need to show the client that we 'see' them (including different parts) and respect their autonomy. More than this, it can be particularly potent when we demonstrate that they impact us, for instance, when we respond actively to any requests or criticisms. Erskine enacts this when his client asked him to listen to the 'little boy' in him and not just the man and that stops him suggesting changes the client could make:

> He said "This therapy is not working". After he repeated his comment a few times I eventually inquired as to what he meant by "not working". I wanted to know his experience of our relationship. He hesitantly said that he needed me to "listen to the little boy ... My mother was always telling me the right way to act. I want you to just listen and be with me". I allowed Andrew's request to impact me. I changed ... I listened". (Erskine, 2021, p. 28)

In the example above, Richard Erskine is explicitly engaging the working alliance and developmentally needed relationship in Clarkson's typology. In the next example, transferential and person-to-person aspects of relationship are highlighted. Here, the therapist (Ken Evans) contains his client's rage, and doesn't react in anger when 'wiped out'. Instead, Evans uses his awareness of his own experience and what seems to be happening 'between' to attune to his client's experience and shows that he is impacted:

> **Therapist:** "Tell me some more about what that was like for you Phillip, to witness your brother get beaten" ... "it must have been really tough for you" ...
>
> At this point there is a dramatic physical change in Phillip's presence, from a sad slumped body posture to an erect and rigid position and with a face contorted with rage and distain ... "You haven't a fucking clue what it was like for me" ...
>
> I imagine I experience something of what it must have been like for him as a child – sarcasm, dismissal, humiliation and a deep sense of being 'wiped out' ...
>
> **Therapist:** "Phillip, I was listening intently to you talk about your father beating up on your brother, and feeling a lot of compassion I reached out to you in your obvious distress. I then experienced you responding to me with sarcasm and angry disdain, which impacted me deeply. I experienced being dismissed by you and feel unseen, fearful and angry. I want to ask you 'Who did this to you?'"
>
> Phillips's posture instantly deflated, as did his seething anger, and with eyes filled with tears he replied sorrowfully, "That's just how it was for me".
> (Evans and Gilbert, 2005, pp. 118–19)

Here, Evans attempts to be attentive to the client's experience, his own, and what is happening between. He makes himself both present and transparent to Phillip, inviting him to recognise his projections. While some therapist self-disclosure is involved (the therapist owns feeling dismissed, unseen, fearful and angry), we can also see how he contains his personal reactive responses. His hurt/anger/shame is not the issue; it's about being in the process and being alert to the source and meanings of those emotions (Finlay, 2016a).

Lynne Jacobs provides another example of person-to-person relating (together with what is perhaps a transpersonal element), one that involves reflexively monitoring and adjusting her approach:

> The patient was argumentative and critical. She claimed to be desperate for help, but disparaged my attempts to understand her and to be helpful. I tended to react with unaware defensiveness by taking a particularly

superior, authoritative stance toward her. The meeting – the momentary I–Thou – occurred after I realized that I was defensive, and decided to be more attentive to my own defensiveness.

The next hour, I found myself again reacting defensively. I began to disclose this to the patient, while still operating from my defensive authoritative stance. Suddenly I realized that *at that moment* I was still protecting myself by pushing against the patient. I brightened and exclaimed, "See! Oh my, I'm doing it right now! Damn it, E –, you are just too good. I give up!" I began laughing at my own absurd attempts to coerce the patient. The patient, surprised, also laughed heartily. She admitted she was very good at what she was doing, and enjoyed it, although she always left feeling bitter and dissatisfied. What ensued was our first authentically cooperative exchange of ideas. Both of us had gained a renewed respect for the anxieties that had driven us into defensive styles at the expense of presence with each other. (Jacobs, 1989, pp. 3–4)

The reference to I–Thou in the above quote relates to the ideas of the phenomenological philosopher Buber, who drew a contrast between I–Thou with I–It relationships. In the authentic, open relationship of I–Thou, each person gives of themself without manipulating the other or controlling the impression being created. The direct experience of such presence with another is comforting (by showing us we are not alone) and threatening (by challenging us to be more). Treating others as 'Thous' rather than 'Its' has important ramifications: Buber saw the Holocaust as a terrifying example of the ethical consequences of seeing others as 'Its'. Ultimately, the I–Thou relationship is mutually revealing. Recognising the value of the other's personhood helps us renew our own.

In a further exploration of this ethical dimension, Kunz presents a fictional dialogue between client and therapist. Here gifts of simplicity, humility and patience are offered as the ethical condition of what makes therapy therapeutic.

Her face says, "I am the one before you. I am here and others are not here ... these problems I will tell you about are unique." Her face does not say, "I'm here to represent that group of people called depressives." ...

The face of the client says, "... I am more vulnerable here than when I'm out on the street. In here I tell you my story. I'm opening up my life to you. I lay bare my suffering. In here I lower my defenses. I trust you will not abuse me. I have no one here to protect me. I am more vulnerable than you. This is not an equal situation ..."

The face of the good therapist responds to her fear, "I will not harm you." ...

The good therapist's gift to her conflict is, "I see you and I witness your goodness and dignity."

The client's face goes on to say, "... I want to believe your face when it expresses back to me, '... Yes, I hear you. I'm not only with you but for you.' ... "You will not use me simply to practice becoming a skilled therapist, not use me to feel good about yourself." (Kunz, 2002)

In this dialogue, Kunz refers implicitly to the work of another phenomenological philosopher, Levinas ([1961] 1969), where concern for the Other is placed at the centre of ethics. The Other is an elusive stranger who can never be fully possessed or understood. The other's 'Face' (their concrete presence) says 'I am Other' and commands that it not be reduced to, and annihilated by, categories and labels. By encountering the Other, I in turn am offered a gift. I am awed; called to Being, I awaken to myself.

Social being

Throughout this book I have emphasised the significance of the social context for the therapeutic relationship. By this I mean that array of cultural elements that both client and therapist bring with them to the therapy room: aspects and attitudes deriving from their backgrounds and social location (class, sex/gender, race, ethnicity, sexuality, disability, age, and so on). If we are to use ourselves therapeutically within the relationship, it's necessary to be aware how our social values and the power we possess by virtue of our position in society impact on and interact with those of the client. Put another way, our way of being as therapists arises in large part from both *micro*-social communications and *macro*-social elements.

One of the most problematic ideas circulating in the therapy field is the notion that a client's issues derive from, and reside within, that single individual. Here, the root of clients' problems is seen to lie in faulty cognitions or in some kind of malfunctioning personality and behaviour. This tendency to give undue weight to individual-based explanations can result in some therapists viewing clients' issues purely as pathological 'problems' to be fixed – with the therapist's role that of offering the 'solution'. If the client could only be taught to think more positively or engage in proper self-care, they'd feel better ...

It's all too easy to overlook factors in the client's wider environment that might be hugely significant – for example, where the client lives in a deprived community or is in an abusive, undermining relationship, and/or that they are struggling to juggle impossible life pressures and demands without adequate external support.

Research over the last 50 years (see Box 10.4) has established that mental distress is invariably linked with wider social factors such as poverty, inequality and/or lack of social support (Kaposi, 2020). Wider systemic/ structural factors – whether micro-family dynamics or macro-sociopolitical

Box 10.4 Research: mental distress and the social context

- A famous series of studies conducted by Brown and Harris (1978, 1989) revealed strong links between depression and lack/inadequacy of social support. They found that the onset of depression invariably occurred as a response to major life events (job loss, for example, or major illness in the family). A total of 90 per cent of women who became depressed in the year leading up to the research had experienced extremely stressful life events. In further studies, Brown and Harris documented the role played by the availability (or otherwise) of close personal support and explored links between depression and historical/familial experiences of neglect, loss and abuse (in other words, cumulative trauma).
- On the basis of a survey carried out in England, McManus et al. (2009) found that men from the lowest income group were 35 times more likely to have depression compared with those in the highest income group.
- Research by Pickett and Wilkinson (2018) indicated that people in the UK and US were more likely to suffer from mental disorders than were people in Germany and Japan. On the basis of these findings, the authors argue that in respect of the relationship between social conditions and mental illness, what matters most is the socioeconomic status of some people relative to that of others in the same culture/society. In other words, perceived inequalities may play a larger role than absolute poverty. The more unequal a society or nation, the greater the importance attached to status and wealth – with a corresponding corrosion of supportive community values.
- On behalf of Psychologists for Social Change, McGrath et al. (2015) highlight the damage inflicted by long-term austerity measures in the UK. In a 'briefing paper' they document a higher incidence of suicide in European countries that have adopted austerity policies (UK, Greece, Portugal and Spain), compared with countries that to a greater extent have protected their welfare states (Iceland and Germany).

realities – must therefore be factored into our therapeutic understandings. Mental health isn't just an individual issue.

Just as we acknowledge the impact of social structures and institutions on our everyday practice, we need to recognise the ways in which our professional power (Proctor, 2002) is also shaped by external structures, including those relating to class, sex/gender, race, ethnicity, disability, sexuality, and so on. The term 'intersectionality' describes the complex ways in which different forms of discrimination are expressed and experienced in everyday life. This results in a kaleidoscopic experience of difference, potency and powerlessness. For example, consider a client from a working-class background who has made a lot of money. How will that client perceive and relate to their middle-class therapist who is struggling financially? If a male client happens to be white, to what extent may he feel himself to be more powerful than his black female therapist?

Within the therapeutic relationship, part of our art lies in our ability to ask questions about the meanings and impact of mutual social positionings and relative levels of 'privilege' (advantage). It is not enough simply to be respectful or demonstrate lip service 'acceptance' of the client's different culture, religion, and so on. We need to ensure that we don't make assumptions based on stereotypical generalisations by enquiring what their ethnicity, race and class means to them and about any impact of their perceptions of our ethnicity, race and class (see Box 2.1). We need to actively acknowledge the impact of people's backgrounds and show real awareness of the relevance of their cultural–historical identities (McKenzie-Mavinga, 2016).

Research suggests that cultural humility and cultural competence are helpful therapeutic modes. Cultural humility specifically is a predictor for a good therapeutic relationship and for positive therapy outcomes (Hook et al., 2013; Duden and Lucienne Martins-Borges, 2020). Research highlights that while we can never be completely competent in understanding another's culture or experience, we can commit to being interested in learning about difference/diversity and we can aim to minimise oppressive power imbalances.

A reflexive, self-critical stance about the impact of our own background and degrees of power is the first step: we need to question our assumptions, biases, prejudices and certainties. Put another way, our therapeutic relationship with clients from diverse backgrounds depends on our ability to cultivate an openness and contain our natural tendency to assume the superiority or 'normality' of our own values and world views (Hook et al., 2013). Equally, it is important to locate the client's world views. To give a concrete example, consider the impact on the therapeutic relationship if a client from a working-class background feels subtly inferior to their therapist who they assume has had a privileged middle-class background.

In practice, however, therapists sometimes find it difficult to engage wider systemic thinking and tend to maintain an undue focus on the individual. Wilcox et al. (2020) (see Box 10.5) argue that if therapists ascribe stress/distress to skill deficits and view clients' problems as lying just within the individual, there is the risk of an implicit denial of oppressive systems (the family, work contexts, institutionalised racism, culture, etc.). If this happens, it becomes impossible to get a full picture of the person and their struggles. In effect, therapists can be seen to implicitly endorse messages like 'pull yourself up by the bootstraps'. Clients who are not improving might

Box 10.5 Research: multicultural competence

Wilcox et al. (2020) conducted multi-method research with 93 counselling trainees and 107 practising therapists in the US. They found that while participants felt generally effective about working with clients from marginalised backgrounds, a substantial proportion failed to address – even minimally – the clients' sociocultural context. The sole exception here was participants' awareness of 'privilege'; such awareness was linked to improved multicultural competence (knowledge and awareness). Otherwise, participants paid attention to clients' intrapsychic processes while tending to pass over the potential influence of sociocultural factors on clients' presenting concerns. They recommend training organisations raise the profile of multicultural training, enabling trainees to understand the sociopolitical realities of clients' lives and conceptualise their clients' presenting concerns in this context.

In a study by Duden and Martins-Borges (2020), 18 psychologists who engage psychotherapy with refugees in Brazil were interviewed about what they saw were the supportive and hindering elements in their work. The qualitative data (analysed thematically) highlighted the importance of adaptability and competent knowledge of wider social factors on the part of psychotherapists. More specifically, participants indicated that a move from knowledge-based cultural-competence towards more flexible notions such as cultural humility was helpful. Participants highlighted the value of continuously decentring from their own values and theoretical assumptions. This was aided by supervision, cultural awareness training and a genuine interest in patients' countries of origin.

be blamed for being 'resistant' and 'non-compliant' in situations where the blockages may have a systemic origin.

Supervisors and trainers have significant roles to play in cultivating increased cultural humility and awareness. Recognising supervision is a cultural encounter (Falicov, 2014), Hook et al. (2016) recommend an 'initiate-invite-instil' approach by which supervisors initiate conversations about cultural diversity, then invite supervisees to consider ramifications while modelling cultural humility that prioritises respectful dialogue. Such an approach is seen to instil this value in supervisees. Conversational questioning can help here – for example, 'How do you think this client's cultural background impacts on their presenting problem?' or 'Is there a possible culture clash with you here?'

The case example in Box 10.6 illustrates the importance of supervisors by means of a horror story: that of a supervisor who not only lacks cultural humility but also shows unhelpful cultural arrogance and ignorance

Box 10.6 Case example: a culturally arrogant supervisor

Supervisor

The supervisor was a Caucasian female in her late 30s with a doctoral degree in clinical psychology. She identified with cognitive-behavioral theory, had supervised at a community mental health centre for several years, and was held in high regard by colleagues for her treatment and supervision work.

Supervisee

The supervisee was an African American female in her late 20s. She was a fifth-year doctoral student in a clinical psychology program.

Client

The client was a married male in his 40s of Mexican ethnicity, with no previous mental health history. The client presented with symptoms of depression and stress. He attributed these to difficulty in protecting his family from what he termed "Americanisation." He described this as dressing and acting in ways that conflicted with his conservative Catholic views and cultural values, and in their building strong friendships with people outside the family.

The supervision process

Supervision focused on two goals: helping the client come to terms with the fact that his wife and daughters were changing and considering how he could better cope with that reality. As treatment progressed, however, the supervisee began to feel as if work with the client was stagnating ... The supervisee wondered how her American cultural views and values might be affecting the work of treatment ...

The supervisee decided to discuss these issues in supervision and brought up the cultural concerns with her supervisor. But the supervisor ... dismissed the supervisee's cultural concerns, saying that "Your client is just being a man ... and a Mexican man at that." The supervisor said that the client's behavior—lacking openness to others' perspectives, wanting to dominate and control, and believing that he was always right—was a reflection of why men, particularly men with a Mexican cultural background, did not go to therapy. Lack of therapeutic progress was attributed to the client's supposedly holding therapy-incongruent cultural values ... From that point forward, the supervisee never brought up matters of culture with this supervisor. (Hook et al., 2016, pp. 159–60) in relation to the client's cultural background. The supervisor reveals further prejudice by making negative judgements about the client and his ability to engage therapy. We can all learn from this 'lesson by negative example'!

Case study

Lynne Jacobs offers the following story to show that relationally minded therapists tailor their presence and levels of self-disclosure to the developmental readiness of the patient/client. 'In that process,' she says, 'therapists can continue to refine their abilities to engage in a dialogue with their patients that is both sensitive to their developmental needs and evocative of their richness as human beings' (Jacobs, 1991):

> I am reminded of a patient I work with who is deeply ashamed of herself and considers herself to be inherently and irreparably defective. She also often believes that no one else in the world has the same problems that she has. In the first few years I was so pained by her sense of shameful isolation that I twice told her things about myself that were similar to problems she was describing. In both instances she became severely distressed, felt impinged on, and insisted that I not ever do that again. She said she needed me to be a "whole," not defective like herself. ...
>
> Four years later she tentatively seeks a connection to my inner world, warts and all, as she begins to feel herself more and more a part of the planet. She now thinks that if I have problems and can function as well as I do, then maybe she can too ... I started out imposing myself too strongly on her, crushing her sense of herself as having her own mind. Then she experienced me as providing the water she could learn to swim in. During that phase I brought myself to her largely through systematic immersion in her world as best she and I could describe it. Now I am more active in bringing in my personal, particular personality, and she is reveling in the experience of engaging deeply as two distinct personalities. She never knew before that we could be different people and yet share the same passion – commitment to her development. (Jacobs, 1991)

Critical reflections

This chapter has emphasised the importance of being a human being in relation with another human being. Use of self is less about applying therapy techniques and more about finding a way to be-with our clients, in patience, curiosity, compassion, caring and challenge, while they go exploring in search of a different path. It involves going beyond knowledge, protocol and skill, to a place of Being, not Doing.

Working relationally with a focus on the therapeutic relationship means privileging the emergent, here-and-now relationship between therapist and client, and flexibly attuning and responding to each client's relational needs (DeYoung, 2003; Spinelli, 2015; Erskine, 2020a). It is about opening to the other while being willing to give of self, and as it is in the service of the client, it remains an ethical undertaking. It also means opening to wider social–cultural factors and influences imbedded in our embodied intersubjective relationships.

The therapist needs to have the courage to stay in 'the process': to be emotionally present to intrapsychic and interpersonal dynamics while being prepared to take some risks towards the co-creation of the therapy. The challenge is to embody ways of 'being-with' naturally and effortlessly, rather than be led by theory or technique (Finlay, 2016a). Then, we need to take up opportunities to reflect and grow. On the basis of their extensive critical review, Hill et al. (2017) conclude that growth through therapy, supervision, reflection and feedback is crucial to the development of expertise.

Throughout this book I've highlighted the ways we use ourselves in therapy: through our spacious hospitality, openness, embodied presence, empathy, attunement, creativity … To sum up, the therapeutic use of self is an ethical, reflexive, creative, relational process that involves being warmly and compassionately present, sensitively attuned and actively nurturing the therapeutic relationship.

While we have our special knowledge and professional skills, these are counterbalanced by the human vulnerability we all carry. Our own woundedness may be a part of the 'selves' we bring to the therapy encounter. I find it interesting (and salutary) to remember that humility, self-criticism, unknowingness and self-doubt also contribute to expertise.

The Danish philosopher Søren Kierkegaard famously said: 'all true helping begins with humbling'. Here, he links humility with being unknowing and needing to strive to understand and value clients' understandings. He emphasises the impact of letting go of our power and authority as we open to meeting the client in their world.

> If one is truly to succeed in leading a person to a specific place, one must first and foremost take care to find them where they are, and begin there … I must understand more than they – but certainly first and foremost understand what they understand. … The helper must first humble themselves under the person they want to help; and thereby understand that to help is not to dominate but to serve … (Kierkegaard, [1848] 1998, p. 45)

Our therapeutic being achieves its greatest potency and resonance when we connect with clients in openness, care and humility, at the relational threshold between their world and our own. At such moments we offer clients the gift of ourselves: our time, our presence, our emotional labour, our loving concern. And as we accompany our clients on their journey, we receive an abundance of gifts and inspiration in turn. It is a privilege and honour to accompany them on their journey.

Discussion questions

1. Which facets of 'use of self' discussed in previous chapters do you prioritise, and how does this impact on the techniques and interventions you engage?
2. Highlighting the complex link between person-centred approaches and politics, Proctor et al. (2006) argue for the need to recognise (and challenge) the ways in which individually focused non-judgemental, unconditional respect can end up obscuring wider structural inequalities. Discuss.
3. Reviewing the material across the book, identify one significant insight you've gained which has surprised or challenged you.

Resources

Book: *The Gift of Therapy* by Irvin Yalom. Yalom's easy-reading tips and insights to the next generation of therapists based on his decades of practice; a 'must read' book.

Book: *The Therapeutic Relationship* by Petruska Clarkson. A classic text detailing different types of therapeutic relationships.

Book: *A Healing Relationship* by Richard Erskine. Erskine deftly lays out the theory of his integrative psychotherapy and demonstrates its practice through powerful but subtle case study dialogues. See also the rich collection of articles on relational theory and processes in integrative psychotherapy by Erskine and colleagues at the Institute for Integrative Psychotherapy: www.integrativetherapy.com/en/articles.php

Book: *Understanding and Treating Chronic Shame* by Patricia DeYoung. Essential reading for therapists engaged in depth relational work.

Academic paper: A new therapy for each patient: evidence-based relationships and responsiveness by J.C. Norcross and B.E. Wampold.

REFERENCES

Ablack, J. (2000) Body psychotherapy, trauma and the Black woman client. *International Journal of Psychotherapy*, 5 (2): 149. Available at: www.baatn. org.uk/wp-content/uploads/Body-psychotherapy-trauma-and-the-Black-woman-client-1.pdf (accessed August 2020).

Abram, D. (1996) *The Spell of the Sensuous: Perception and Language in a More than Human World*. New York: Random House.

Adams, M. (2014) *The Myth of the Untroubled Therapist: Private Life, Professional Practice*. Hove: Routledge.

Alexander, F. and French, F. (1946) *Psychoanalytic Therapy: Principles and Application*. New York: Ronald Press.

Amari, N. (2020) The use of self in counseling psychology and Buber's 'Turning'. *The Humanistic Psychologist*. Advance online publication: http://dx.doi. org/10.1037/hum0000174

American Counseling Association (ACA) (n.d.) *Taskforce on Counselor Wellness and Impairment*. Available at: www.counseling.org/wellness_taskforce/index. htm (accessed July 2020).

Amis, K. (2017) *Boundaries, Power and Ethical Responsibility in Counselling and Psychotherapy*. London: Sage.

Anderson, H. and Goolishian, H. (1992) The client is the expert: a not-knowing approach to therapy, in S. McNamee and K.J. Gergen (eds), *Therapy as Social Construction*. London: Sage Publications, pp. 25–39.

Appel-Opper, J. (2012) Psychotherapy of the relational living body: from physical resonances to embodied interventions and experiences, in C. Young (ed.), *About Relational Body Psychotherapy*. Galashiels: Body Psychotherapy Publications. Excerpt available at: www.idet.paris/psychotherapy-of-the-relational-living-body-with-julianne-appel-opper (accessed October 2020).

Appel-Opper, J. (2019) English smiles, Italian shoulders, and a German therapist. *International Body Psychotherapy Journal: The Art and Science of Somatic Praxis*, 18 (2): 28–39. Available at: www.ibpj.org/issues/IBPJ-Volume-18-Number-2-2019.pdf (accessed October 2020).

Ardito, R.B. and Rabellino, D. (2011) Therapeutic alliance and outcome of psychotherapy: historical excursus, measurements, and prospects for research. *Frontiers in Psychology*, 2: 270. Available at: https://doi.org/10.3389/ fpsyg.2011.00270

Atiyeh, S. (2017) Bringing Syrian hospitality into your counseling practice. *Blog post*, 8 November: https://ct.counseling.org/2017/11/bringing-syrian-hospitality-counseling-practice/# (accessed September 2020).

Atwood, G.E. and Stolorow, R.D. (2014) *Structures of Subjectivity: Explorations in Psychoanalytic Phenomenology and Contextualism* (2nd edn). London: Routledge.

Audet, C.T. and Everall, R.D. (2010) Therapist self-disclosure and the therapeutic relationship: a phenomenological study from the client perspective, *British Journal of Guidance & Counselling*, 38 (3): 327–42. DOI: 10.1080/03069885.2010.482450

Axline, V. (1964) *Dibs: In Search of Self.* New York: Ballantine Books.

Balmforth, J. (2009) "The weight of class": clients' experiences of how perceived differences in social class between counsellor and client affect the therapeutic relationship. *British Journal of Guidance and Counselling*, 37 (3): 75–386.

Barker, M-J. (2017–2019) *Gender, Sexual, and Relationship Diversity (GSRD)*. Lutterworth, Leicestershire: British Association for Counselling and Psychotherapy. Available at: www.bacp.co.uk/media/5877/bacp-gender-sexual-relationship-diversity-gpacp001-april19.pdf (accessed October 2020).

Barr, A. (2006) *An investigation into the extent to which psychological wounds inspire counsellors and psychotherapists to become wounded healers, the significance of these wounds on their career choice*. Unpublished dissertation, University of Strathclyde, Glasgow.

Barsness, R.E. (ed.) (2017) *Core Competencies in Relational Psychoanalysis: A Guide to Practice, Study, and Research*. London: Routledge.

Bazzano, M. (2015) Therapy as unconditional hospitality. *Psychotherapy and Politics International*. Downloaded from: http://manubazzano.com/wp-content/uploads/2020/11/Therapy-as-Unconditional-Hospitality.pdf (accessed May 2021).

Beck, A.T. (1967) *Depression: Clinical, Experimental, and Theoretical Aspects*. New York: Harper & Row.

Berg, H., Antonsen, P. and Binder, P.-E. (2017) Sincerely speaking: why do psychotherapists self-disclose in therapy?—A qualitative hermeneutic phenomenological study. *Nordic Psychology*, 69 (3): 143–59. Available at: https://doi.org/10.1080/19012276.2016.1198272

Berne, E. (1961) *Transactional Analysis in Psychotherapy: A Systematic Individual and Social Psychiatry*. New York: Grove Press.

Bion, W.R. (2005) *The Tavistock Seminars 1976–1979*. London: Karnac.

Blatner, A. (2003) Using creativity to explore in psychotherapy. *Psychiatric Times*. Available at: www.psychiatrictimes.com/view/using-creativity-explore-psychotherapy (accessed September 2020).

Blevins, T.L. (2010) *Humor in therapy: expectations, sense of humor, and perceived effectiveness*. Doctoral dissertation, Auburn University, Alabama.

Bond, P. (2020) Wounded healer therapists: a legacy of developmental trauma. *European Journal for Qualitative Research in Psychotherapy*, 10: 68–81. Retrieved from: https://ejqrp.org/index.php/ejqrp/article/view/93

Branson, D.C. (2019) Vicarious trauma, themes in research, and terminology: a review of literature. *Traumatology*, 25 (1): 2–10. DOI: 10.1037/trm0000161

Bravata, D.M., Watts, S.A., Keefer, A.L., Madhusudhan, D.K., Taylor, K.T., Clark, D.M., Nelson, R.S., Cokley, K.O. and Hagg, H.K. (2020) Prevalence, predictors, and treatment of impostor syndrome: a systematic review. *Journal of General Internal Medicine*, 35 (4): 1252–75. DOI: 10.1007/s11606-019-05364-1

British Association for Counselling and Psychotherapy (2018) *Good Practice in Action 088: Self-care for the Counselling Professions*. Lutterworth, Leicestershire: Available at: www.bacp.co.uk/media/3939/bacp-self-care-fact-sheet-gpia088-jul18.pdf (accessed October 2020).

British Psychological Society (2020) *Position paper: racial and social inequalities: taking the conversations forward*. Available at: www.bps.org.uk/sites/www.bps.org.uk/files/Member%20Networks/Divisions/DCP/Racial%20and%20Social%20Inequalities%20in%20the%20times%20of%20Covid-19.pdf (accessed October 2020).

Brown, G. and Harris, T. (1978) *Social Origins of Depression: A Study of Psychiatric Disorder in Women*. London: Tavistock Publications.

Brown, G. and Harris, T. (1989) *Life Events and Illness*. London: The Guilford Press.

Brown, G., Kainth, K., Matheson, C., Osborne, J., Trenkle, A. and Adlam, J. (2011) An hospitable engagement?: open-door psychotherapy with the socially excluded. *Psychodynamic Practice*, 17 (3): 307–24. DOI: 10.1080/14753634. 2011.587605

Buber, M. ([1923] 1958) *I and Thou* (trans. R.G. Smith). New York: Charles Scribner's Sons.

Buber, M. ([1951] 1965) *The Knowledge of Man: A Philosophy of the Interhuman* (Introduction, M.S. Friedman, trans. M.S. Friedman and R.G. Smith). New York: Harper & Row.

Bugental, J.F.T. (1978) *Psychotherapy and Process*. New York: McGraw-Hill.

Casement, P. (1985) *On Learning from the Patient*. London: Routledge.

Casement, P. (1990) *Further Learning from the Patient*. London: Routledge.

Cassels, T.G., Chan, S., Chung, W. and Birch, S.A.J. (2010) The role of culture in affective empathy: cultural and bicultural differences. *Journal of Cognition and Culture*, 10 (3–4): 309–26. Available at: https://doi. org/10.1163/156853710X531203

Castonguay, L.G. and Hill, C.E. (2012) *Transformation in Psychotherapy: Corrective Experiences across Cognitive, Behavioral, Humanistic and Psychodynamic Approaches*. Washington DC: American Psychological Association.

Chidiac, M.A. and Denham-Vaughan, S. (2007) The process of presence: energetic availability and fluid responsiveness. *British Gestalt Journal*, 16 (1): 9–19.

Chopik, W.J., O'Brien, E.D. and Konrath, S.H. (2017) Differences in empathic concern and perspective taking across 63 countries. *Journal of Cross-Cultural Psychology*, 48 (1): 23–38. DOI: 10.1177/0022022116673910

Cigolla, F. and Brown, D. (2011) A way of being: bringing mindfulness into individual therapy. *Psychotherapy Research*, 21 (6): 709–21.

Clarkson, P. (2003) *The Therapeutic Relationship* (2nd edn). London: Whurr Publishers.

Colosimo, K.A. and Pos, A.E. (2015) A rational model of expressed therapeutic presence. *Journal of Psychotherapy Integration*, 25 (2): 100–14.

Cooper, M. (2001) Embodied empathy, in S. Haugh and T. Merry (eds), *Empathy*. Ross-on-Wye: PCCS Books. pp. 218–19.

Cooper, M. (2007) Humanizing psychotherapy. *Psychotherapy Journal of Contemporary Psychotherapy*, 37 (1): 11–16.

Cooper, M. (2008) *Essential Research Findings in Counselling and Psychotherapy: The Facts are Friendly*. Los Angeles, CA: Sage Publications.

Cooper, M. (2009) Welcoming the Other: actualising the humanistic ethic at the core of counselling psychology practice. *Counselling Psychology Review*, 24 (3): 119–29.

Cooper, M., Mearns, D., Stiles, W.B., Warner, M. and Elliott, R. (2004) Developing self-pluralistic perspectives within the person-centered and experiential approaches: a round-table dialogue. *Person-Centered and Experiential Psychotherapies*, 3 (3): 176–91. Available at: http://search.ebscohost.com/login. aspx?direct=true&db=psyh&AN=2007-06508-004&site=ehost-live

Csikszentmihalyi, M. (1992) *Flow: The Psychology of Happiness*. London: Rider Press.

Cuseglio, R. (2019) After the flood: reflections of a wounded healer's countertransference in adolescent treatment. *Clinical Social Work Journal*. DOI: 10.1007/s10615-019-00716-0

Cvetovac, M.E. and Adame, A.L. (2017) The wounded therapist: understanding the relationship between personal suffering and clinical practice. *The Humanistic Psychologist*, 45 (4): 348–66. DOI: 10.1037/hum0000071

Dana, D.D. (2020) *The Polyvagal Theory in Therapy: Engaging the Rhythm of Regulation, Polyvagal Exercises for Safety and Connection: 50 Client-Centred Practices and Befriending the Nervous System*. New York: W.W. Norton.

D'Arcy, J., Reynolds, W., Stiles, W.B. and Hanley, T. (2015) The online calming effect: does the internet provide a more comfortable modality for conducting psychotherapy?, in G. Riva, B.K. Wiederhold and P. Cipresso (eds), *The Psychology of Social Networking: Identity and Relationships in Online Communities*. Warsaw/Berlin: De Gruyter Open. pp. 17–28.

Derrida, J. (2000) 'Hospitality', *Angelaki*, 5 (3): 3–18, DOI: 10.1080/09697250020034706.

Devlin, A.S., Donovan, S., Nicolov, A., Nold, O., Packard, A. and Zandan, G. (2009) "Impressive?" Credentials, family photographs, and the perception of therapist qualities. *Journal of Environmental Psychology*, 29: 503–12. DOI: 10.1016/j.jenvp.2009.08.008

Dewane, C.J. (2006) Use of self: a primer revisited. *Clinical Social Work Journal*, 34 (4): 543–58.

DeYoung, P.A. (2003) *Relational Psychotherapy: A Primer*. New York: Brunner–Routledge.

DeYoung, P.A. (2015) *Understanding and Treating Chronic Shame: A Relational and Neurobiological Approach*. New York: Routledge.

Dobrin, A. (2014) *What it means to be gracious: the gracious person is kind and tactful. Blog post*. Available at: www.psychologytoday.com/gb/blog/am-i-right/201402/what-it-means-be-gracious (accessed June 2020).

Duden, G.S. and Martins-Borges, L. (2020) Psychotherapy with refugees: supportive and hindering elements. *Psychotherapy Research*. DOI: 10.1080/10503307.2020.1820596

Edwards, J.K. and Bess, J.M. (1998) Developing effectiveness in the therapeutic use of self. *Clinical Social Work Journal*, 26 (1): 89–105. Available at: https://doi.org/10.1023/A:1022801713242

Eger, E.E. (2017) *The Choice*. New York: Scribner.

Elliott, R., Bohart, A.C., Watson, J.C. and Murphy, D. (2018) Therapist empathy and client outcome: an updated meta-analysis. *Psychotherapy*, 55: 399–410.

Erskine, R.G. (2008) Cooperation, relationship, and change. *Transactional Analysis Journal*, 38 (1): 31–5. DOI: 10.1177/036215370803800105. Available at: www.integrativetherapy.com/en/articles.php?id=58 (accessed June 2020).

Erskine, R.G. (2011) *Attachment, relational-needs, and psychotherapeutic presence*. Available at: www.integrativetherapy.com/en/articles.php?id=73 (accessed September 2014).

Erskine, R.G. (2015) *Relational Patterns, Therapeutic Presence: Concepts and Practice of Integrative Psychotherapy*. London: Karnac.

Erskine, R.G. (2020a) Compassion, hope and forgiveness in the therapeutic dialogue. *International Journal of Integrative Psychotherapy*, 11: 1–13.

Erskine, R.G. (2020b) Relational withdrawal, attunement to silence: psychotherapy of the schizoid process. *International Journal of Integrative Psychotherapy*, 11: 14–29.

Erskine, R.G. (2021) *A Healing Relationship: Commentary on Therapeutic Dialogues*. Bicester: Phoenix Publishing House.

Erskine, R.G. and Trautmann, R.L. (2003) Resolving intrapsychic conflict: psychotherapy of parent ego states, in C. Sills and H. Hargaden (eds), *Ego States: Key Concepts in Transactional Analysis, Contemporary Views*. London: Worth Publishing. pp. 109–34.

Erskine, R.G., Moursund, J.P. and Trautmann, R.L. (1999) *Beyond Empathy: A Therapy of Contact-in-Relationship*. London: Sage/Karnac.

Essig, T. (2019) *How to make remote psychotherapy work better for you: a consumer's guide*. Available at: www.forbes.com/sites/toddessig/2019/02/26/how-to-make-remote-psychotherapy-work-better-for-you-a-consumers-guide/#1c24e0dd7398 (accessed July 2020).

Evans, K.R. and Gilbert, M.C. (2005) *An Introduction to Integrative Psychotherapy*. Basingstoke: Palgrave Macmillan.

Falicov, C.J. (2014) Psychotherapy and supervision as cultural encounters: the multidimensional ecological comparative framework, in C.A. Falender, E.P. Shafranske and C.J. Falicov (eds) *Multiculturalism and Diversity in Clinical Supervision: A Competency-Based Approach*. Washington, DC: American Psychological Association. pp. 29–58.

Farber, S.K. (2017) (ed.) *Celebrating the Wounded Healer Psychotherapist: Pain, Post-Traumatic Growth and Self-Disclosure*. London: Routledge.

Finlay, L. (1998) *The life world of the occupational therapist: meaning and motive in an uncertain world*. Unpublished PhD thesis. Milton Keynes: The Open University.

Finlay, L. (2004) *The Practice of Psychosocial Occupational Therapy* (3rd edn). Cheltenham: Nelson Thornes.

Finlay, L. (2008) A dance between the reduction and reflexivity: explicating the 'phenomenological attitude'. *Journal of Phenomenological Psychology*, 39: 1–32.

Finlay, L. (2014) Embodying research. *Person-Centered & Experiential Psychotherapies*, in K. Krycka (ed.), special issue on embodiment, 13 (1): 4–18.

Finlay, L. (2015) Sensing and making sense: embodying metaphor in relational-centred psychotherapy. *The Humanistic Psychologist*, 43 (4): 338–53.

Finlay, L. (2016a) *Relational Integrative Psychotherapy: Engaging Process and Theory in Practice*. Chichester: Wiley.

Finlay, L. (2016b) 'Therapeutic presence' as embodied, relational 'being'. *International Journal of Psychotherapy*, 20 (2).

Finlay, L. (2016c) Clarifying the adult ego state: toward an integrating–integrated 'adult'. *International Journal of Integrative Psychotherapy*, 7: 60–84.

Finlay, L. (2019) *Practical Ethics in Counselling and Psychotherapy: A Relational Approach*. Los Angeles, CA: Sage Publications.

Finlay, L. (forthcoming) Phenomenological 'use of self' in integrative psychotherapy: applying philosophy to practice. *International Journal of Integrative Psychotherapy*.

Finlay, L. and Evans, K. (2009) *Relational-centred Research for Psychotherapists: Exploring Meanings and Experience*. Chichester: Wiley-Blackwell.

Fisher, J. (2017) *Healing the Fragmented Selves of Trauma Survivors: Overcoming Internal Self-Alienation*. New York: Routledge.

Flückiger, C., Del Re, A.C., Wampold, B.E. and Horvath, A.O. (2018) The alliance in adult psychotherapy: a meta-analytic synthesis. *Psychotherapy*, 55 (4): 316–40. Available at: http://dx.doi.org/10.1037/pst0000172

Foley, G.N. and Gentile, J.P. (2010) Nonverbal communication in psychotherapy. *Psychiatry*, 7 (6): 38–44. Available at: www.ncbi.nlm.nih.gov/pmc/articles/PMC2898840/ (accessed August 2020).

Frettingham, S. (2020) *Personal communication*.

Geller, S., Pos, A. and Colosimo, K. (2012) Therapeutic presence: a fundamental common factor in the provision of effective psychotherapy. *Psychotherapy Bulletin*, 47: 6–13.

Geller, S.M. and Greenberg, L.S. (2002) Therapeutic presence: therapists' experience of presence in the psychotherapy encounter. *Person-Centered and Experiential Psychotherapies*, 1 (1–2): 71–86. Available at: https://doi.org/10.10 80/14779757.2002.9688279

Geller, S.M. and Greenberg, L.S. (2012) *Therapeutic Presence: A Mindful Approach to Effective Therapy*. Washington, DC: American Psychological Association.

Geller, S.M. and Porges, S.W. (2014) Therapeutic presence: neurophysiological mechanisms mediating feeling safe in therapeutic relationships. *Journal of Psychotherapy Integration*, 24 (3): 178–92.

Geller, S.M., Greenberg, L.S. and Watson, J.C. (2010) Therapist and client perceptions of therapeutic presence: the development of a measure. *Psychotherapy Research*, 20: 599–610.

Gelso, C.J. and Hayes, J.A. (2007) *Countertransference and the Therapist's Inner Experience: Perils and Possibilities*. Mahwah, NJ: Lawrence Erlbaum Associates.

Gendlin, E.T. (1981) *Focusing* (2nd edn). New York: Bantam Books.

Gendlin, E.T. (1996) *Focusing-oriented Psychotherapy: A Manual of the Experiential Method*. New York: Guilford Press.

Gendlin, E.T. (online source) Retrieved from: www.scoop.it/t/focusing-gr/p/43344181/eugene-gendlin-introduces-focusing-pt-1-international-conference-toronto-2000 (accessed October 2012).

Germer, C. (2021) *A comprehensive overview of self-compassion in therapy*. Available at: www.compassionintherapy.com/stream/chris-germer-2/ (accessed January 2021).

Gibertoni, C. de S. (2013) An occupational therapy perspective on Freud, Klein and Bion. In L. Nicholls, J.C. Piergrossi, C. de S. Gibertoni and M.A. Daniel (eds) *Psychoanalytic Thinking in Occupational Therapy*. Chichester: Wiley.

Gilbert, P. (2010) *Compassion Focused Therapy*. Hove: Routledge.

Goetz, J.L., Keltner, D. and Simon-Thomas, E. (2010) Compassion: an evolutionary analysis and empirical review. *Psychological Bulletin*, 136: 351–74. DOI: 10.1037/a0018807

Goffman, E. (1990) *The Presentation of Self in Everyday Life*. London: Penguin.

Goldstein, S.E. (2020) Hear us!: seven women diagnosed with borderline personality disorder describe what they need from their therapy relationships. *Qualitative Psychology*, 7 (2): 132–52. DOI: 10.1037/qup0000174

Greenberg, L.S. (2015) *Emotion-focused Therapy: Coaching Clients to Work through their Feelings* (2nd edn). Washington, DC: American Psychological Association. https://doi.org/10.1037/14692-000

Hart, T. (1999) The refinement of empathy. *Journal of Humanistic Psychology*, 39 (4): 111–25.

Hayes, J.A. (2002) Playing with fire: countertransference and clinical epistemology. *Journal of Contemporary Psychotherapy*, 32: 93–100.

Henretty, J.R. and Levitt, H.M. (2010) The role of therapist self-disclosure in psychotherapy: a qualitative review. *Clinical Psychology Review*, 30 (1): 63–77. DOI: 10.1016/j.cpr.2009.09.004

Heron, J. (2001) *Helping the Client: A Creative Practical Guide* (5th edn). London: Sage Publications.

Hill, C.E., Spiegel, S.B., Hoffman, M.A., Kivlighan, D.M. Jr and Gelso, C.J. (2017) Therapist expertise in psychotherapy revisited. *The Counseling Psychologist*, 45: 7–53. DOI: 10.1177/0011000016641192

Hook, J.N., Davis, D.E., Owen, J., Worthington, E.L. Jr and Utsey, S.O. (2013) Cultural humility: measuring openness to culturally diverse clients. *Journal of Counseling Psychology*, 60: 353–66.

Hook, J.N., Watkins, C.E., Davis, D.E., Owen, J., van Tongeren, D.R. and Marciana, J.R. (2016) Cultural humility in psychotherapy supervision. *The American Journal of Psychotherapy*, 7: 149–66. DOI: 10.1176/appi. psychotherapy.2016.70.2.149

Hycner, R. ([1991] 1993) *Between Person and Person: Toward a Dialogical Psychotherapy*. Highland, NY: Gestalt Journal Press.

Hycner, R. and Jacobs, L. (1995) *The Healing Relationship in Gestalt Therapy: A Dialogic/Self Psychology Approach*. Highland, NY: Gestalt Journal Press.

Ingham, E. (2018) *The (physically) wounded healer: the impact of a physical disability on training and development as a counselling psychologist: a case study*. Available at: www.semanticscholar.org/6ab1/dc2af555f523999f1fa96d2135c1a4b888ef.pdf (accessed June 2020).

Innocente, G.M. (2015) *Client–clinician texting: an expansion of the clinical holding environment*. Doctoral thesis (DSW), University of Pennsylvania. Available at: www.repository.upenn.edu/cgi/viewcontent.cgi?article=1074&context=edissertations_sp2 (accessed June 2020).

International Society for the Study of Trauma and Dissociation (ISSTD) (2011) Guidelines for treating Dissociative Identity Disorder in adults (3rd revision). *Journal of Trauma and Dissociation*, 12: 115–87.

Jackson, S. (2001) The wounded healer. *Bulletin of the History of Medicine*, 75: 1–36. DOI: 10.1353/bhm.2001.0025

Jacobs, L. (1989) Dialogue in gestalt theory and therapy (first published in *The Gestalt Journal*, 12 (1)). Available at: www.gestaltpsychotherapie.de/jacobs1.pdf (accessed June 2020).

Jacobs, L. (1991) The therapist as 'Other': the patient's search for relatedness. (Presented at Martin Buber's Contribution to the Humanities conference, October, 1991.) http://www.gestaltpsychotherapie.de/jacobs2.pdf

Joyce, P. and Sills, C. (2018) *Skills in Gestalt Counselling & Psychotherapy* (4th edn). London: Sage Publications.

Jung, C.G. ([1954] 2014) *Volume Sixteen: The Practice of Psychotherapy* (2nd edn). Translated from the German by R.F.C. Hill. Hove, East Sussex: Routledge.

Jung, C.G. (1921) Psychological types. *The Collected Works of C.G. Jung, Vol. 6*. Bollingen Series XX. Princeton, NJ: Princeton University Press.

Kapitan, L. (2003) *Re-enchanting Art Therapy: Transformational Practices for Restoring Creative Vitality*. Springfield, IL: Charles C. Thomas.

Kaposi, D. (2020) Individual or social problems?, in N. Moller, A. Vossler, D.W. Jones and D. Kaposi (eds), *Understanding Mental Health and Counselling*. London: Sage Publications. pp. 551–76.

Karkou, V., Aithal, S., Zubala, A. and Meekums, B. (2019) Effectiveness of dance movement therapy in the treatment of adults with depression: a systematic review with meta-analyses. *Frontiers in Psychology*, 10: 936. DOI: 10.3389/fpsyg.2019.00936

Kierkegaard, S. ([1848] 1998) The point of view for my work as an author (trans/eds, H.V. Hong and E.H. Hong). Princeton, NJ: Princeton University Press.

Knox, R., Murphy, D., Wiggins, S. and Cooper, M. (2013) *Relational Depth: New Perspectives and Developments*. London: Palgrave Macmillan.

Kottler, J.A. (2017) *On Being a Therapist* (5th edn). New York: Oxford University Press.

Kottler, J.A. (2018) *The Secrets of Exceptional Counsellors*. Alexandria, VA: American Counseling Association.

Kottler, J.A. and Carlson, J. (2009) *Creative Breakthroughs in Therapy: Tales of Transformation and Astonishment*. Hoboken, NJ: John Wiley.

Kottler, J.A. and Carlson, J. (2014) *On Being a Master Therapist: Practicing What You Preach*. Hoboken, NJ: Wiley.

Krug, O.T. (2009) James Bugental and Irvin Yalom: two masters of existential therapy cultivate presence in the therapeutic encounter. *Journal of Humanistic Psychology*, 49: 329–54.

Kuhnke, J.L. (2020) Art-based activities and adverse events: an autobiographical inquiry. *European Journal for Qualitative Research in Psychotherapy*, 10: 82–92.

Kuhnke, J.L. (2021) Reflexivity and an arts-based inquiry during COVID times. *European Journal for Qualitative Research in Psychotherapy*, 11: 13–21.

Kunz, G. (2002) *What makes therapy therapeutic: meaning-focused therapy. An address delivered at Orientation Retreat for the Graduate Program in Counseling Psychology at Trinity Western University on September 14, 2002* Available at: www.meaning.ca/article/what-makes-therapy-therapeutic/ (accessed May 2021).

Lamprecht, L. (2013) *Therapeutic letter writing as relationally responsive practice*. In paper/workshop presentation at the International Conference: The Challenge of Establishing a Research Tradition for Gestalt Therapy. Cape Cod, MA, 17–20 April. pp. 39–53.

Larner, G. (1995) The real as illusion: deconstructing power in family therapy. *Journal of Family Therapy*, 17: 191–217.

Lemma, A. (2017) *The Digital Age on the Couch: Psychoanalytic Practice and New Media*. London: Routledge.

Levinas, E. ([1961] 1969) *Totality and Infinity*. Pittsburgh: Duquesne University Press.

Levy, F.J. (ed.) (1995) *Dance and Other Expressive Art Therapies: When Words are not Enough*. New York: Routledge.

Levy, F.J. (2014) Integrating the arts in psychotherapy: opening the doors of shared creativity. *American Journal of Dance Therapy*, 36: 6–27. DOI: 10.1007/s10465-014-9171-8

Lewin, R.A. (1996) *Compassion: The Core Value that Animates Psychotherapy*. Northvale, NJ: Jason Aronson.

Loewenthal, D. (ed.) (2015) *Critical Psychotherapy, Psychoanalysis and Counselling: Implications for Practice*. Basingstoke: Palgrave Macmillan.

Madison, G. (2009) *Therapists are human, too! Blog post*. Available at: www.goodtherapy.org/blog/therapists-are-human-too/ (accessed May 2020).

Mandić, M. (2016) *A psychotherapist's lived experience of care: a hermeneutic-phenomenological study. Unpublished PhD dissertation, Regent's School of Psychotherapy and Psychology*, Regent's University, London.

May, R. (1983) *The Discovery of Being: Writings in Existential Psychology*. New York: W.W. Norton.

McGrath, L., Griffin, V. and Mundy, E. (2015) *The Psychological Impact of Austerity: A Briefing Paper. Psychologists for Social Change*. Available at: https://psychagainstausterity.files.wordpress.com/2015/03/paa-briefing-paper.pdf (accessed February 2018).

McKenzie-Mavinga, I. (2016) *The Challenge of Racism in Therapeutic Practice: Engaging with Oppression in Practice and Supervision*. London: Palgrave.

McManus, S., Meltzer, S., Brugha, T., Bebbington, P. and Jenkins, R. (eds) (2009) *Adult Psychiatric Morbidity in England, 2007: Results of a Household Survey*. Leeds: NHS digital.

McNeel, J.R. (1976) The Parent interview. *Transactional Analysis Journal*, 6 (1): 61–8. DOI: 10.1177/036215377600600114

McWilliams, N. (2017) Core competency two: therapeutic stance/attitude, in R.E. Barsness (ed.), *Core Competencies in Relational Psychoanalysis: A Guide to Practice, Study, and Research*. London: Routledge. pp. 87–104.

Mearns, D. and Cooper, M. (2005) *Working at Relational Depth in Counselling and Psychotherapy*. London: Sage Publications.

Merleau-Ponty, M. ([1945] 1962) (trans. C. Smith) *Phenomenology of Perception*. London: Routledge & Kegan Paul.

Miller, S.D., Duncan, B.L. and Hubble, M.A. (2005) Outcome-informed clinical work, in J.C. Norcross and M.R. Goldfried (eds), *Oxford series in clinical psychology. Handbook of Psychotherapy Integration*. Oxford University Press. pp. 84–102. Available at: https://doi.org/10.1093/med:ps ych/9780195165791.003.0004

Mitchell, E. (2020) "Much more than second best": therapists' experiences of videoconferencing psychotherapy. *European Journal of Qualitative Research in Psychotherapy*, 10: 121–35.

Mitchell, L.R. (2016) *Creativity as Co-Therapists: The Practitioner's Guide to the Art of Psychotherapy*. New York: Routledge.

Moller, N. and Tischner, I. (2019) Young people's perception of fat counsellors: "How can THAT help me?". *Qualitative Research in Psychology*, 16 (1): 34–53.

Mosey, A. (1986) *Psychosocial Components of Occupational Therapy*. New York: Raven Press.

Moursund, J.P. and Erskine, R.G. (2004) *Integrative Psychotherapy: The Art and Science of Relationship*. Victoria, Australia: Thomson/Brooks-Cole.

Moyers, B. (1989) *A World of Ideas: Conversations with Thoughtful Men and Women about American Life Today and the Ideas Shaping Our Future*. New York: Doubleday.

Murphy, B.C. and Dillon, C. (1998) *Interviewing in Action: Process and Practice*. Pacific Grove, CA: Brooks/Cole.

Nasar, J. and Devlin, A. (2011) Impressions of psychotherapists' offices. *Journal of Counseling Psychology*, 58: 310–20. DOI: 10.1037/a0023887

Ng, C.T. and James, S. (2013) Counselor empathy or 'having a heart to help'? An ethnographic investigation of Chinese clients' experience of counseling. *The Humanistic Psychologist*, 41 (4): 333–49.

Niblock, S. (2020) *UKCP updates from your Chair and Chief Executive, August 2020*. Blog post: www2.psychotherapy.org.uk/webmail/585663/242013566/c6e538ba6af4427cc50d3a9d6654ba7fbf7d59dbe52217dfdbd5ea9d503fb998 (accessed September 2020).

Nissen-Lie, H.A. (2020) *Humility and self-doubt are hallmarks of a good therapist*. Available at: www.aeon.co/ideas/humility-and-self-doubt-are-hallmarks-of-a-good-therapist (accessed November 2020).

Nissen-Lie, H.A., Rønnestad, M.H., Høglend, P.A., Havik, O.E., Solbakken, O.A., Stiles, T.C., Monsen, J.T. (2017) Love yourself as a person, doubt yourself as a therapist? *Clinical Psychology and Psychotherapy*, 24 (1): 48–60. DOI: 10.1002/cpp.1977

Norcross, J.C. (ed.) (2011) *Psychotherapy Relationships that Work: Evidence-based Responsiveness* (2nd ed.). Oxford: Oxford University Press. https://doi.org/10.1093/acprof:oso/9780199737208.001.0001

Norcross, J.C. and Karpiak, C.P. (2017) Our best selves: defining and actualizing expertise in psychotherapy. *The Counseling Psychologist*, 45 (1): 48–60. DOI: 10.1177/0011000016655603

Norcross, J.C. and Wampold, B.E. (2018) A new therapy for each patient: evidence-based relationships and responsiveness. *Journal of Clinical Psychology*, 74 (11): 1889–1906. DOI: 10.1002/jclp.22678

Noricks, J. (2011) *Parts Psychology: A Trauma-based, Self-state therapy for Emotional Healing in Counseling and Psychotherapy. Case Studies in Normal Dissociation.* Los Angeles, CA: New University Press.

Nouwen, H.J.M. (1972) *The Wounded Healer: Ministry in Contemporary Society.* New York: Doubleday.

Nouwen, H.J.M. (1998) *Reaching Out.* London: Fount, HarperCollins.

Ogden, J. and Fisher, P. (2015) *Sensorimotor Psychotherapy: Interventions for Trauma and Attachment.* New York: W.W. Norton.

Orbach, S. (2003) Part I: There is no such thing as a body. The John Bowlby Memorial Lecture 2003. *British Journal of Psychotherapy*, 20 (1): 3–15. Available at: https://onlinelibrary-wiley-com.libezproxy.open.ac.uk/doi/pdfdirect/10.1111/j.1752-0118.2003.tb00110.x

Orbach, S. (2004) What can we learn from the therapist's body? *Attachment & Human Development*, 6 (2): 141–50. DOI: 10.1080/14616730410001695349

Paul, S. and Charura, D. (2015) *An Introduction to the Therapeutic Relationship in Counselling and Psychotherapy.* London: Sage.

Pearson, M. and Wilson, H. (2012) Soothing spaces and healing places: is there an ideal counselling room design? *Psychotherapy in Australia*, 18 (3): 46–53.

Pickering, J. (2019) *The Search for Meaning in Psychotherapy: Spiritual Practice, the Apophatic Way and Bion.* London: Routledge.

Pickett, K. and Wilkinson, R. (2010) Inequality: an underacknowledged source of mental illness and distress. *The British Journal of Psychiatry*, 197 (6): 426–8.

Pinto-Coelho, K.G., Hill, C.E. and Kivlighan, D.M. (2016) Therapist self-disclosure in psychodynamic psychotherapy: a mixed methods investigation. *Counselling Psychology Quarterly*, 29 (1): 29–52. DOI: 10.1080/09515070.2015.1072496

Porges, S. (2011) *The Polyvagal Theory: Neurophysiological Foundations of Emotions, Attachment, Communication and Self-Regulation.* New York: W.W. Norton.

Proctor, G. (2002) *The Dynamics of Power in Counselling and Psychotherapy: Ethics, Politics and Practice.* Ross-on-Wye: PCCS Books.

Proctor, G., Cooper, M., Sanders, P. and Malcom, B. (2006) *Politicizing the Person-Centred Approach: An Agenda for Social Change.* Ross-on-Wye: PCCS Books.

Public Health England (2020) *Disparities in the Risk and Outcomes of Covid-19.* London: Crown copyright. Available at: www.gov.uk/government/publications/covid-19-review-of-disparities-in-risks-and-outcomes (accessed October 2020).

Reinkraut, R. (2008) Moral awareness and therapist use of self. *Journal of Pedagogy, Pluralism, and Practice*, 4 (1): 12–24. Available at: https://digitalcommons.lesley.edu/jppp/vol4/iss1/4

Reupert, A. (2008) A trans-disciplinary study of the therapist's self. *European Journal of Psychotherapy and Counselling*, 10 (4): 369–83.

Rice, L.N. and Greenberg, L.S. (1990) Fundamental dimensions in experiential therapy: new directions in research, in G. Lietaer, J. Rombauts and R. Van Balen (eds), *Client-centered and experiential psychotherapy in the Nineties.* Leuven: Leuven University Press. pp. 397–414.

Richard, A.M.P. (2012) The wounded healer: can we do better than survive as therapist? *International Journal of Psychoanalytic Self Psychology*, 7 (1): 131–8. DOI: 10.1080/15551024.2011.606967

Rogers, C.R. (1969) *Freedom to Learn.* Columbus, OH: Merrill.

Rogers, C.R. (1980) *A Way of Being.* Boston, MA: Houghton Mifflin.

Rogers, C.R. (1986) Client-centered therapy, in I.L. Kutash and A. Wolf (eds), *Psychotherapist's Casebook: Theory and Technique in the Practice of Modern Therapies*. San Francisco, CA: Jossey-Bass.

Rogers, C.R. (1995) *A Way of Being*. Boston, MA: Houghton-Mifflin.

Rowan, J. (1990) *Subpersonalities: The People Inside Us*. London: Routledge.

Rowan, J. (2002) Three levels of empathy. *Self & Society*, 30 (4): 20–7.

Rowan, J. (2006) *Dialogue and the transpersonal in therapy*. PhD thesis, Middlesex University. Available at: http://eprints.mdx.ac.uk/13427/

Rowan, J. and Cooper, M. (1999) *The Plural Self: Multiplicity in Everyday Life*. London: Sage Publications.

Rowan, J. and Jacobs, M. (2002) *The Therapist's Use of Self*. Buckingham: Open University Press.

Rugsaken, K. (2006) *Body speaks: body language around the world*. Available at: https://nacada.ksu.edu/Resources/Clearinghouse/View-Articles/Body-Language-Around-the-World.aspx

Russell, G.I. (2020) Remote working during the pandemic: A Q & A with Gillian Isaacs Russell: questions from the editor and editorial board of the BJP. *British Journal of Psychotherapy*, 3 (3): 364–74.

Safran, J.D. (2018) *Therapeutic alliance ruptures: research sheds light on what to do when therapy isn't working*. Blog post. Available at: www.psychologytoday.com/us/blog/straight-talk/201801/therapeutic-alliance-ruptures (accessed December 2020).

Safran, J.D., Muran, J.C., Wallner Samstag, L. and Stevens, C. (2001) Repairing therapeutic alliance ruptures. *Psychotherapy*, 38: 406–12.

Samuelson, E. (2017) Soaring above the ashes of the past. In S.K. Farber (ed.) *Celebrating the Wounded Healer Psychotherapist*. London: Routledge. pp. 180–4.

Satir, V. (1967) *Conjoint Family Therapy: A Guide to Theory and Technique*. Palo Alto, CA: Science and Behavior Books.

Satir, V. ([1987] 2013) The therapist story, in M. Baldwin (ed.), *The Use of Self in Therapy* (3rd edn). New York: Routledge. pp. 19–27.

Satir, V. (2000) The therapist story, in M. Baldwin (ed.) *The Use of Self in Therapy*. New York: The Haworth Press. pp. 17–27.

Sayre, G. and Kunz, G. (2005) Enduring intimate relationships as ethical and more than ethical: inspired by Emmanuel Levinas and Martin Buber. *Journal of Theoretical and Philosophical Psychology*, 25 (2): 224–37. Available at: https://doi.org/10.1037/h0091260

Schneider, K.J. (2008) *Existential–Integrative Psychotherapy: Guideposts to the Core of Practice*. New York: Routledge.

Schneider, K.J. (2009) *Awakening to Awe: Personal Stories of Profound Transformation*. Lanham, MD: Jason Aronson.

Schore, A.N. (1994) *Affect Regulation and the Origin of the Self: The Neurobiology of Emotional Development*. Mahwah, NJ: Erlbaum.

Schore, A.N. (2003) *Affect Regulation and the Repair of the Self*. New York: W.W. Norton.

Schwartz, A. (2015) *Natural vagus nerve stimulation*. Blog post. Available at: www.drarielleschwartz.com/natural-vagus-nerve-stimulation-dr-arielle-schwartz/#.XuxdV2hKg2w (accessed May 2021).

Schwartz, A. (2020) *Online therapy sessions: focusing on somatic psychology and parts work*. Available at: www.nscience.uk/product/online-therapy-sessions-focussing-on-somatic-psychology-parts-work/ (accessed June 2020).

Schwartz, R.C. (2001) *Introduction to the Internal Family Systems Model*. Oak Park, IL: Trailhead Publishers.

Segal, Z.V., Williams, J.M.G. and Teasdale, J.D. (2013) *Mindfulness-based Cognitive Therapy for Depression* (2nd edn). New York: The Guilford Press.

Seth, P. (2017) *Being opened: a hermeneutic phenomenological enquiry into the existential psychotherapist's lived experience of wonder*. PhD thesis, Middlesex University. Available at: http://eprints.mdx.ac.uk/22613/

Shallcross, L. (2011) *Working outside the box. Counseling Today*. Available at: www.ct.counseling.org/2011/02/working-outside-the-box/# (accessed June 2020).

Shaw, R. (2003) *The Embodied Psychotherapist: The Therapist's Body Story*. Hove: Psychology Press.

Simpson, S., Richardson, L., Pietrabissa, G., Castelnuova, G. and Reid, C. (2020) Videotherapy and therapeutic alliance in the age of Covid-19. *Clinical Psychology & Psychotherapy*, 1–13. DOI: 10.1002/cpp.2521

Sleater, A.M. and Scheiner, J. (2020) Impact of the therapist's "use of self". *The European Journal of Counselling Psychology*, 8 (1): 118–43. DOI: 10.5964/ejcop.v8i1.160

Smith, R. (2021) The emotional impact of research: a reflexive account of a counsellor-turned-PhD researcher's experience of vicarious trauma. *European Journal for Qualitative Research in Psychotherapy*, 11: 22–32.

Soth, M. (2018) *Embodied countertransference*. Available at: www.researchgate.net/publication/322918578_Embodied_Countertransference (accessed June 2020).

Soto, A., Smith, T.B., Griner, D., Rodriguez, M.D. and Bernal, G. (2019) Cultural adaptations and multicultural competence, in J.C. Norcross and B.E. Wampold (eds), *Psychotherapy Relationships that Work: Volume 2: Evidence-Based Therapist Responsiveness*. New York: Oxford. pp. 86–132.

Speedy, J. (2016) Ghosts, traces, sediments, and accomplices in psychotherapeutic dialogue with Sue, Grace and Jane Speedy, in N.K. Denzin and M.D. Giardina (eds), *Qualitative Inquiry Outside the Academy*. Abingdon: Routledge. pp. 268–76.

Spinelli, E. (1997) *Tales of Un-knowing: Therapeutic Encounters from an Existential Perspective*. London: Duckworth.

Spinelli, E. (2015) *Practising Existential Therapy: The Relational World* (2nd edn). London: Sage Publications.

Spring, C. (2010) A brief guide to working with dissociative identity. Blog post. Available at: www.information.pods-online.org.uk/a-brief-guide-to-working-with-dissociative-identity-disorder/ (accessed July 2020).

Stern, D.N. (1985) *The Interpersonal World of the Infant*. New York: Basic Books.

Stern, D.N. (2004) *The Present Moment in Psychotherapy and Everyday Life*. New York: W.W. Norton.

Stoll, J., Müller, J.A. and Trachsel, M. (2020) Ethical issues in online psychotherapy: a narrative review. *Frontiers in Psychiatry*, 10: 993. DOI: 10.3389/fpsyt.2019.00993

Stolorow, R.D. (2014) Undergoing the situation: emotional dwelling is more than empathic understanding. *International Journal of Psychoanalytic Self Psychology*, 9 (1): 80–3. DOI: 10.1080/15551024.2014.857750

Stone, D. (2008) Wounded healing: exploring the circle of compassion in the helping relationship. *Humanistic Psychologist*, 36 (1): 45–51. DOI: 10.1080/08873260701415587

Stone, H. and Stone, S.L. (1989) *Embracing Our Selves: The Voice Dialogue Method*. Novato, CA: Nataraj Publishing.

Stone, H. and Stone, S. (1993) *Embracing Your Inner Critic: Turning Self-Criticism into a Creative Asset*. San Francisco, CA: Harper San Francisco.

Stone, M. (2006) The analyst's body as tuning fork: embodied resonance in countertransference. *Journal of Analytical Psychology*, 51 (1): 109–124. DOI: 10.1111/j.1465-5922.2006.575_1.x

Stone, S. (2005) *One secret of graceful aging: separating from primary selves.* Available at: www.voicedialogueinternational.com/articles/One_Secret_Of_Graceful_Aging.htm (accessed July 2020).

Storr, A. (1990) *The Art of Psychotherapy* (2nd edn). Oxford: Butterworth-Heinemann.

Suler, J. (2000) *Psychotherapy in cyberspace: a five dimensional model of online and computer-mediated psychotherapy.* Available at: www.usr.rider.edu/~suler/psycyber/therapy.html (accessed July 2020).

Suler, J. (2004) The online disinhibition effect: the impact of the internet, multimedia and virtual reality on behavior and society. *CyberPsychology & Behavior*, 7: 321–6. DOI: 10.1089/1094931041291295

Sussman, M.B. (1992) *A Curious Calling: Unconscious Motivations for Practicing Psychotherapy.* Lanham, MD: Jason Aronson.

Sussman, M.B. (1995) *Intimations of mortality*, in M.B. Sussman (ed.), *A Perilous Calling: The Hazards of Psychotherapy Practice.* New York: John Wiley. pp. 15–25.

Sussman, M.B. (2007) *A Curious Calling: Unconscious Motivations for Practicing Psychotherapy* (2nd edn). Plymouth: Rowman & Littlefield Publishers.

Symons, C. (2020) Context of practice: boundaries and ethics, in N. Moller, A. Vosser, D.W. Jones and D. Kaposi (eds) *Understanding Mental Health and Counselling.* London: Sage.

Thériault, A. and Gazzola, N. (2008) Feelings of incompetence among experienced therapists. *European Journal of Qualitative Research in Psychotherapy*, 3: 19–29.

Thériault, A. and Gazzola, N. (2010) Therapist feelings of incompetence and suboptimal processes in psychotherapy. *Journal of Contemporary Psychotherapy*, 40: 233–43. DOI: 10.1007/s10879-010-9147-z

Todres, L. (2007) *Embodied Enquiry: Phenomenological Touchstones for Research, Psychotherapy and Spirituality.* Basingstoke: Palgrave Macmillan.

Tosone, C. (2013) Virtual intimacy in the therapeutic space: help or hindrance, in E. Ruderman and C. Tosone (eds), *Contemporary Clinical Practice: The Holding Environment under Assault.* New York: Springer. pp. 41–9.

Treisman, K. (2017) *A Therapeutic Treasure Box for working with Children and Adolescents with Developmental Trauma.* London: Jessica Kingsley.

UKCP (2017) *UKCP's diversity and equalities statement.* Available at: www.psychotherapy.org.uk/wp-content/uploads/2017/11/Diversity-and-equalities-statement.pdf

van der Hart, O., Nijenhuis, E.R.S. and Steele, K. (2006) *The Haunted Self: Structural Dissociation and the Treatment of Chronic Traumatization.* New York: W.W. Norton.

van der Kolk, B.A. (2014) *The Body keeps the Score: Brain, Mind, and Body in the Healing of Trauma.* New York: Penguin.

van Deurzen-Smith, E. (1997) *Everyday Mysteries: Existential Dimensions of Psychotherapy.* London: Routledge.

van Deurzen, E. and Adams, M. (2011) *Skills in Existential Counselling and Psychotherapy.* Los Angeles, CA: Sage.

van Manen, M. (2014) *Phenomenology of Practice.* Walnut Creek, CA: Left Coast Press. Available at: www.maxvanmanen.com/files/2014/10/MvM-Phen-of-Practice-113.pdf

Vieira, E.M., Castelo Branco, P.C. and Ribeiro, G.D.P.D. (2020) Becoming an emergency psychologist: alterity and presence in a comprehensive not-knowing relationship. *Theory & Psychology*, 30 (5): 690–702. DOI: 10.1177/0959354320943298

Watkins, J.G. and Watkins, H.H. (1997) *Ego States: Theory and Therapy*. New York: W.W. Norton.

Weinberg, H. and Rolnick, A. (2020) *Theory and Practice of Online Therapy: Internet-delivered Interventions for Individuals, Groups, Families, and Organization*. New York: Routledge.

Wertz, F. (2005) Phenomenological research methods for counseling psychology. *Journal of Counseling Psychology*, 52 (2): 167–77.

Westland, G. (2009) Considerations on communications – both verbal and non-verbal in body psychotherapy. *Body, Movement and Dance in Psychotherapy*, 4 (2): 121–34. Available at: www.cbpc.org.uk/articles/considerations-on-communications-both-verbal-and-non-verbal-in-body-psychotherapy/ (accessed September 2020).

Wilcox, M.M., Franks, D.N., Taylor, T.O., Monceaux, C.P. and Harris, K. (2020) Who's multiculturally competent?: everybody and nobody: a multimethod examination. *The Counseling Psychologist*, 48 (4): 466–97. DOI: 10.1177/0011000020904709

Williamson, R. (2013) *Exploring the therapeutic self*. Unpublished doctoral thesis, City University London. Available at: www.openaccess.city.ac.uk/id/eprint/2393/1/Williamson,_Rosannav2.pdf (accessed June 2020).

Winnicott, D.W. (1971) *Playing and Reality*. London: Pelican Books.

Wosket, V. (2017) *The Therapeutic Use of Self: Counselling Practice, Research and Supervision*. Abingdon: Routledge.

Yalom, I.D. (n.d.) *Autobiographical note*. Available at: www.yalom.com/biography (accessed May 2020).

Yalom, I.D. (1989) *Love's Executioner*. London: Penguin.

Yalom, I.D. (2002) *The Gift of Therapy: An Open Letter to a New Generation of Therapists and their Patients* (revised and updated). London: Piatkus.

Yalom, I.D. and Elkin, G. (1974) *Every Day Gets a Little Closer*. New York: Basic Books.

Yalom, V. and Yalom, M.-H. (2010) Peter Levine on somatic experiencing. *Psychotherapy.Net*. Available at: www.psychotherapy.net/interview/interview-peter-levine (accessed June 2020).

Yontef, G.M. (1993) *Awareness, Dialogue, and Process: Essays in Gestalt Therapy*. Highland, NY: Gestalt Journal Press.

Zerubavel, N. and Wright, M.O. (2012) The dilemma of the wounded healer. *Psychotherapy*, 49 (4): 482–91. DOI: 10.1037/a0027824

Ziv-Beiman, S. (2013) Therapist self-disclosure as an integrative intervention. *Journal of Psychotherapy Integration*, 23 (1): 59–74. DOI: 10.1037/a0031783

Ziv-Beiman, S. and Shahar, G. (2016) Therapeutic self-disclosure in integrative psychotherapy: when is this a clinical error? *Psychotherapy*, 53 (3): 273–7. DOI: 10.1037/pst0000077

Žvelc, G. and Žvelc, M. (2021) *Integrative Psychotherapy: A Mindfulness and Compassion-oriented Approach*. Abingdon: Routledge.

Žvelc, G., Javanoska, K. and Žvelc, M. (2020) Development and validation of the relational needs satisfaction scale. *Frontiers in Psychology*, 1:901. DOI: 10.3389/fpsyg.2020.00901

INDEX

Note: Page numbers followed by "*n*" indicate notes.

www.ingramcontent.com/pod-product-compliance
Lightning Source LLC
Chambersburg PA
CBHW080557030426
42336CB00019B/3222